CH00536667

"How does one write a simple and clear treatment of one of the most complex and challenging doctrines? I'm not entirely sure, but that is precisely what Andy Naselli has done. This book provides an accessible and careful treatment of predestination that will serve pastors, laypeople, and all those who want to learn more about the wonders of God's glory in election. Take, read, and be stirred to worship."

Steven Lee, Pastor for Preaching and Vision, The North Church, Mounds View, Minnesota

Predestination

SHORT STUDIES IN SYSTEMATIC THEOLOGY

Edited by Graham A. Cole and Oren R. Martin

The Atonement: An Introduction, Jeremy Treat (2023)

The Attributes of God: An Introduction, Gerald Bray (2021)

The Church: An Introduction, Gregg R. Allison (2021)

The Doctrine of Scripture: An Introduction, Mark D. Thompson (2022)

Faithful Theology: An Introduction, Graham A. Cole (2020)

Glorification: An Introduction, Graham A. Cole (2022)

The Holy Spirit: An Introduction, Fred Sanders (2023)

Justification: An Introduction, Thomas R. Schreiner (2023)

The Person of Christ: An Introduction, Stephen J. Wellum (2021)

Predestination: An Introduction, Andrew David Naselli (2024)

The Trinity: An Introduction, Scott R. Swain (2020)

Predestination

An Introduction

Andrew David Naselli

WHEATON, ILLINOIS

Predestination: An Introduction

© 2024 by Andrew David Naselli

Published by Crossway
      1300 Crescent Street
      Wheaton, Illinois 60187

Cover design: Jordan Singer

First printing 2024

Printed in the United States of America

Trade paperback ISBN: 978-1-4335-7314-9
ePub ISBN: 978-1-4335-7317-0
PDF ISBN: 978-1-4335-7315-6

Library of Congress Cataloging-in-Publication Data

Names: Naselli, Andrew David, 1980– author.
Title: Predestination : an introduction / Andrew David Naselli.
Description: Wheaton, Illinois : Crossway, 2024. | Series: Short studies in systematic theology | Includes bibliographical references and indexes.
Identifiers: LCCN 2023011170 (print) | LCCN 2023011171 (ebook) | ISBN 9781433573149 (trade paperback) | ISBN 9781433573156 (pdf) | ISBN 9781433573170 (epub)
Subjects: LCSH: Predestination.
Classification: LCC BT809 .N48 2024 (print) | LCC BT809 (ebook) | DDC 202/.2—dc23/eng/20230804
LC record available at https://lccn.loc.gov/2023011170
LC ebook record available at https://lccn.loc.gov/2023011171

Crossway is a publishing ministry of Good News Publishers.

VP		33	32	31	30	29	28	27	26	25	24
15	14	13	12	11	10	9	8	7	6	5	4	3	2	1

To Phil Gons,
chosen by God

Contents

Illustrations xi

Series Preface. xiii

Introduction. 1

PART 1
VESSELS OF MERCY
What Does the Bible Teach about Election?

1   What Is the Goal of Election? 23

2   When Did God Choose to Save Some Humans? 37

3   Did God Choose to Save Individuals? 43

4   Did God Choose to Save Individuals Based on
    Foreseen Faith? 51

5   Is Unconditional Election Unfair? 69

6   Do We Have Free Will? 79

7   Does Election Contradict God's Desire That All
    Humans Be Saved? 111

8   How Does God Accomplish His Plan to Save
    Individuals? 121

9   How Do I Know If God Has Elected Me? 137

10 Did God Elect Babies Who Die? 143

PART 2
VESSELS OF WRATH
What Does the Bible Teach about Reprobation?

11 Who Ultimately Causes Reprobation? 153

12 How Does God Accomplish Reprobation? 169

13 What Is the Result of Reprobation? 181

14 What Is the Goal of Reprobation? 185

15 Who Deserves Blame for Reprobation? 199

Conclusion 205
Exult in God as You Take in the View

Acknowledgments 207

Appendix 209
Chapter Summary Questions and Answers

Further Reading 213

General Index 217

Scripture Index 229

Illustrations

Tables

0.1   Two Ways to Respond to Predestination 4

0.2   Defining *Predestination*, *Election*, and *Reprobation* 7

0.3   Distinguishing the Synonyms *Election* and *(Positive)*
Predestination 9

0.4   Comparing Arminianism and Calvinism 11

0.5   How TULIP Is Misleading 14

0.6   Three Levels of Predestination's Importance 18

3.1   Four Kinds of Election 43

4.1   Foreknowledge according to Conditional and
Unconditional Election 52

5.1   Arminianism versus Calvinism on God's Special Grace .. 74

6.1   Incompatibilism versus Compatibilism 88

6.2   Four Possibilities for Whether Humans Are Morally Free
to Choose What God Wants 92

6.3   Doctrinal Tensions 104

7.1   Biblical Examples That Distinguish Two Ways That God
Wills 113

7.2   Terms That Distinguish Two Ways That God Wills.... 115

7.3   What Does God Value More Highly Than Saving All
      Humans without Exception? 117

8.1   Analogies for How Regeneration Enables and Causes
      Faith 124

11.1 Two Views on Double Predestination................... 160

11.2 Eternal Death and Eternal Life in Romans 6:23........ 162

11.3 Two Views on the Logical Order of Different Aspects of
      God's Decree 164

12.1 Ultimate, Proximate, and Efficient Causes............. 177

14.1 Doxologies in Books That Highlight God's Wrath and
      Power and Mercy 191

Figures

6.1   How Our Choices, Desires, and Heart Relate............95

6.2   Evangelism That Assumes Incompatibilism 97

8.1   Christ's Nine Saving Events............................ 122

Series Preface

The ancient Greek thinker Heraclitus reputedly said that the thinker has to listen to the essence of things. A series of theological studies dealing with the traditional topics that make up systematic theology needs to do just that. Accordingly, in each of these studies, a theologian addresses the essence of a doctrine. This series thus aims to present short studies in theology that are attuned to both the Christian tradition and contemporary theology in order to equip the church to faithfully understand, love, teach, and apply what God has revealed in Scripture about a variety of topics. What may be lost in comprehensiveness can be gained through what John Calvin, in the dedicatory epistle of his commentary on Romans, called "lucid brevity."

Of course, a thorough study of any doctrine will be longer rather than shorter, as there are two millennia of confession, discussion, and debate with which to interact. As a result, a short study needs to be more selective but deftly so. Thankfully, the contributors to this series have the ability to be brief yet accurate. The key aim is that the simpler is not to morph into the simplistic. The test is whether the topic of a short study, when further studied in depth, requires some unlearning to take place. The simple can be amplified. The simplistic needs to be corrected. As editors, we believe that the volumes in this series pass that test.

While the specific focus varies, each volume (1) introduces the doctrine, (2) sets it in context, (3) develops it from Scripture, (4) draws the various threads together, and (5) brings it to bear on the Christian life. It is our prayer, then, that this series will assist the church to delight in her triune God by thinking his thoughts—which he has graciously revealed in his written word, which testifies to his living Word, Jesus Christ—after him in the powerful working of his Spirit.

Graham A. Cole and Oren R. Martin

Introduction

Why I Love Predestination

An advertisement for an energy bar pictures two triumphant climbers at the tip of a mountain peak, basking in the glorious view. The caption over the photo reads, "You've never felt more alive. You've never felt more insignificant."[1] Why do we love seeing grandeur and feeling small? Because God made us for God. That's why I love what the Bible teaches about predestination.

An Invitation to Hike Up a Mountain

When you arduously hike up a mountain, it is satisfying to take in the breathtaking panoramic view at the top. God designed us so that we complete our joy by seeing God's beauty, savoring him, praising him, and then sharing our joy with others. In this book I invite you to let me share my joy with you. The hike is not easy, but it's worth it because the view at the top is awe-inspiring. The more you know about God and his ways, the deeper and sweeter will be your praise.

Who Is This Book For?

This book's target audience is thoughtful Christians—both pastors and laypeople—who want to study what the Bible teaches

---

1. See Andy Naselli, "God Is Supreme," *Andy Naselli* (blog) November 6, 2021, https://andynaselli.com/god-is-supreme.

about predestination. I wrote it with several types of Christians in mind, including my students at Bethlehem College and Seminary, the members of my church (to whom I preached the gist of this book in four sermons), my wife (a homemaker and homeschooling mom), and my oldest daughter (who was thirteen when I drafted it). My main audience is not professional academics, but I attempt to be academically responsible. I aim to explain a complex topic simply but not simplistically.

What Is Helpful to Know Upfront about Predestination As We Prepare to Study It?

I'll attempt to orient us by answering six questions.

1. What If I Am Anxious or Fearful about Studying Predestination?

My wife, Jenni, was initially anxious about my writing this book. Here is what she wrote after reading a draft of it:

> When Andy told me that he was planning to study predestination in order to write his next book, I honestly felt trepidation. I firmly believe and rejoice in the sovereignty of God, but the doctrine of predestination and especially reprobation felt very frightening to me, especially because some people I love are not believers. The thought of digging into that doctrine felt frightening—like digging into a dark hole. I wasn't sure I would like what I found.
>
> But each time I come back to Andy's book, I come away with a completely different emotion. My heart is filled with grateful worship to God. There is nothing in me that caused God to choose me. I am amazed that the God of the universe chose me before the foundation of the world. The doctrine of predestination—rather than frightening me—has changed my heart and caused me to worship and love our good God even more. And that was surprising to me.

Friend, if you think predestination is hard to understand and even harder to treasure, you're not alone. Many Christians have struggled with being assured that they are God's elect. And most of us have loved ones who are rejecting Christ.

If you are anxious or fearful about studying predestination, take courage. All Scripture is God-breathed and "profitable for teaching, for reproof, for correction, and for training in righteousness, that the man of God may be complete, equipped for every good work" (2 Tim. 3:16–17). That's true for what God says about predestination. These precious truths are gifts from the all-good, all-powerful, all-wise God to humble us, comfort us, and satisfy us with himself.[2]

Many people avoid talking about predestination or gloss over it or misinterpret it to fit with what they already presuppose. We are born with a self-centered view of the universe instead of a God-centered one. We naturally think, "It's all about me." We need a Copernican revolution so that our "felt reality" matches reality.[3] My goal in this book is to clearly and faithfully explain and apply what God says about predestination.

2. How Should We Talk about Such a Controversial and Emotional Issue?

When I told friends that I was writing a book on predestination—that is, election and reprobation—some would pause long enough for me to read the thought bubble above their heads: "Wow, that's brave. Election is controversial. And reprobation is frightening. That's heavy stuff."

---

2. John Calvin, a French pastor-theologian in the 1500s, reminds us that in Scripture "nothing is omitted that is both necessary and useful to know, so nothing is taught but what is expedient to know." John Calvin, *Institutes of the Christian Religion*, ed. John T. McNeill, trans. Ford Lewis Battles, 2 vols., Library of Christian Classics (Philadelphia: Westminster, 1960), 3.21.3 (924).

3. Joe Rigney, "Submit Your Felt Reality to God," Desiring God, May 19, 2022, https://www.desiringgod.org/.

Sometimes Christians passionately disagree with each other about predestination. For many of us, our convictions about predestination are deep. We feel strongly about how to interpret and systematize and apply what the Bible says about predestination.

So how should we talk about an issue that is often controversial and emotional? Carefully, reasonably, charitably, even-handedly, patiently, humbly, convictionally, straightforwardly, soberly, joyfully.

It is pitiful how we can take a Bible teaching that should result in humility, praise, and comfort and instead talk about it with sinful pride, divisiveness, and anxiety (see table 0.1).

Table 0.1   Two Ways to Respond to Predestination

The Right Way to Respond to Predestination	The Wrong Way to Respond to Predestination
Be humbled.	Be proud.
Praise God.	Be divisive.
Feel comforted.	Feel anxious.

We self-centered sinners routinely rebel against God's brilliant designs. We can turn a blessing into a wicked mess—like indulging in sexual activity outside of marriage or misusing authority to oppress others. Let's not turn the blessing of predestination on its head.

Predestination is a teaching that God has revealed to us for his glory and our good. To talk about predestination in a humble way does not mean that we shrug our shoulders and decline to address it in detail since Christians disagree about it. To talk about predestination in a humble way means that we unreservedly affirm and cherish whatever God has revealed. We must not be embarrassed about what the Bible teaches. It does not honor God to say, "The Bible teaches that, but I don't like it," or, "The Bible says that, but it can't really mean that." We do not have the authority to judge what God has revealed. And if we feel the need to apologize for something God has said, then we must repent of our arrogance. If we have a problem understanding the nature and rationale of what God has revealed in Scripture, then the problem is with *us*—not with God's word.[4] We must be aware that sin has affected even our thought processes and that we are finite creatures who think we are a lot smarter than we really are. We think we know better than God does, and we don't like it if we are not in control.

So let's approach predestination on our knees and with open hands. Let's not stand *over* the word of God as if we are the judge. Instead, let's kneel *under* the word of God as humble learners. And let's be committed to believe and cherish whatever God reveals.

> This is the one to whom I will look:
>> he who is humble and contrite in spirit
>> and trembles at my word. (Isa. 66:2)

3. What Do Predestination, Election, and Reprobation Mean?

Predestination may be contentious and alarming for some Christians, but we must not ignore it because it is all over the Bible. The Bible refers to God's people as "the elect" (Matt. 24:22, 24; 24:31; Mark 13:20, 22, 27; Luke 18:7; 2 Tim. 2:10) and "God's elect" (Rom. 8:33; Titus 1:1). What does that mean?

---

4. To clarify, (1) the Bible itself is without error, but (2) a human's *interpretation* of the Bible is not necessarily without error. On interpreting the Bible, see Andrew David Naselli, *How to Understand and Apply the New Testament: Twelve Steps from Exegesis to Theology* (Phillipsburg, NJ: P&R, 2017).

When addressing a controversial topic, it is crucial to define key terms clearly. I repeatedly use the words *predestination, election,* and *reprobation* in this book, so I will define those keywords here at the beginning.

In the New Testament, *predestine* translates *proōrizō*, which occurs six times (Acts 4:28; Rom. 8:29–30; 1 Cor. 2:7; Eph. 1:5, 11). *Proōrizō* means "decide upon beforehand, *predetermine*."[5] It is an action that God does. God predetermines whatever takes place (Eph. 1:11; cf. Acts 4:28), and for God to predestine a person means for him to predetermine a person's destiny.[6] While it is valid to use *predestination* for everything God decrees,[7] I am using *predestination* specifically regarding a person's eternal destiny—similar to what Paul writes in 1 Thessalonians 5:9: "God has not *destined* us for wrath, but [God has destined us] for obtaining salvation through our Lord Jesus Christ" (NASB).[8] (See table 0.2.)

---

5. Frederick W. Danker, Walter Bauer, William F. Arndt, and F. Wilbur Gingrich, eds., *Greek-English Lexicon of the New Testament and Other Early Christian Literature,* 3rd ed. (Chicago: University of Chicago Press, 2000), 873 (προορίζω; hereafter cited as BDAG).

6. "Person" includes both humans and angels. Aquinas rightly asserts, "Predestination applies to angels." Thomas Aquinas, *Summa Theologiae: Prima Pars, 1–49,* trans. Laurence Shapcote, Latin/English Edition of the Works of St. Thomas Aquinas 21 (Green Bay, WI: Aquinas Institute, 2017), q. 23, a. 1 (254). Angels are either elect (1 Tim. 5:21) or evil (2 Pet. 2:4; Jude 6). Cf. C. Fred Dickason, *Angels: Elect and Evil,* 2nd ed. (Chicago: Moody Press, 1995), 42–45. This book focuses on the predestination of humans.

7. E.g., "*Predestination* and *election* are not synonyms, although they are closely related. Predestination has to do with God's decrees concerning anything. A specific type of predestination is election, which has to do with God's choosing certain people in Christ to be adopted into the family of God, or, in simple terms, to be saved." R. C. Sproul, *Everyone's a Theologian: An Introduction to Systematic Theology* (Orlando, FL: Reformation Trust, 2014), 222.

8. Elsewhere (in contrast to the previous footnote), Sproul defines *predestination* the way I do in this book. E.g., "We may define *predestination* broadly as follows: From all eternity God decided to save some members of the human race and to let the rest of the human race perish. God made a choice—he chose certain individuals to be saved unto everlasting blessedness in heaven, and he chose others to pass over, allowing them to suffer the consequences of their sins, eternal punishment in hell." R. C. Sproul, *Grace Unknown: The Heart of Reformed Theology* (Grand Rapids, MI: Baker, 1997), 141. See also R. C. Sproul, *Chosen by God* (Wheaton, IL: Tyndale House, 1986), 23.

Table 0.2   Defining *Predestination*, *Election*, and *Reprobation*

Predestination
God predetermined the destiny of certain individuals for salvation (election) and others for condemnation (reprobation).

Election	Reprobation
God sovereignly and graciously chose to save individual sinners:	God sovereignly and justly chose to pass over nonelect sinners and punish them:
"vessels of mercy, which [God] has prepared beforehand for glory" (Rom. 9:23)	"vessels of wrath prepared for destruction" (Rom. 9:22)
"the elect" (Rom. 11:7)	"the rest" (Rom. 11:7)
Jesus's sheep (John 10:27–29)	not Jesus's sheep (John 10:26)
positive predestination for eternal life	negative predestination for eternal death
with distinct goals (see chap. 1)	with distinct goals (see chap. 14)
in accordance with God's love, mercy, and grace	in accordance with God's wrath, power, and justice

Predestination means that *God predetermined the destiny of certain individuals for salvation and others for condemnation*. Predestination has two parts: choosing to save some (election) and choosing not to save others (reprobation).

Election is positive predestination: *God sovereignly and graciously chose to save individual sinners*. God predestined certain individuals (i.e., predetermined their destiny) for salvation.

Reprobation is negative predestination: *God sovereignly and justly chose to pass over nonelect sinners and punish them*.[9]

---

9. Some theologians label two aspects of God's decree of reprobation as *preterition* and *precondemnation*. (1) *Preterition* means that God sovereignly and justly chose to pass over nonelect sinners. He did not choose to save certain individual sinners; he chose to leave some sinners to themselves in their sins; he chose to withhold grace. God did not choose to pass over some sinners in the same way that he chose to save some sinners (see chap. 11), and his choice to pass over some sinners is based on his sovereign will (see chap. 7). (2) *Precondemnation* (or *predamnation*) means that God sovereignly and justly chose to hold accountable the sinners he passed over by punishing them. God will

God predestined certain individuals (i.e., predetermined their destiny) for condemnation. (*Proörizō* does not refer specifically to reprobation, but other destine-words do. See 1 Pet. 2:8; cf. Rom. 9:22; Jude 4.) The word *reprobation* does not appear in the Bible, but it is a common label that theologians use for a reality that I believe the Bible teaches.[10]

The range of meanings for *election* and (positive) *predestination* overlaps. They can function as synonyms. What distinguishes them is that election emphasizes the *who* and predestination emphasizes the *what*.[11] That is, election emphasizes that God chose *us*, and predestination emphasizes what God chose us *for*—"to be conformed to the image of his Son" (Rom. 8:29) and "for adoption to himself as sons" (Eph. 1:5). But we should not overemphasize this distinction between the *who* and the *what* because (1) God chose us *for* something—"that we should be holy and blameless" (Eph. 1:4)—and (2) God "predestined *us*" (Eph. 1:5; cf. Rom. 8:29–30). (See table 0.3.)

---

execute his decree when he righteously condemns people for their sins; hell is what sinners deserve. E.g., see Francis Turretin, *Institutes of Elenctic Theology*, ed. James T. Dennison Jr., trans. George Musgrave Giger, 3 vols. (Phillipsburg, NJ: P&R, 1992–1997), 1:380–82; Peter Sammons, *Reprobation and God's Sovereignty: Recovering a Biblical Doctrine* (Grand Rapids, MI: Kregel Academic, 2022), 121–27.

10. I offer you the same invitation John Piper does: "I invite you to penetrate through words into reality. *Providence* is a word not found in the Bible. In that sense, it is like the words *Trinity*, *discipleship*, *evangelism*, *exposition*, *counseling*, *ethics*, *politics*, and *charismatics* [and I would add *reprobation*]. People who love the Bible and believe that it is God's word want to know what the Bible teaches, not just what it says. They want to know the *reality* being presented, not just the *words* that were written. . . . The task of a teacher is not just to read the Bible to his hearers, but to *explain* it. And explaining means using other words besides the ones in the text. Throughout the history of the church, heretics have frequently insisted on using only Bible words in defending their heresy." John Piper, *Providence* (Wheaton, IL: Crossway, 2021), 15–16; emphasis original.

11. See Geerhardus Vos, *Reformed Dogmatics*, ed. and trans. Richard B. Gaffin Jr., 5 vols. (Bellingham, WA: Lexham, 2013–2016), 1:112; Harold W. Hoehner, *Ephesians: An Exegetical Commentary* (Grand Rapids, MI: Baker Academic, 2002), 199, 228.

Table 0.3   Distinguishing the Synonyms *Election* and *(Positive) Predestination*

Election	(Positive) Predestination
Emphasizes the *who*: God chose *us*.	Emphasizes the *what*: God predestined us *for* something.
Includes the *what*: God chose us *for* something.	Includes the *who*: God predestined *us*.

I think "those whom he predestined" (Rom. 8:30) are synonymous with "God's elect" (Rom. 8:33), and I agree with Doug Moo that "chose" and "predestined" are "essentially equivalent" in Ephesians 1:4–5.[12]

In this book I use the terms *predestination, election,* and *reprobation* as shorthand for what I believe the Bible teaches. I am not being creative. This is the standard way that Reformed theologians use those three terms. For example, John Calvin explains,

> We call predestination God's eternal decree, by which he compacted with himself what he willed to become of each man. For all are not created in equal condition; rather, eternal life is foreordained for some, eternal damnation for others.

12. Douglas J. Moo, *A Theology of Paul and His Letters: The Gift of the New Realm in Christ*, Biblical Theology of the New Testament (Grand Rapids, MI: Zondervan, 2021), 272. A more form-based translation of Ephesians 1:4–5 is "*he chose* us in him before the foundation of the world, . . . *having predestined* us for adoption as sons." Most translations break up the single sentence of 1:3–14 into several English sentences and begin a new sentence in 1:5. For example, the ESV begins 1:5, "He predestined us." If the participle *proörizō* (*predestine*) modifies the verb "he chose," then it is not clear how God's predestining relates to his choosing—e.g., contemporaneous time (God chose us *when* he predestined us), antecedent time (God chose us *after* he predestined us), means (God chose us *by* predestining us), cause (God chose us *because* he predestined us), manner (God chose us *in a predestining manner*), purpose (God chose us *for the purpose of* predestining us), or result (God chose us *with the result that* he predestined us). I am not convinced that Paul intended to communicate such a precise relation between "he chose" and "having predestined." I think Paul is using the terms here as synonyms to emphasize God's sovereign choice. His stylistic variation is similar to saying, "he *loved* us . . . having *cherished* us" or "she *hugged* me . . . having *embraced* me." The participle ("having predestined us") restates and emphasizes the main idea ("he chose us") as Paul continues his prayer of praise, which he intended people to read and hear aloud. He is using a common rhetorical style of his day. See S. M. Baugh, *Ephesians*, Evangelical Exegetical Commentary (Bellingham, WA: Lexham, 2015), 83 (and 62–70).

Therefore, as any man has been created to one or the other of these ends, we speak of him as predestined to life or to death.[13]

Similarly, J. I. Packer explains, "It has become usual in Protestant theology to define God's predestination as including both his decision to save some from sin (election) and his decision to condemn the rest for their sin (reprobation), side by side."[14]

4. What Are the Two Main Ways Theologians Have Understood Predestination?

If you walk into a room where two people are hours into a deep conversation, it would be responsible and respectful for you to have a basic understanding of what they are talking about before you weigh in on the conversation. As we consider predestination, it is helpful to remember that we are entering a conversation that theologians have been carrying on for centuries, so before we continue that conversation, it would be responsible and respectful to have a basic understanding of what some influential theologians have argued.

Specifically, it would be helpful to be familiar with the two major positions on predestination—commonly called *Arminianism* and *Calvinism*. Those labels are common nicknames or shorthand for different ways of thinking about predestination. Authors have written entire books on how Augustine (354–430) or John Calvin (1509–1564) or Jacob Arminius (1560–1609) or John Wesley (1703–1791) understood election. We are not focusing on historical theology in this book, but we should value it and benefit from it. So let's get our bearings by surveying the

---

13. Calvin, *Institutes*, 3.21.5 (926).

14. J. I. Packer, *Concise Theology: A Guide to Historic Christian Beliefs* (Wheaton, IL: Tyndale House, 1993), 38. Cf. Turretin, *Institutes of Elenctic Theology*, 1:332–33; Robert Letham, *Systematic Theology* (Wheaton, IL: Crossway, 2019), 173–74; Wayne Grudem, *Systematic Theology: An Introduction to Biblical Doctrine*, 2nd ed. (Grand Rapids, MI: Zondervan, 2020), 1520.

two main ways theologians have understood predestination in the context of larger theological frameworks.[15]

Instead of focusing primarily on Arminius and Calvin, I am focusing on the mainstream teaching in the Arminian and Calvinist traditions without getting sidetracked on intramural debates. Table 0.4 compares Arminianism and Calvinism on six issues.

Table 0.4   Comparing Arminianism and Calvinism

Issue	Arminianism	Calvinism
God's sovereignty	God's sovereignty is general. God is in charge of everything, but he does not ordain everything. For example, God does not ordain sin; he allows sin to preserve man's free will.	God's sovereignty is meticulous. God is in charge of everything, and he ordains everything— even sin.
Man's depravity	As a result of Adam's fall, man is radically depraved and thus cannot repent and believe in Jesus without God's special grace. (God gives that special grace to everyone; Arminians call it prevenient grace.)[a]	As a result of Adam's fall, man is radically depraved and thus cannot repent and believe in Jesus without God's special grace. (God gives that special grace to only some people—the elect; this grace is effective and invincible.)

15. Historical theology typically focuses on four broad periods of church history: (1) the early church (1st c.–600), (2) the Middle Ages (600–1500), (3) the Reformation and post-Reformation (1500–1750), and (4) the modern period (1750–present). For a concise survey of predestination in these four periods, see Gregg R. Allison, *Historical Theology: An Introduction to Christian Doctrine—A Companion to Wayne Grudem's "Systematic Theology"* (Grand Rapids, MI: Zondervan, 2011), 453–73. See also Peter Sammons, *Reprobation: From Augustine to the Synod of Dort—The Historical Development of the Reformed Doctrine of Reprobation*, Reformed Historical Theology 63 (Göttingen: Vandenhoeck & Ruprecht, 2020); David Gibson and Jonathan Gibson, eds., *Chosen Not for Good in Me: Unconditional Election in Historical, Biblical, Theological, and Pastoral Perspective* (Wheaton, IL: Crossway, forthcoming), esp. chaps. 1–10 (the book title is provisional).

(Table 0.4 continued)

Issue	Arminianism	Calvinism
God's election	God's election is conditional. God chose to save sinners he foresaw would freely choose to believe in Christ.	God's election is unconditional. God sovereignly chose to save individual sinners based on his forelove.
Christ's atonement	The intention of Christ's atonement is general—that is, it provides salvation for all people without exception. Christ's atonement provides payment for the sins of all people, but God applies it to only those who repent and believe (i.e., the elect).	The intention of Christ's atonement is definite—that is, it provides and accomplishes salvation for only the elect. Christ's atonement provides payment for the sins of only the elect, and God applies it to only the elect.
The Spirit's grace and man's will	The Spirit's saving grace is universal and ultimately resistible—that is, every individual receives prevenient grace and can reject it. Man has a free will in the sense that he can make equally alternative choices in the same circumstances. So man is equally free to choose or reject Christ. Theologically, repentance and faith precede and cause regeneration.	The Spirit's saving grace is particular and ultimately irresistible—that is, it is persuasively effective for the elect. Man has a free will in the sense that he chooses what he most wants. The Spirit does not force a man to repent and believe against his will; the Spirit transforms a man's heart with the result that he wants to repent and believe. Theologically, regeneration precedes and causes repentance and faith.
The believer's perseverance	Genuine believers can finally fall away from the faith. They can fail to continue in the faith and thus will not be eternally saved.	Genuine believers (i.e., the elect) cannot finally fall away from the faith. Believers continue in the faith (perseverance) because God preserves them as eternally secure (preservation).

a. On prevenient grace, see the end of chap. 5.

God's sovereignty (the first issue in table 0.4) is the overarching category.[16] Everything follows from how you define God's sovereignty. If God's sovereignty is meticulous and not merely general—that is, if God is in charge of everything and ordains everything—then it follows that God also ordains every human's eternal destiny. It's an argument from the greater to the lesser. If I can pick up a refrigerator, then I can pick up a gallon of milk that's in the refrigerator. If God ordains everything, then he ordains a man's salvation.

The final five issues in table 0.4 correspond to the popular Calvinist acronym TULIP:

T̲otal depravity
U̲nconditional election
L̲imited atonement
I̲rresistible grace
P̲erseverance of the saints

The origin of the TULIP acronym is unknown. "The five points of Calvinism" were originally a five-point response to Arminians. In 1610, Arminius's followers presented a Remonstrance (a written protest) in the Netherlands containing five points that objected to John Calvin's *Institutes* and arguably to Reformed confessions. The Synod at Dort (1618–1619) unanimously condemned the Remonstrance and responded to it with their own five-point answer, and that five-point structure persists.[17] The popular TULIP acronym is misleading (see table 0.5),[18] but it is so memorable and well-known that Calvinists still use it.

---

16. This is why some systematic theologies organize predestination under the doctrine of God. Predestination is an aspect of God's sovereign decree. Other systematic theologies organize predestination under the doctrine of salvation since predestination concerns whom God chose to save. Theological topics are organically connected, and theologians may responsibly address predestination under the doctrine of God or salvation.

17. For a concise and accessible commentary on the Canons of Dort, see Kevin DeYoung, *Grace Defined and Defended: What a 400-Year-Old Confession Teaches Us about Sin, Salvation, and the Sovereignty of God* (Wheaton, IL: Crossway, 2019).

18. Cf. Roger Nicole, "Calvinism: The Five Points," 1974; repr., *Reformed Faith and Practice* 1 (2016): 62–68; Kenneth J. Stewart, *Ten Myths About Calvinism: Recovering the Breadth of the Reformed Tradition* (Downers Grove, IL: InterVarsity Press, 2011),

Table 0.5 How TULIP Is Misleading

TULIP	More Accurate (Less Misleading)	Explanation
Total depravity	Man's pervasive corruption	*Total* may sound like *absolute* or *utter*. The point is not depravity's *depth* (as if every person is as wicked as he possibly can be) but depravity's *breadth*. Every aspect of a person is corrupt. Man is radically (i.e., at the *root*) corrupted in the sense that evil pollutes his whole being—body, will, mind, conscience, etc. The corruption is all-pervasive—like salt permeating sea water or chlorine permeating pool water. Pervasive (or radical) corruption describes man's condition, and total inability describes the result of that condition. That is, unregenerate man cannot repent and believe in Jesus apart from God's special grace.
Unconditional election	The Father's sovereign election	*Unconditional* may sound like *arbitrary*—as if God the Father selected individuals randomly and whimsically (e.g., flipping a coin or picking names out of a hat). The point is that before God created the world he sovereignly chose to save specific individuals by name without basing his choice on any human conditions. The all-wise God has reasons for everything he does, and we don't know what all of them are.
Limited atonement	Christ's definite atonement	*Limited* may sound like *tiny, weak, sparse, defective.* But Christ's atonement is global, powerful, lavish, perfect. The point is that Christ did not die for everyone in the same way. Christ definitively provided and accomplished redemption for particular individuals—the same individuals whom the Father elected (sovereign election) and whom the Spirit regenerates (effective grace). The members of the triune God do not work contrary to each other but in a unified way to accomplish the same goals.

TULIP	More Accurate (Less Misleading)	Explanation
Irresistible grace	The Spirit's effective grace	*Irresistible* may sound like what a robber does (*attack, force, steal*) or what a prostitute does (*tempt, allure, seduce*). Further, *irresistible* may sound like it is *impossible to resist* God's grace. Of course, it is possible to resist God's grace (Acts 7:51). The point is that it is impossible to *ultimately* resist God's special saving grace. It's effective (i.e., it successfully produces the result that God intends) because it's invincible (i.e., it's too powerful to defeat or overcome). When God's Spirit causes a man to be born again, he gives spiritual life to a man who was spiritually dead; he changes that man's heart by effectively calling him so that he willingly (not reluctantly or protestingly) comes to Christ. Regeneration is not a joint effort in which the Spirit contributes his part and we contribute ours; the Spirit's effective grace is entirely one-sided—like when Jesus cried, "Lazarus, come out!" (John 11:43).
Perseverance of the saints	God's preservation of the saints	*Perseverance* may sound like a believer's activity is the key. The point is that believers persevere *because God preserves them*. (Those who claim to be neither Calvinists nor Arminians typically like this teaching—or at least a truncated version of it: "Once saved, always saved.") We work out our salvation because God works in us the willing and the working (Phil. 2:12–13).

TULIP presents a logical order according to Calvinism:

- It starts with man's desperate need to be saved (T), and the rest explains how God saves his people.
- God the Father chose to save specific individuals without basing his choice on the condition of faith (U).
- God the Son atoned particularly for those individuals the Father chose to save (L).
- God the Spirit effectively calls them to himself (I).
- God enables them to persevere until they die or Christ returns (P).

J. I. Packer summarizes Calvinism in three words: "*God saves sinners.*"[19]

This introductory chapter to a concise book on predestination is not the place to explain in depth the complexities and nuances of Arminianism and Calvinism. Many other resources helpfully argue for Arminianism[20] or for Calvinism.[21] The purpose of this short survey is to orient us to how predestination is part of larger frameworks for understanding

---

75–98, 291–92; Richard A. Muller, *Calvin and the Reformed Tradition: On the Work of Christ and the Order of Salvation* (Grand Rapids, MI: Baker Academic, 2012), 58–62; Douglas Wilson, "Triune Grace – Douglas Wilson | Reformed Basics #6," Christ Church, February 2, 2021, YouTube Video https://www.youtube.com/.

19. J. I. Packer, *A Quest for Godliness: The Puritan Vision of the Christian Life* (Wheaton, IL: Crossway, 1990), 130; emphasis original. Cf. Jonah 2:9: "Salvation belongs to the LORD."

20. E.g., Jerry L. Walls and Joseph R. Dongell, *Why I Am Not a Calvinist* (Downers Grove, IL: InterVarsity Press, 2004); Roger E. Olson, *Arminian Theology: Myths and Realities* (Downers Grove, IL: IVP Academic, 2006); Olson, *Against Calvinism* (Grand Rapids, MI: Zondervan, 2011); F. Leroy Forlines, *Classical Arminianism: A Theology of Salvation*, ed. J. Matthew Pinson (Nashville: Randall House, 2011); J. Matthew Pinson, *40 Questions about Arminianism*, 40 Questions (Grand Rapids, MI: Kregel Academic, 2022).

21. E.g., Thomas R. Schreiner and Bruce A. Ware, eds., *The Grace of God, the Bondage of the Will*, 2 vols. (Grand Rapids, MI: Baker, 1995); Robert A. Peterson and Michael D. Williams, *Why I Am Not an Arminian* (Downers Grove, IL: InterVarsity Press, 2004); John Piper, *Five Points: Toward a Deeper Experience of God's Grace*, in *The Collected Works of John Piper*, ed. David Mathis and Justin Taylor, 14 vols. (Wheaton, IL: Crossway, 2017), 8:543–620; Shawn D. Wright, *40 Questions about Calvinism*, 40 Questions (Grand Rapids, MI: Kregel Academic, 2019); Curt Daniel, *The History and Theology of Calvinism* (Darlington, UK: Evangelical Press, 2020).

how God saves sinners. Arminians and Calvinists agree on many evangelical doctrines, but they fundamentally differ on predestination.

You have probably figured it out by now, but I'll say it in case you are still wondering: I am a Calvinist. I use the term *Calvinism* as theological shorthand. I do not follow John Calvin in a proud or partisan way (see 1 Cor. 1:12) or in every way, but I am convinced that Calvinism faithfully expresses what the Bible teaches. My goal in this book is not to explain and defend what *John Calvin* wrote about predestination—though I essentially agree with him.[22] My goal is to explain and defend what *the Bible* teaches about predestination.

5. How Important Is Predestination?

Some Bible teachings are more important than other Bible teachings. Paul writes, "I delivered to you as of *first importance* what I also received" (1 Cor. 15:3). "First importance" implies that although everything in the Bible is important, not everything is *equally* important. Some doctrines are *more* important than others. That is why Jesus could refer to "the weightier matters of the law" (Matt. 23:23). We can distinguish at least three levels of importance (see table 0.6).[23]

---

22. See Calvin, *Institutes*, 3.21–24 (920–87). Cf. Fred H. Klooster, *Calvin's Doctrine of Predestination*, 2nd ed. (Grand Rapids, MI: Baker, 1977); Donald Sinnema, "Calvin's View of Reprobation," in *Calvin for Today*, ed. Joel R. Beeke (Grand Rapids, MI: Reformation Heritage Books, 2009), 115–36; Joel R. Beeke, "Calvin on Sovereignty, Providence, and Predestination," *Puritan Reformed Journal* 2, no. 2 (2010): 77–105; Beeke, *Debated Issues in Sovereign Predestination: Early Lutheran Predestination, Calvinian Reprobation, and Variations in Genevan Lapsarianism*, Reformed Historical Theology 42 (Göttingen: Vandenhoeck & Ruprecht, 2017), 83–162; Paul Helm, "Predestination," in *John Calvin: For a New Reformation*, ed. Derek W. H. Thomas and John W. Tweeddale (Wheaton, IL: Crossway, 2019), 449–70; David Gibson, "Mercy on Every Side: Calvin's Misunderstood Doctrine of Election," Desiring God, August 18, 2020, https://www.desiringgod.org/.

23. On distinguishing the importance of Bible teachings, see R. Albert Mohler Jr., "A Call for Theological Triage and Christian Maturity," *Albert Mohler* (blog), July 12, 2005, https://albertmohler.com/. Cf. Naselli, *How to Understand and Apply the New Testament*, 295–96.

Table 0.6   Three Levels of Predestination's Importance

Level		Labels		
1	First-level issues	Essential for the Christian faith	Dogma	Funda-mental teachings
2	Second-level issues	Crucial for church health but not essential for the Christian faith	Doctrine	Denomi-national distinctives
3	Third-level issues	Important but not essential for the Christian faith or crucial for church health	Disputable matters	Matters of conscience

You do not have to affirm the Calvinist view of predestination in order to be a Christian (level 1). But predestination is not merely a matter of conscience (level 3). I think affirming the Bible's teaching on predestination is crucial for a church to be robustly healthy (level 2).

My church has two statements of faith—one that the pastors (also called elders) affirm and one that the members affirm. The Elder Affirmation of Faith upholds Calvinism (without using that word), and the Member Affirmation of Faith upholds basic Christianity (plus credobaptism). An Arminian may be a *member* of our church but not a *pastor* of our church, and members know that our church teaches in accord with the Elder Affirmation of Faith. We think it is crucial that our pastors and other teachers be aligned on predestination because it directly affects how we make disciples. It affects what and how we preach and teach and sing and pray and counsel.

6. How Will We Explore What the Bible Teaches about Predestination?

This book attempts to answer specific questions regarding what the Bible teaches about predestination. Part 1 addresses election (chaps. 1–10), and part 2 addresses reprobation (chaps. 11–15):

1. What is the goal of election?
2. When did God choose to save some humans?
3. Did God choose to save individuals?
4. Did God choose to save individuals based on foreseen faith?
5. Is unconditional election unfair?
6. Do we have free will?
7. Does election contradict God's desire that all humans be saved?
8. How does God accomplish his plan to save individuals?
9. How do I know if God has elected me?
10. Did God elect babies who die?
11. Who ultimately causes reprobation?
12. How does God accomplish reprobation?
13. What is the result of reprobation?
14. What is the goal of reprobation?
15. Who deserves blame for reprobation?

I crafted and arranged these questions as I studied what the Bible teaches about predestination. This is my attempt to synthesize and organize both what the Bible explicitly teaches and what we may reasonably infer.[24] Such correlating or systematizing is doing systematic theology.[25]

---

24. I am approaching predestination both inductively and deductively. I ask questions in all the chapter titles and then explore the answers (inductive), and I summarize what I have inductively discovered by making assertions and supporting them with Bible passages (deductive). In my research I began with questions and Bible passages and then let those passages lead to answers, but this book would be at least three times longer if I argued entirely inductively.

25. On my theological method, see Naselli, *How to Understand and Apply the New Testament*; Jason S. DeRouchie, Oren R. Martin, and Andrew David Naselli, *40 Questions about Biblical Theology*, 40 Questions (Grand Rapids, MI: Kregel Academic, 2020). Cf. Layton Talbert, "Levels of Systematic Theology and the Role of Logic," *Journal of Biblical Theology and Worldview* 1, no. 2 (2021): 4–22.

PART 1

Vessels of Mercy

What Does the Bible Teach about Election?

A man is drowning in the ocean, and a lifeguard saves him with his paddle board.

A toddler is trapped in her burning home, and a fireman saves her by cradling her in his arms as he rushes through the flames and smoke.

A pregnant woman's infant son has the umbilical cord wrapped tightly around his neck, and a doctor saves him with an emergency C-section.

An American woman is held hostage by a terrorist, and a Navy SEAL rescues her.

To save a person means to rescue that person from harm or danger.

The ultimate danger is eternal punishment for rebelling against God. That is what we deserve in order for justice to be served. In this life we protest against injustice because we deeply desire that justice be served. God is just, so he punishes all sin perfectly and completely. And *God sovereignly and graciously chose to save individuals*. The Bible calls that *election*.

1

What Is the Goal of Election?

Why begin with the *goal* of election? Because we can better understand what we see if we know what the goal is. I can better understand why men are using dynamite to blow up part of a mountain if I know that their goal is to build a tunnel for a highway through that part of the mountain. If I did not understand their goal, I would not understand the reason for the explosions. Similarly, if we understand God's goal for election, then we can better understand what happens that leads to that goal.[1]

But it is rather difficult to summarize only one goal for election. My favorite tweet by John Piper explains why: "God never does only one thing. In everything he does he is doing thousands of things. Of these we know perhaps half a dozen."[2] That is about how many goals of election God has revealed to us in

---

1. Cf. John Piper, *Providence* (Wheaton, IL: Crossway, 2021), 24.
2. John Piper (@JohnPiper), Twitter, December 18, 2009, 1:01 p.m., https://twitter .com/JohnPiper/status/6803509843.

Scripture. I'll attempt to summarize them in a single statement after we work through them.

Election has a reputation for being impractical, esoteric, divisive, and scary. But that is not how God talks about election. God has revealed at least eight of his overlapping goals of election. The first six goals are different ways of saying that God's goal is *to save us*; the final two goals are negative and positive ways of expressing that the ultimate goal of election is *to praise God's glorious grace*.

Goal 1: To Save Us on the Day of the Lord

Paul thanks God that he chose to save the Thessalonian believers: "We ought always to give thanks to God for you, brothers beloved by the Lord, because God chose you as the firstfruits *to be saved*, through sanctification by the Spirit and belief in the truth" (2 Thess. 2:13). God chose us "for salvation" (NASB, CSB, NET)—that is, to save us from our sins and the judgment we deserve. In the context of Paul's letters to the Thessalonians, this salvation likely refers to when God saves us on the day of the Lord (cf. 1 Thess. 2:16; 5:8–10; 2 Thess. 2:10).[3] The day of the Lord is when God will decisively judge and defeat his enemies and deliver and vindicate his people.

Practical application. Election encourages us that God loves us and that our future salvation on judgment day depends on God's choice, not our effort. We are "beloved by the Lord" (2 Thess. 2:13). God will not finally deliver and vindicate us as a result of our earning his favor. God will finally deliver and vindicate us because he chose us. God chose us in order to save us.

---

3. Cf. Jeffrey A. D. Weima, *1–2 Thessalonians*, Baker Exegetical Commentary on the New Testament (Grand Rapids, MI: Baker Academic, 2014), 551.

Goal 2: That We Should Be Holy and Blameless

Paul praises God because "he [God the Father] chose us in him [Christ] before the foundation of the world, *that we should be holy and blameless before him*" (Eph. 1:4). One goal of election is that when we stand before God we will be morally pure and blameless.

"Blameless" recalls Old Testament sacrifices of animals "without blemish" (e.g., Lev. 4:3, 23, 28, 32) and Christ's ultimate substitutionary sacrifice (Heb. 9:14; 1 Pet. 1:19). For us to be holy and blameless is a goal of election in that God not only frees us from sin's penalty and enslaving power but also will ultimately free us from sin's very presence in our hearts (cf. 1 Cor. 1:8; Col. 1:22; Phil. 1:9; 1 Thess. 3:13; Jude 24). Christ plans to "present the church to himself in splendor, without spot or wrinkle or any such thing, that she might be *holy and without blemish*" (Eph. 5:27; cf. 2 Cor. 11:2; Rev. 19:7–8).[4]

Practical application. Election encourages us that we will be holy and blameless before God. Can you imagine what it will be like to be completely free from our sins? We can praise God now for this glorious work he will do.

Election also motivates us to be holy and blameless now. The New Testament portrays God's saving and sanctifying work with three tenses:

- You have been saved (past). You are being saved (present). You will be saved (future).
- You have been sanctified (past). You are being sanctified (present). You will be sanctified (future).

Sometimes God reasons that you must *become what you are*: you are holy, so become holy (e.g., Rom. 6:13; 1 Cor. 5:7;

---

4. "Holy and without blemish" in Ephesians 5:27 translates the same words that "holy and blameless" translate in 1:4.

6:11, 17). Sometimes God reasons that you must *become what you will be*: you will be holy, so become holy. Ephesians 1:4 fits here. God chose us so that at the day of Christ we would be holy and blameless. That implies that we should become increasingly holy and blameless now (cf. Phil. 2:15). We are no longer in bondage to sin's enslaving power (Rom. 6), and we must put our sin to death (Col. 3).

Goal 3: To Be Conformed to the Image of God's Son

"Those whom he [God] foreknew he also predestined *to be conformed to the image of his Son*, in order that he [the Son] might be the firstborn among many brothers" (Rom. 8:29). One goal of election is to conform us to the "image" or likeness or appearance of God's Son. It includes our moral character and our physical bodies. We currently have bodies like Adam's natural, earthy body, but when Christ returns, our bodies will be like Christ's supernatural, heavenly body (cf. 1 Cor. 15:45–49). Christ "will transform our lowly body to be like his glorious body" (Phil. 3:21).

Practical application. Election encourages us that we will be conformed to the image of God's Son. Election also motivates us to be conformed to the image of God's Son now. We must live in the present in light of the future. Because we know that God will conform us to the image of his Son, we should be and behave like the Son now (cf. 1 Cor. 15:49; 2 Cor. 3:18; 4:16–5:9; Col. 3:10).

Goal 4: For Adoption as Sons to God

Paul praises God because "in love he predestined us *for adoption to himself as sons* through Jesus Christ" (Eph. 1:4–5). One goal for election is for our adoption as sons to God.

The phrase "for adoption . . . as sons" translates a single Greek word that refers to "those who believe in Christ and are accepted by God as God's children . . . with full rights."[5] In its Greco-Roman context, this custom guaranteed that an adopted son had all the rights and privileges of a natural-born son. A man who headed a household would adopt a male not related by blood and become his father just as if the boy were his biological son.[6] That beautifully pictures what God did for us when we were "sons of disobedience" and "children of wrath" (Eph. 2:2, 3). God has legally adopted us (Rom. 8:14–17; Gal. 4:5–7), and we await the culmination of that adoption when God will redeem our bodies (Rom. 8:23).

One of the privileges of adoption to sonship is that we become heirs (Rom. 8:17; cf. Gal. 3:29; 4:7). We obtain an inheritance. That is likely what Paul highlights in Ephesians 1:11: "*In him we have obtained an inheritance*, having been [because we were (CSB)] predestined according to the purpose of him who works all things according to the counsel of his will."[7] If we become heirs *because* God predestined us, then a goal of predestination is that we become heirs. But what do we inherit? It is not clear in Ephesians 1:11, 14, or 18. But 5:5 suggests that

---

5. BDAG 1024 (υἱοθεσία).

6. Does this adoption *as sons* exclude females? No. That is why some translations say "adoption as sons *and daughters*" (NASB) or "adopt us as his children" (NIrV) or "adopt us into his own family" (NLT). But those translations fail to capture that Paul is referring to a Greco-Roman practice in which the head of a household adopted a male as his son with all the rights that a natural-born son would have. Sons had the privilege of inheriting property. Sonship language (and not merely *children* language, as Paul uses in Rom. 8:16–17) also preserves the "sons-in-the-Son solidarity that shapes Pauline theology." David B. Garner, *Sons in the Son: The Riches and Reach of Adoption in Christ* (Phillipsburg, NJ: P&R, 2016), 52. In this adoption metaphor, women get to be *sons*, just as in the marriage metaphor, men get to be a *bride* (Eph. 5:22–32). On how the background for Paul's adoption metaphor includes both Greco-Roman adoption and Israelite divine sonship, see Joshua A. Maurer, "Adoption in Romans: Destined to Be Conformed to the Image of His Son" (Wheaton College, PhD diss., 2022), 44–126.

7. I say "likely" because "we have obtained an inheritance" could instead mean something like "we were allotted to God as his portion" in the sense that "we are God's inheritance" or "we were also chosen" (NIV). But that is less likely because this sentence (Eph. 1:3–14) later distinguishes us from the inheritance: the Holy Spirit is "the guarantee of our inheritance until we acquire possession of it" (1:14). See Frank Thielman, *Ephesians*, Baker Exegetical Commentary on the New Testament (Grand Rapids, MI: Baker Academic, 2010), 72–73.

the inheritance is God's end-time kingdom: "Everyone who is sexually immoral or impure, or who is covetous (that is, an idolater), has no *inheritance in the kingdom of Christ and God*" (cf. 1 Cor. 6:9–10; 15:50; Gal. 5:21). More specifically, the inheritance is God himself: "we are children of God, and if children, then heirs—*heirs of God* and fellow heirs with Christ" (Rom. 8:16–17). God chose us *for himself*. God chose us *for God*.[8]

Practical application. Election encourages us that we are secure as sons who belong to God. We deeply long to belong—to be loved, to have a home, to be part of a family, to be part of something great and meaningful. What ultimately satisfies that desire is being adopted as a son of God. That is what God predestined us for.

Goal 5: To Obey the Gospel and Be Sprinkled with Christ's Blood

Peter addresses his first letter, "*To those who are elect* exiles of the Dispersion in Pontus, Galatia, Cappadocia, Asia, and Bithynia, according to the foreknowledge of God the Father, in the sanctification of the Spirit, *for obedience* to Jesus Christ and *for sprinkling with his blood*" (1 Pet. 1:1–2). A more form-based translation of those final two phrases is "for obedience and sprinkling of the blood of Jesus Christ."[9] In other words, Peter describes the purpose of election with two phrases: "[1] to be obedient and [2] to be sprinkled with the blood of Jesus Christ" (CSB). To be elect for *obedience* and *sprinkling* most

---

8. Cf. Trevor J. Burke, *Adopted into God's Family: Exploring a Pauline Metaphor*, New Studies in Biblical Theology 22 (Downers Grove, IL: IVP Academic, 2006), 98.

9. Form-based Bible translations prioritize reproducing the form of the Hebrew or Greek in English (e.g., NASB, ESV). Another approach prioritizes reproducing the meaning in natural English (e.g., NLT). Cf. Andrew David Naselli, *How to Understand and Apply the New Testament: Twelve Steps from Exegesis to Theology* (Phillipsburg, NJ: P&R, 2017), 50–81.

likely refers to the moment of conversion when (1) the Spirit enables a sinner to obey the gospel—to repent and believe in Christ—and (2) Christ cleanses and forgives the repenting and believing sinner. The Old Testament background is that Israelites entered the old covenant by pledging to obey God and were sprinkled with blood from burnt offerings (Ex. 24:3–8). Similarly, we enter the new covenant by obeying the gospel and are sprinkled with Christ's blood (cf. Heb. 10:22; 12:24).[10] So one goal of election is that we would obey the gospel and be sprinkled with the blood of Jesus Christ—that is, for our *conversion* and *forgiveness*.

Practical application. Election encourages us that our conversion and forgiveness depend on God's choice, not our effort. God does not convert and cleanse us as a result of our earning his favor. God converts and cleanses us because he chose us; that is, he chose us in order to convert and cleanse us.

Goal 6: That We May Be with Jesus to See His Glory

Jesus prayed, "Father, I desire that they also, whom you have given me, *may be with me where I am, to see my glory that you have given me* because you loved me before the foundation of the world" (John 17:24). Jesus does not say, "The Father *chose* you so that you may be with me to see my glory." So what is my warrant for saying that one goal of *election* is that we may be with Jesus to see his glory? My warrant is twofold:

1. The people whom the Father gave the Son refers to those whom the Father chose (i.e., the elect).[11] Jesus repeatedly (and exclusively) prays for them here (17:2, 6–9, 20, 24). The reason

10. See D. A. Carson, "1 Peter," in *Commentary on the New Testament Use of the Old Testament*, ed. G. K. Beale and D. A. Carson (Grand Rapids, MI: Baker Academic, 2007), 1016–17; Thomas R. Schreiner, *1 and 2 Peter and Jude*, 2nd ed., Christian Standard Commentary (Nashville: B&H, 2020), 51–54.

11. Cf. D. A. Carson, *The Gospel according to John*, Pillar New Testament Commentary (Grand Rapids, MI: Eerdmans, 1991), 569.

people come to Jesus is that the Father previously gave them to Jesus (6:37, 39, 65; 10:29; 17:6, 9, 24; 18:9).

2. There is a logical connection between the people the Father gave Jesus (i.e., the elect) and being with Jesus. Imagine that my mom said to me, "Andy, I desire that my grandchildren, whom you have driven to South Carolina, may be with me at my home to spend time with me." (Okay, she wouldn't say it just like that, but work with me—I'm trying to parallel John 17:24.) In other words, one of my goals for driving my daughters to South Carolina is that they may be with Grandma to enjoy her presence. Similarly, one of the goals for the Father's giving the elect to Jesus is that they may be with Jesus to see his glory. That is what makes the new heavens and the new earth supremely pleasurable. You get to be with Jesus when you "enter into the joy of your master" (Matt. 25:23).

John Piper asks a piercing question:

> If you could have heaven, with no sickness, and with all the friends you ever had on earth, and all the food you ever liked, and all the leisure activities you ever enjoyed, and all the natural beauties you ever saw, all the physical pleasures you ever tasted, and no human conflict or any natural disasters, could you be satisfied with heaven if Christ were not there?[12]

The gospel is good news not merely because God will rescue us from hell and because we can enjoy the pleasures of heaven. It is good news ultimately because we can enjoy God himself like we never could in our shackles of sin. The new heavens and new earth will be so satisfying because we get to enjoy the triune God more and more. Forever!

---

12. John Piper, *God Is the Gospel: Meditations on God's Love as the Gift of Himself*, in *The Collected Works of John Piper*, ed. David Mathis and Justin Taylor, 14 vols. (Wheaton, IL: Crossway, 2017), 6:262.

Practical application. Election exhilarates us that we will be with Jesus to see his glory. Nothing could be more happy, more satisfying, more awesome, more wonderful than being with the exalted Jesus. And King Jesus wants us to be with him so that we will see his glory that the Father has given him. We love to see the glory of places on this earth (my favorites include the Sunset Cliffs in San Diego, California; the Grand Canyon in Arizona; the Rocky Mountains in Colorado; and the North Shore in Minnesota). We love to marvel at beauty and grandeur. The most beautiful and grandest marvel we can imagine on earth or in outer space is but a shadow compared to the glory of the exalted King Jesus. We get to be with King Jesus to see his glory because God chose us.

Goal 7: To Shame the Mighty So That No Human Might Boast[13]

Paul tells the Corinthians (note the ABC-ABC pattern),

Consider your calling, brothers:

[a] not many of you were wise according to worldly standards,
　[b] not many were powerful,
　　[c] not many were of noble birth.

[a′] But God *chose* what is foolish in the world *to shame the wise*;
　[b′] *God chose* what is weak in the world *to shame the strong*;
　　[c′] *God chose* what is low and despised in the world, even things that are not, to bring *to nothing things that are, so that no human being*

---

13. This section updates Andrew David Naselli, "1 Corinthians," in *Romans–Galatians*, vol. 10 of *ESV Expository Commentary* (Wheaton, IL: Crossway, 2020), 235.

> *might boast in the presence of God.* (1 Cor.
> 1:26–29)

Paul says three times: "God chose . . . God chose . . . God chose." God sovereignly chose people in such a way that he enables them to believe and ensures that they do.

God chose mostly low-status people—not the mighty. When God sovereignly called the Corinthian believers, most of them were uneducated, noninfluential, and socially disdained—not the wise, influential, or highborn whom the worldly wise people would expect (cf. James 2:5).

For what purpose did God choose mostly low-status people? To shame, confound, and invalidate the mighty: the wise, influential, and highborn. This is how God has chosen his people throughout history—for example, by skipping the patriarchs' firstborns and by selecting Israel (Deut. 7:6–8; 9:4–6).

For what purpose did God choose mostly low-status people to shame, confound, and invalidate the mighty? "So that no human being might boast in the presence of God" (1 Cor. 1:29). God chose mostly low-status people so that the elect cannot boast in themselves. If God chose primarily the mighty, they might proudly presume that God had chosen them because of their high status.

Practical application. Election humbles us so that we cannot boast that God chose us because of our status or accomplishments or character or abilities. God did not choose us because we earned his favor. Election is 100 percent a gracious gift from God. "By grace you have been saved through faith. And this [being saved by grace through faith] is not your own doing; it is the gift of God, not a result of works, *so that no one may boast*" (Eph. 2:8–9). This illustrates the principle in 1 Corinthians 4:7: "What do you have that you did not receive? If then you received it, why do you boast as if you did not receive it?"

If God chose you, then don't boast that you somehow earned your salvation.

Goal 8: To Praise God's Glorious Grace and God's Glory

When you think of reasons to praise God for blessing you in Christ with every spiritual blessing, what comes to mind? You might reply, "God forgives my sins, declares me to be righteous, and redeems me." You should certainly praise God for those spiritual blessings. But how often do we think about praising God for choosing to save us? That is the very first blessing Paul specifies in his opening prayer in Ephesians 1:3–14: "Blessed be the God and Father of our Lord Jesus Christ, who has blessed us in Christ with every spiritual blessing in the heavenly places" (1:3). What is the evidence—the first specific basis—that Paul gives for praising God for blessing us in Christ? "Even as [for (NIV, CSB, NET)] *he chose us* in him before the foundation of the world" (1:4a). Praise God *because* he chose us.

Of the many goals for election, this one is *ultimate*:

In love he predestined us for adoption to himself as sons through Jesus Christ, according to the purpose of his will, *to the praise of his glorious grace*, with which he has blessed us in the Beloved. (Eph. 1:4b–6; cf. 2:7)

In him we have obtained an inheritance, having been predestined according to the purpose of him who works all things according to the counsel of his will, *so that we who were the first to hope in Christ might be to the praise of his glory*. (Eph. 1:11–12)

A more form-based translation of the first part of 1:6 is "to the praise of the glory of the grace of him." The word "glory" probably describes "grace," which is why translations say "glorious grace" (ESV, NIV, CSB, NLT).[14] God's grace (i.e., his undeserved kindness) is glorious in that it manifests his glory. What is God's glory in this sense? God's *holiness* is his God-ness (there is no one like him!), and God's *glory* is his holiness on display. God's holiness is who God is, and God's glory displays who God is (cf. 2 Cor. 4:4–6).[15] God predestined us so that we would "be to the praise of his glory" (Eph. 1:12).

God designed us to praise him, and he designed us to get a satisfying delight in praising him. We most glorify God when he most satisfies us.[16] This is what God made us for. God's ultimate goal for choosing to save us is so that we would praise his glorious grace and praise his glory. If you did something for the ultimate goal that others would praise you, you would be conceited. Only God can do this without being a megalomaniac because only God is intrinsically praiseworthy. It is actually *loving* for God to pursue our praise because praising God brings us the most joy.[17]

Above we considered the goal of election that we be conformed to the image of God's Son. What is the purpose of that goal? "Those whom he [God] foreknew he also predestined to be conformed to the image of his Son, *in order that he* [the Son] *might be the firstborn among many brothers*" (Rom. 8:29). The

---

14. I hope that is the correct reading because my wife and I named our second daughter Gloria Grace based on this passage!

15. Or one could say that God's glory is both intrinsic (i.e., the essence of God) and extrinsic (i.e., God displays his intrinsic glory). See Christopher W. Morgan and Robert A. Peterson, *The Glory of God and Paul: Text, Themes and Theology*, New Studies in Biblical Theology 58 (Downers Grove, IL: IVP Academic, 2022), 9–13. It is challenging to define God's glory because Scripture speaks of God's glory in at least seven distinct senses (5–8).

16. See the works of John Piper, especially his signature book, *Desiring God: Meditations of a Christian Hedonist*, 4th ed. (Colorado Springs, CO: Multnomah, 2011).

17. See John Piper, "Why God Is Not a Megalomaniac in Demanding to Be Worshiped," Desiring God, November 20, 2008, https://www.desiringgod.org/; Sam Storms, "Praise: The Consummation of Joy," Desiring God, November 17, 2013, https://www.desiringgod.org/; Walter J. Schultz, "Jonathan Edwards' Argument That God's End in Creation Must Manifest His Supreme Self-Regard," *Jonathan Edwards Studies* 4, no. 1 (2014): 81–103; Piper, *Providence*, 39–45, 53–56.

purpose of conforming us to the image of God's Son is that the Son will be "the firstborn"—that is, the first and most honored among God's resurrected children.

Practical application. Election motivates us to praise God's glorious grace and God's glory. That is the ultimate goal for which God chose us: "You are *a chosen race*, a royal priesthood, a holy nation, a people for his own possession, *that you may proclaim the excellencies of him who called you out of darkness into his marvelous light.* Once you were not a people, but now you are God's people; once you had not received mercy, but now you have received mercy" (1 Pet. 2:9–10). Ultimately, there are only two human races: the human race in Adam and the "chosen race" (cf. Isa. 43:21) in Christ.[18] God's ultimate goal for choosing us is that we would proclaim his excellencies—that is, that we would praise him. "From him [source] and through him [means] and to him [goal] are all things"; therefore, "To him be glory forever" (Rom. 11:36). "Not to us, O Lord, not to us, but to your name give glory" (Ps. 115:1). The goal of election is for God to save us so that we praise him for his glorious grace.

Responding with a Prayer

We praise you, Father, because you chose us in Christ before the foundation of the world that we should be holy and blameless before you. We praise you because you predestined us for adoption to yourself as sons through Jesus Christ to the praise of your glorious grace. Amen.

---

18. Cf. Andrew David Naselli, "What the Bible Teaches about Ethnic Harmony," *Midwestern Journal of Theology* 19, no. 2 (2020): 21–24.

2

When Did God Choose to Save Some Humans?

When exactly did God choose to save certain people? Does it occur at some point after a person's birth? Or while a person is a baby in the womb? Or before a person is conceived?

Paul explicitly answers this question: "The God and Father of our Lord Jesus Christ . . . chose us in him *before the foundation of the world*" (Eph. 1:3–4). What does that mean?

"Before the Foundation of the World" = Before God Created the World

The phrase "before the foundation of the world [Gk. *pro katabolēs kosmou*]" occurs two other times in the Bible (John 17:24; 1 Pet. 1:20), and both refer to when God the Father loved or foreknew God the Son:

1. Jesus prays, "Father, . . . you loved me *before the foundation of the world* [Gk. *pro katabolēs kosmou*]" (John 17:24). "Before the foundation of the world" refers to *before creation*. Jesus had just prayed, "Father, glorify me in your

own presence with the glory that I had with you *before the world existed*" (17:5). That harmonizes with the first line of the Gospel of John: "In the beginning was the Word" (1:1)—that is, prior to creation the Word already existed (cf. Gen. 1:1).

2. Peter describes Christ: "He was foreknown *before the foundation of the world* [Gk. *pro katabolēs kosmou*]" (1 Pet. 1:20). God the Father foreknew Christ *prior to creation.*

So when Paul says that God "chose us in him before the foundation of the world" (Eph. 1:4), he means that God chose us in Christ before creation—not merely before our choosing Christ; not merely before our birth; not merely before our conception; not merely before our parents or grandparents or great-grandparents. God chose us before he created the heavens and the earth.

So in Ephesians 1:4, John 17:24, and 1 Peter 1:20, "before the foundation of the world" means *before God created the world* or *prior to creation.* Do other passages that use the phrase "the foundation of the world" confirm this understanding? The phrase "the foundation of the world" (without the Greek word *pro* [*before*] in front of it) appears seven other times in the New Testament (Matt. 13:35; 25:34; Luke 11:50; Heb. 4:3; 9:26; Rev. 13:8; 17:8). These passages also refer to when God initially created the world.[1] The two passages in Revelation are especially significant for predestination:

1. "And all who dwell on earth will worship it [the beast], everyone whose name has not been written *before the foundation of the world* [Gk. *apo katabolēs kosmou*] in the book of life of the Lamb who was slain" (Rev. 13:8).

---

1. The only passage that may seem to be ambiguous is Luke 11:50–51: "the blood of all the prophets, shed *from the foundation of the world* . . . from the blood of Abel to the blood of Zechariah." The NET captures the sense of this phrase well: "the blood of all the prophets that has been shed *since the beginning of the world.*" The idea is that murdering has occurred throughout human history *from the beginning of time*—starting with Abel in Genesis and extending to Zechariah in the book of Chronicles at the end of the Hebrew canon. Translating the preposition as "since" (NASB, NIV, CSB, NET) may indicate that more clearly than "from."

2. "And the dwellers on earth whose names have not been written in the book of life *from the foundation of the world* [Gk. *apo katabolēs kosmou*] will marvel to see the beast, because it was and is not and is to come" (Rev. 17:8).

Those two passages say that before "the foundation of the world"—that is, prior to creation—God wrote the names of certain individuals (and not others) in "the book of life" (cf. Rev. 21:27).

In Matthew 25:34, Jesus explains, "The King will say to those on his right, 'Come, you who are blessed by my Father, inherit the kingdom prepared for you *from the foundation of the world* [Gk. *apo katabolēs kosmou*].'" This promise makes good sense in light of other passages that say God chose people prior to creation—people "purchased of old" or from the beginning of time (Ps. 74:2). God "saved us and called us" according to "his own purpose and grace, which he gave us in Christ Jesus *before the ages began*" (2 Tim. 1:9).[2]

So "the foundation of the world" refers to *when God initially created the world* or *at creation*. It refers to the beginning of creation, to the world's starting point.

God Chose to Save Humans before He Created the World

The universe is everything that is not God. Only God is eternal, infinite, and self-existent. God created the universe, so there

---

2. 2 Thessalonians 2:13 may also be relevant, but it depends on which Greek manuscripts accurately communicate what God breathed out. The CSB (cf. the ESV note, NASB, NET) reads, "We ought to thank God always for you, brothers and sisters loved by the Lord, because *from the beginning* [Gk. *ap archēs*] *God has chosen you for salvation* through sanctification by the Spirit and through belief in the truth." But it seems slightly more likely that the reading in the ESV (also NIV, NLT) is correct: "We ought always to give thanks to God for you, brothers beloved by the Lord, because *God chose you as the firstfruits* [Gk. *aparchēn*] *to be saved*, through sanctification by the Spirit and belief in the truth." Cf. Gordon D. Fee, *The First and Second Epistles to the Thessalonians*, New International Commentary on the New Testament (Grand Rapids, MI: Eerdmans, 2009), 301–2; Jeffrey A. D. Weima, *1–2 Thessalonians*, Baker Exegetical Commentary on the New Testament (Grand Rapids, MI: Baker Academic, 2014), 550–51.

was a time when the universe did not yet exist. What was God doing prior to creation?

Theologians commonly distinguish between the immanent (or ontological) Trinity and the economic (or functional) Trinity. The immanent Trinity is who God is apart from how he relates to creation, and the economic Trinity is who God is as he relates to creation.[3] Almost everything God reveals about himself in the Bible regards how he relates to creation, so we know relatively little about what God was doing prior to creation.

Jesus prayed, "Father, glorify me in your own presence with the glory that I had with you before the world existed" (John 17:5). Prior to creation the Father, the Son, and the Spirit shared the divine glory. Prior to creation the triune God was infinitely glorious; no other being yet existed, and thus no other being saw God's glorious holiness. Prior to creation the triune God decided to create the universe and to save certain individuals and not others. That is when God chose to save humans: "before the foundation of the world."

Paul writes, "We impart a secret and hidden wisdom of God, *which God decreed before the ages* for our glory" (1 Cor. 2:7). "Decreed" translates *proörizō*. Before God created the world, he decreed or "predestined" (NASB, CSB) or "destined" (NIV) or "determined" (NET) a wise plan for us. God "saved us and called us to a holy calling, not because of our works but because of *his own purpose* and grace, *which he gave us in Christ Jesus before the ages began*" (2 Tim. 1:9).

---

3. The immanent Trinity is "the Trinity in itself, or the three persons as they relate to one another without regard to creation," and the economic Trinity is "the Trinity as revealed in creation and salvation, acting in our world, in human history." Robert Letham, *The Holy Trinity: In Scripture, History, Theology, and Worship*, 2nd ed. (Phillipsburg, NJ: P&R, 2019), 579, 581; cf. Scott R. Swain, *The Trinity: An Introduction*, Short Studies in Systematic Theology (Wheaton, IL: Crossway, 2020), 105–20.

Responding with a Prayer

Thank you, God, for choosing to save me before you created the world. It is humbling and encouraging that I am part of "the eternal purpose that [you have] realized in Christ Jesus our Lord" (Eph. 3:11). Amen.

3

Did God Choose to Save Individuals?

Election is positive predestination—that is, *God's sovereign and gracious choice to save individual sinners.* God predestined certain individuals (i.e., predetermined their destiny) for salvation.

That is how I define *election* in the introduction above. Now I need to back up and clarify that I am defining a specific aspect of election.

- Election is either corporate or individual:
  - *Corporate* election is choosing a group of people.
  - *Individual* election is choosing specific individuals.
- Election is either to serve or to save.

So there are at least four kinds of election (see table 3.1).

Table 3.1   Four Kinds of Election

	Corporate Election	Individual Election
Election to Serve	1. Corporate election to serve (Israel)	2. Individual election to serve (e.g., the Messiah, Cyrus)
Election to Save	3. Corporate election to save (elect Israelites, elect Gentiles, all God's people as a group)	4. Individual election to save (each individual believer)

1. Corporate Election to Serve

God chose the people of Israel. This corporate election is not for salvation but for special favor and service. Moses tells Israel, "The LORD has chosen you to be a people for his treasured possession, out of all the peoples who are on the face of the earth" (Deut. 14:2; cf. Isa. 41:8–9). The Lord refers to his people as "my chosen people, / the people whom I formed for myself / that they might declare my praise" (Isa. 43:20–21; cf. Isa. 65:9, 15, 22; Ps. 106:5). The Lord refers to "Israel my chosen" (Isa. 45:4; cf. Ps. 105:6, 43; 1 Chron. 16:13). Paul preaches in a Jewish synagogue, "The God of this people Israel chose our fathers" (Acts 13:17).

2. Individual Election to Serve

God elected the Messiah—not to be saved but to save others. The Lord refers to the Messiah as "my servant . . . / *my chosen*, in whom my soul delights" (Isa. 42:1; quoted in Matt. 12:18). The Father refers to Jesus as chosen: "A voice came out of the cloud, saying, 'This is my Son, *my Chosen One*; listen to him!'" (Luke 9:35; cf. 23:35). Peter twice describes Christ as "*chosen* and precious" (1 Pet. 2:4, 6).

Another example of individual election to serve is Cyrus, the pagan king of Persia. As far as we know, God did not choose to save Cyrus; God chose Cyrus to accomplish a specific task—to deliver his chosen people Israel from exile so that they could return to Jerusalem and rebuild the temple. Isaiah does not use one of the words for election for Cyrus, but he uses the concept of election. Before Cyrus was born, Isaiah recorded that God

"says of Cyrus, 'He is my shepherd,
    and he shall fulfill all my purpose';
saying of Jerusalem, 'She shall be built,'
    and of the temple, 'Your foundation shall be laid.'"
        (Isa. 44:28)

God said to Cyrus,

"I call you by your name,
    I name you, though you do not know me." (Isa. 45:4)

3. Corporate Election to Save

Three examples of God's choosing to save groups are most prominent in Scripture:

1. Elect Israelites. God chose to save only some Israelites. Paul describes the remnant of ethnic Israelites—the spiritual Israel within physical Israel (Rom. 9:6–8)—as a group whom God "foreknew" (11:2) and as a group whom God chose to save: "a remnant, chosen by grace" (11:5); "the elect" (11:7); "as regards election, they are beloved for the sake of their forefathers" (11:28).

2. Elect Gentiles. James refers to a subset of Gentiles as chosen by God: "Simeon has related how God first visited the Gentiles, to take from them [select from among the Gentiles (NET)] a people for his name" (Acts 15:14).

3. All the Elect. Peter refers to God's people as a group as "a chosen race" (1 Pet. 2:9).

4. Individual Election to Save

The topic of this book is this fourth kind of election—individual election to save. The New Testament emphasizes that God chose to save *individuals*.[1]

> Jesus explains, "No *one* [singular] knows the Father except the Son and anyone to *whom* [singular] the Son chooses to reveal him" (Matt. 11:27).
>
> The Father gave specific individuals to the Son, and God will save each and every one of them. Jesus explains,

---

1. Choosing individuals is not unique to the New Testament. The people of Israel prayed, "You are the LORD, the God who chose Abram" (Neh. 9:7). The psalmist refers to Moses as the Lord's "chosen one" (Ps. 106:23). The Lord refers to David as "my chosen one" (Ps. 89:4; cf. 2 Sam. 6:21; Ps. 78:70). The Lord says, "O Zerubbabel . . . I have chosen you" (Hag. 2:23).

"*All that* [singular—*everyone whom*] the Father gives me will come to me, and *whoever* [singular—*the one who*] comes to me I will never cast out. . . . For this is the will of my Father, that *everyone who* [singular] looks on the Son and believes in him should have eternal life, and I will raise *him* [singular] up on the last day" (John 6:37, 40). Similarly, in Jesus's high priestly prayer, he thanks the Father for giving him authority "to give eternal life to all whom you have given him" (John 17:2; cf. 17:6–9, 20, 24; Heb. 2:13). A more form-based way to translate that is "so that *everyone whom* [singular] you have given to him, he may give to them eternal life" (cf. CSB, NET). The NLT translates, "He gives eternal life to *each one* you have given him."[2]

Luke reports, "As many as [all who (NIV, CSB, NET, NLT)] were appointed to eternal life believed" (Acts 13:48). If you as an individual believe in Christ, you believe because God appointed you as an individual to eternal life.

Paul refers to individuals in Romans 9:18–19, 21: "So then he has mercy on *whomever* [singular] he wills, and he hardens *whomever* [singular] he wills. You will say to me then, 'Why does he still find fault? For *who* [singular] can resist his will?' . . . Has the potter no right over the clay, to make out of the same lump *one* [singular] vessel for honorable use and *another* [singular] for dishonorable use?"

Paul tells the church in Rome, "Greet Rufus, *chosen* in the Lord" (Rom. 16:13). The individual man Rufus is "chosen." We can say that about every single person who is part of the elect. The group as a whole is chosen, and each individual in that group is chosen.

---

2. Cf. Bruce A. Ware, "Divine Election to Salvation: Unconditional, Individual, and Infralapsarian," in *Perspectives on Election: Five Views*, ed. Chad Owen Brand (Nashville: B&H Academic, 2006), 42–43.

God wrote the names of individuals in the book of life
before he created the world: "And all who dwell on
earth will worship it, *everyone whose* [singular] *name*
[singular] has not been written before the foundation
of the world in the book of life of the Lamb who was
slain" (Rev. 13:8).

Does the Bible Teach the Arminian View of Corporate Election?

Both Arminians and Calvinists believe that God chose to save
individuals as well as a group of people. Calvinists believe that
the New Testament emphasizes that God chose to save *individuals*, but some (not most) Arminians argue that God chose
to save primarily a *group* of people. Here is how some Arminians argue that corporate election is primary:

God elected Christ as Savior, and he elected primarily
a *group* of people (rather than specific individuals) in
Christ. Each individual decides whether or not he or she
will be united to Christ, God's elect one. A person who
decides to be united to Christ becomes elect. God foresaw
in eternity past that such persons would freely choose
Christ. The decisive reason some individuals become elect
and others do not is that some freely respond to God's
invitation to repent and believe in Christ and others do
not. When God elects an individual, he elects that person
for a specific task; individual election is for service, not
salvation.[3]

---

3. I am summarizing the book that makes the strongest case for corporate election
and against individual election: William W. Klein, *The New Chosen People: A Corporate
View of Election*, 2nd ed. (Eugene, OR: Wipf and Stock, 2015). E.g., Klein writes, "*When
the issue is 'election to salvation,' the NT writers speak of election only in corporate
terms*. . . . Does this mean that individuals are NOT elect unto salvation? Of course they
are! But these ones are elect *because of their membership in the elect people of God*.
They obtain their status as chosen because they belong to [the] body of chosen ones,
not because God specifically chose them for that position" (269–70; emphasis original).

Other Arminians do not hold the above view but instead emphasize individual conditional election. They think that the above view of corporate election is an unconvincing attempt to counter individual unconditional election (which Calvinists affirm).[4]

Did God elect *primarily a group of people* (rather than specific individuals) in Christ, then foresee in eternity past that some individuals would freely choose Christ, and then elect those individuals for service? No. We should reject the Arminian view of corporate election for at least seven reasons.

1. The Arminian view of corporate election is incompatible with unconditional election (see chap. 4). In the corporate election view, faith results in election, but the Bible teaches that election results in God-enabled faith (Eph. 1:3–14; 2:1–10).[5] Or as Bruce Ware puts it, "Effectual calling requires individual election."[6] The proof texts I cite in the following reasons are compelling in light of the scriptural framework of the Father's sovereign election, Christ's definite atonement, and the Spirit's effective grace. The persons of the Trinity are united in what they intend and how they act (see the introduction to chap. 8).

2. The Arminian view of corporate election emphasizes that God chose a group of people in Christ, but the New Testament emphasizes that God chose to save *individuals* (see the previous section above: "4. Individual Election to Save").[7]

See also Brian J. Abasciano, "Clearing Up Misconceptions about Corporate Election," *Ashland Theological Journal* 41 (2009): 59–90.

4. Cf. Jack W. Cottrell, "Conditional Election," in *Grace for All: The Arminian Dynamics of Salvation*, ed. Clark H. Pinnock and John D. Wagner (Eugene, OR: Resource, 2015), 75–76; J. Matthew Pinson, *40 Questions about Arminianism*, 40 Questions (Grand Rapids, MI: Kregel Academic, 2022), 283–91.

5. See S. M. Baugh, *Ephesians*, Evangelical Exegetical Commentary (Bellingham, WA: Lexham, 2015), 165–70.

6. Ware, "Divine Election to Salvation," 45.

7. Cf. Thomas R. Schreiner, "Does Romans 9 Teach Individual Election unto Salvation? Some Exegetical and Theological Reflections," *Journal of the Evangelical Theological Society* 36 (1993): 25–40; Schreiner, "Corporate and Individual Election in Romans 9: A Response to Brian Abasciano," *Journal of the Evangelical Theological Society* 49

3. The New Testament emphasizes that God chose *us*. When Paul says that God the Father "chose us *in him* [Gk. *en autō*]" (Eph. 1:4)—that is, in Christ—Paul does not say that God chose *Christ* and that then we chose to be in Christ and are therefore elect. God chose us in Christ in the sense that he chose us by means of Christ or through Christ's work on our behalf; Christ accomplished the salvation that our election entails (see chap. 8). God "predestined us . . . *through* Jesus Christ" (1:5). We are "in Christ Jesus" *because* God chose us (1 Cor. 1:27–30).

4. God "predestined us for adoption to himself as sons" (Eph. 1:5), and God adopts particular individuals. If adoption is individual, so is election.

5. God foreknows, calls, justifies, and glorifies particular individuals (Rom. 8:29–30). If foreknowledge, calling, justification, and glorification are individual, so is election (i.e., positive predestination).

6. If the corporate election view is true, then it is logically possible for God to elect a group of people in Christ and for no individuals to freely choose Christ. Thus, God could elect a group of people with no individuals in it other than Christ.

But God chose individuals, and those individuals constitute a group. Consider two illustrations: (1) Luke 6:13: "When day came, [Jesus] called his disciples and *chose* from them twelve, whom he named apostles." This illustrates how choosing works. There was a group of disciples, and Jesus chose twelve individuals from that group to form a subgroup. (2) John 13:18: "I am not speaking of all of you; I know whom I have chosen." Jesus chose the twelve to be his disciples, but he is distinguishing Judas from the other eleven. Jesus chose a group, and he

(2006): 373–86; Cornelis P. Venema, "'Jacob I Loved, but Esau I Hated': Corporate or Individual Election in Paul's Argument in Romans 9?," *Mid-America Journal of Theology* 26 (2015): 7–58.

thought of that group as composed of specific individuals. This is why God sometimes refers to elect individuals as an elect group. Peter writes,

> You [i.e., you individual Christians I am collectively addressing] are *a chosen race*, a royal priesthood, a holy nation, a people for his own possession, that you may proclaim the excellencies of him who called you out of darkness into his marvelous light. Once you were not a people, but now you are God's people; once you had not received mercy, but now you have received mercy. (1 Pet. 2:9–10; cf. 5:13)[8]

7. Election is not just for service but for salvation. Granted, sometimes God chooses primarily for service (see John 6:70; 13:18). But Paul writes, "God chose you . . . *to be saved*" (2 Thess. 2:13; cf. 1 Pet 1:1–2). "God has not destined us for wrath, but [God has destined us] *for obtaining salvation* through our Lord Jesus Christ" (1 Thess. 5:9 NASB). God appointed individuals "to eternal life" (Acts 13:48). God chose "those who are poor in the world *to be rich in faith* and *heirs of the kingdom*" (James 2:5).

Responding with a Prayer

Thank you, Father, for choosing to save *me*. You didn't choose to save merely a group but each and every individual in that group. And one of the ways you describe your people is *chosen:* "They will make war on the Lamb, and the Lamb will conquer them, for he is Lord of lords and King of kings, and those with him are called and *chosen* and faithful" (Rev. 17:14). I am who you say I am. I am *chosen*—chosen by you. Thank you.

---

8. Similarly, "the elect lady and her children" and "the children of your elect sister" (2 John 1, 13) likely refer to specific local churches. See Robert W. Yarbrough, *1–3 John*, Baker Exegetical Commentary on the New Testament (Grand Rapids, MI: Baker Academic, 2008), 334, 359.

4

Did God Choose to Save Individuals Based on Foreseen Faith?

What is the basis of God's election? God's foreknowledge.[1] Arminians and Calvinists agree about that:

"Those whom he foreknew he also predestined" (Rom. 8:29).

"Those who are elect exiles . . . according to the foreknowledge of God the Father." (1 Pet. 1:1–2)

What is controversial is *how to define God's foreknowledge*. There are two basic (and mutually exclusive) ways to explain how God's foreknowledge is the basis of God's election (see table 4.1).

---

1. Parts of this chapter update Andrew David Naselli, "Chosen, Born Again, and Believing: How Election, Regeneration, and Faith Relate to Each Other in the Gospel According to John," *Master's Seminary Journal* 32, no. 2 (2021), 275–76, 279–80.

Table 4.1   Foreknowledge according to Conditional and
Unconditional Election

Conditional Election (Arminianism)	Unconditional Election (Calvinism)
Foreknowing = fore*seeing*. God's foreknowledge is his knowledge of what humans would freely choose. (Names for this view include *prescience, foreseen faith*, and *simple foreknowledge*.)	Foreknowing = fore*loving*. God's foreknowledge is his personal loving commitment to specific individuals.
God foresaw that specific individuals would first freely choose to believe in him, and then afterward he chose to save those individuals.	God intimately knew and loved specific individuals beforehand— that is, he personally committed himself to certain individuals before those individuals even existed. Those are the individuals God chose.
Election is conditional. It depends on whether a human freely chooses Christ.	Election is unconditional. It does not depend on any human condition but solely on God's sovereign good pleasure.
God chose to save specific individuals because he foresaw that they would choose to trust him.	Specific individuals choose to trust God because God chose to save them.
The decisive factor in election is what a human freely chooses.[a]	The decisive factor in election is what God freely chooses.

a. Some Arminians protest describing their view with the word *decisive* like this. See my footnote on table 5.1 at the end of chap. 5 below.

Grant Osborne, an Arminian New Testament scholar, explains, "Arminian theology accepts the doctrine of predestination but asserts that it occurs on the basis of foreknowledge (Rom 8:29; 1 Pet 1:2)—that is, God knew beforehand who would respond to the Spirit's convicting power via faith-decision, and he chose them."[2] But the Bible never says that

2. Grant R. Osborne, "The Gospel of John," in Grant R. Osborne, Philip Wesley Comfort, Wendell C. Hawley, *The Gospel of John and 1–3 John*, Cornerstone Biblical Commentary 13 (Carol Stream, IL: Tyndale House, 2007), 97. See also John Miley, *Sys-*

our faith is the basis of election. Such a view presupposes what the Bible does not say. To the contrary, the Bible repeatedly emphasizes that the basis of election is God and not man. At least seven arguments support unconditional election and refute conditional election.

1. God's Sovereign Choice Is Decisive[3]

Romans 9 is the most important passage in the Bible on election and reprobation because it most clearly explains predestination and directly addresses the most common objections. Romans 9 is the decisive passage God used to help me as a college student to see and savor what God reveals about predestination. Similarly, when John Piper was in graduate school, he fought against the view of predestination I argue for in this book. But after arduously studying Romans 9, he surrendered and wrote, "Romans 9 is like a tiger going about devouring free-willers like me." Piper later reflected, "That was the end of my love affair with human autonomy and the ultimate self-determination of my will. My worldview simply could not stand against the Scriptures, especially Romans 9."[4]

Paul's main idea in Romans 9:6–13 is that God unconditionally elected only some Israelites: "not all who are descended from Israel belong to Israel" (9:6).[5] In other words, not all physical Israelites (the first "Israel" in that sentence) are part of the elect remnant

---

tematic Theology, 2 vols. (New York: Hunt and Eaton, 1892–1893), 2:262–63; H. Orton Wiley, *Christian Theology*, 3 vols. (Kansas City, MO: Beacon Hill, 1940), 2:334–78.

3. Some content in this section is adapted from Andrew David Naselli, *From Typology to Doxology: Paul's Use of Isaiah and Job in Romans 11:34–35* (Eugene, OR: Pickwick, 2012), 14–15; used by permission of Wipf and Stock Publishers, www.wipf andstock.com.

4. John Piper, "The Absolute Sovereignty of God: What Is Romans Nine About?," Desiring God, November 3, 2002, https://www.desiringgod.org/.

5. Chaps. 4–6 of this book follow Romans 9:6–29: chap. 4 = Rom. 9:6–13; chap. 5 = Rom. 9:14–18; chap. 6 = Rom. 9:19–23. Part of this section updates Andrew David Naselli, *Romans: A Concise Guide to the Greatest Letter Ever Written* (Wheaton, IL: Crossway, 2022), 116–19.

of Israelites (the second "Israel"—a subdivision within the larger group). Not everyone who is part of physical or ethnic Israel is also part of spiritual Israel (Rom. 9:7; quoting Gen. 21:12). The first "Israel" refers to "the children of the flesh" (i.e., by physical descent). The second "Israel" refers to "the children of the promise" (Rom. 9:8)—that is, to *specific* physical Israelites (i.e., the "spiritual" Israel or remnant *within* physical Israel) whom God has chosen and called without any preconditions (cf. Gal. 3:7).

What Paul says next emphasizes that election is the sovereign choice of God:

> And not only so, but also when Rebekah had conceived children by one man, our forefather Isaac, though they were not yet born and had done nothing either good or bad—*in order that God's purpose of election might continue, not because of works but because of him who calls*—she was told, "The older will serve the younger." As it is written, "Jacob I loved, but Esau I hated." (Rom. 9:10–13)

Before the twins Jacob and Esau were in Rebekah's womb, God chose Jacob and rejected Esau (Gen. 25:23; Mal. 1:2–3). The purpose is explicit: "in order that God's purpose of election might continue" (Rom. 9:11). Thus, Paul argues, God's promises to Israelites have not failed because he has fulfilled them with reference to individual election. God never promised to save every single physical Israelite. Nor has God ever chosen his spiritual people on the basis of ethnicity. The basis is always his sovereign grace—"not because of works but because of him who calls" (9:11). God is entirely sovereign and righteous in choosing to save specific Israelites. Election is based on "God's purpose" (9:11)—not on what God foresaw a human would choose or do.[6]

---

6. Cf. John Piper, *The Justification of God: An Exegetical and Theological Study of Romans 9:1–23*, 2nd ed. (Grand Rapids, MI: Baker Academic, 1993), 56–72.

That is why when some Gentiles believed in Jesus, the Bible says, "As many as were *appointed to eternal life* believed" (Acts 13:48). God describes people who believe in Jesus as those whom he had *destined* for eternal life.[7]

Paul's prayer in Ephesians 1:3–14 highlights God's sovereign plan to predestine his people: "In love he predestined us for adoption to himself as sons through Jesus Christ, *according to the purpose* [*eudokia*; good pleasure (NASB, CSB)] *of his will.* . . . In him we have obtained an inheritance, having been predestined *according to the purpose* [*prothesis*; plan (CSB)] *of him who works all things according to the counsel of his will*" (Eph. 1:4–5, 11). I don't know how precisely we can distinguish God's good pleasure (delight), plan (aim), will (choice), and counsel (wise decision) regarding election, but this rhetoric unmistakably emphasizes that the basis of election is God's sovereign plan (cf. 2 Tim. 1:9). God's will—not man's will—is decisive.

The Gospel of John provides further evidence that God's sovereign choice is decisive. People come to Jesus because the Father previously gave them to the Son (John 6:39, 65; 10:29; 17:6, 9, 24; 18:9). A man does not have the ability to come to Jesus on his own initiative (6:44, 63–65). The decisive cause of one's coming to Jesus is the Father's drawing him or her (6:44). D. A. Carson argues, "The combination of [John 6] v. 37a and v. 44 prove that this 'drawing' activity of the Father cannot be reduced to what theologians sometimes call 'prevenient grace' dispensed to every individual, for this 'drawing' is selective, or else the negative note in v. 44 is meaningless."[8] Whether a person believes in Jesus ultimately depends on whether God

---

7. Schnabel translates *tetagmenoi* as "destined." Eckhard J. Schnabel, *Acts*, Zondervan Exegetical Commentary on the New Testament (Grand Rapids, MI: Zondervan, 2012), 589.

8. D. A. Carson, *The Gospel According to John*, Pillar New Testament Commentary (Grand Rapids, MI: Eerdmans, 1991), 293. On prevenient grace, see chap. 5 below.

enables a person to believe (12:37–40). Robert Peterson rightly infers from the logic of John 6, "Election precedes faith and results in faith. For this reason, it is incorrect to maintain that election is based on God's foreseeing people's faith."[9] Bruce Ware rightly infers from the logic of John 17, "The unconditional election of the Father, then, accounts for the subsequent faith and salvation of those to whom the Son grants eternal life."[10]

2. The Basis for Election Is God's Forelove

God Chose Us Based on His Gracious Love

God predestined us "in love" (Eph. 1:4–5). That is, God chose us because he loved us.[11] But why did he love us? More pointedly, Why did he love us *and not others* in this way? We don't know because God doesn't tell us. But we must eliminate the view that God loved us because we deserve his love. Election is God's *undeserved* kindness, God's *gracious* love. We should be able to say with Charles Spurgeon,

> I believe the doctrine of election, because I am quite certain that, if God had not chosen me, I should never have chosen Him; and I am sure He chose me before I was born, or else He never would have chosen me afterwards; and He must have elected me for reasons unknown to me, for I never

9. Robert A. Peterson, *Election and Free Will: God's Gracious Choice and Our Responsibility*, Explorations in Biblical Theology (Phillipsburg, NJ: P&R, 2007), 61.

10. Bruce A. Ware, "Divine Election to Salvation: Unconditional, Individual, and Infralapsarian," in *Perspectives on Election: Five Views*, ed. Chad Owen Brand (Nashville: B&H Academic, 2006), 7.

11. "In love" could go with either (1) what comes before (i.e., "holy and blameless *in love* before him" [CSB; cf. NET]) or (2) what comes after (i.e., "*In love* he predestined us" [ESV, NIV; cf. NASB]). Even if the first option is correct, "One does not need ἐν ἀγάπῃ ["in love"] to modify προορίσας ["he predestined"] in order to show that God's predestination is based in love; the very act of predestination is a demonstration of God's love." Harold W. Hoehner, *Ephesians: An Exegetical Commentary* (Grand Rapids, MI: Baker Academic, 2002), 183.

could find any reason in myself why He should have looked upon me with special love.[12]

The reason God loved us in eternity past is not that we are inherently more lovable. What God says to Israel applies to all his people:

> You are a people holy to the LORD your God. The LORD your God has chosen you to be a people for his treasured possession, out of all the peoples who are on the face of the earth. *It was not because you were more in number than any other people that the Lord set his love on you and chose you*, for you were the fewest of all peoples, but *it is because the Lord loves you* and is keeping the oath that he swore to your fathers, that the Lord has brought you out with a mighty hand and redeemed you from the house of slavery, from the hand of Pharaoh king of Egypt. (Deut. 7:6–8; cf. 4:37; 10:15)

This is similar to how parents love their children, even when their children are not lovable. I tell my daughters, "There is nothing you can do to make me stop loving you."

Note how Paul describes the Thessalonian believers: "We know, brothers *loved by God*, that he has chosen you" (1 Thess. 1:4). "We ought always to give thanks to God for you, brothers *beloved by the Lord*, because God chose you as the firstfruits to be saved" (2 Thess. 2:13). Note how Paul connects God's love and God's choice. God chose us *because* he loved us. We are elect *because* God loved us.[13]

---

12. C. H. Spurgeon, *C. H. Spurgeon Autobiography*, vol. 1, *The Early Years, 1834–1859*, ed. Susannah Spurgeon, Joseph Harrald, and Banner of Truth Trust, rev. ed. (1898; repr., Carlisle, PA: Banner of Truth, 1962), 166. This is part of a chapter titled "A Defence of Calvinism," 163–75.

13. See G. K. Beale, *1–2 Thessalonians*, IVP New Testament Commentary 13 (Downers Grove, IL: InterVarsity Press, 2003), 225.

God Chose Us Based on His Good Pleasure

God did not choose us in a cold and mechanical way. "He predestined us . . . according to the *purpose* [good pleasure (NASB, CSB)] of his will" (Eph. 1:5). The word "purpose" translates a word that means "state or condition of being favored, *favor, good pleasure.*"[14] It "refers to the pleasure and delight in one's heart that forms the basis for decision making and action."[15] God predestined us according to *the good pleasure* of his will. "This is what he wanted to do, and it gave him great pleasure" (NLT). Election pleases God.[16]

God Chose Us Based on His Grace

The basis of election is not what a human freely chooses to do. The basis of election is God's grace: "At the present time there is a remnant, *chosen by grace*. But if it is by grace, it is *no longer on the basis of works*; otherwise grace would no longer be grace" (Rom. 11:5–6). God "saved us and called us to a holy calling, *not because of our works* but *because of his own purpose and grace*, which he gave us in Christ Jesus before the ages began" (2 Tim. 1:9).

3. The Questions in Romans 9:14 and 9:19 Presuppose Unconditional Election[17]

Paul anticipates that what he teaches in Romans 9:6–13—that is, that God's sovereign choice is decisive—may provoke some

---

14. BDAG 404 (εὐδοκία).

15. Clinton E. Arnold, *Ephesians*, Zondervan Exegetical Commentary on the New Testament (Grand Rapids, MI: Zondervan, 2010), 83.

16. See John Piper, *The Pleasures of God: Meditations on God's Delight in Being God*, in *The Collected Works of John Piper*, ed. David Mathis and Justin Taylor, 14 vols. (Wheaton, IL: Crossway, 2017), 2:469–99.

17. This section updates Andrew David Naselli, *How to Understand and Apply the New Testament: Twelve Steps from Exegesis to Theology* (Phillipsburg, NJ: P&R, 2017), 224–26.

to object that it would not be right for God to act this way. So in Romans 9:14–23 Paul answers two objections (9:14, 19):

1. *It's not fair for God to choose to save individuals unconditionally* (9:14–18). This first objection is a wrong inference of 9:6–13.
2. *It's not fair for God to blame people for doing what he ordained they would do* (9:19–23). This second objection is a wrong inference of 9:15–18. In other words, the objection is that *God cannot justly blame people; it's not fair for God to treat humans as morally responsible and culpable since no one resists his sovereign will.*

If the way you explain Romans 9:6–18 does not logically lead to the objections in 9:14 and 9:19 ("Is there injustice on God's part? . . . Why does he still find fault? For who can resist his will?"), then you are not saying what Paul says in 9:6–18. The conditional election view certainly does not lead to the objections in 9:14 and 9:19. Those who affirm conditional election explain it in such a way that intentionally does not lead to those two objections. And when those who affirm conditional election critique unconditional election, they reject it with the precise logic that Paul anticipates and refutes in 9:14 and 9:19: they argue that (1) it's not fair for God to save individuals unconditionally and (2) it's not fair for God to blame people since no one resists his sovereign will.[18]

---

18. E.g., see John Wesley, "Predestination Calmly Considered," in *The Works of John Wesley*, 3rd ed. (London: Wesleyan Methodist Book Room, 1872), 204–59. Wesley repeatedly argues that unconditional election is false "because it necessarily implies unconditional reprobation" (211; cf. 207, 255, 256), which "flatly contradicts, indeed utterly overthrows, the Scripture account of the justice of God" (221). "If man be capable of choosing good or evil, then he is a proper object of the justice of God, acquitting or condemning, rewarding or punishing. But otherwise he is not. A mere machine is not capable of being either acquitted or condemned" (233–34; cf. 216–29, 232). See also Jacobus Arminius, *Arminius and His Declaration of Sentiments: An Annotated Translation with Introduction and Theological Commentary*, ed. and trans. W. Stephen Gunter (Waco, TX: Baylor University Press, 2012), 113–16. For a robust argument that Calvinism does

The phrase "By no means" in 9:14 is further evidence for what I argue in the previous paragraphs. Paul writes, "What shall we say then? Is there injustice on God's part? *By no means!*" (9:14). "By no means!" translates *mē genoito*, a phrase Paul uses as a standalone reply thirteen times.[19] Translations render it in various ways:

- May it never be! (NASB)
- By no means! (usually ESV, sometimes NIV)
- Certainly not! (sometimes ESV and NIV)
- Not at all! (sometimes NIV)
- Absolutely not! (CSB, usually NET, sometimes NIV and NLT)
- Of course not! (usually NLT)
- Never! (sometimes ESV, NIV, NET, and NLT)
- God forbid. (KJV)

Here's how Paul uses that phrase:

1. He asserts a truth.
2. He raises a question about or an objection to that truth by stating a seemingly logical implication.
3. Then he says *mē genoito*, which essentially implies, "Right premise but outrageous conclusion!"

In Romans 9:6–13, Paul argues that God unconditionally elects individuals. If God unconditionally elects individuals, then that raises one of the most common objections to that truth: *But that's not fair!* (9:14). The objection is that it's unfair for God to choose individuals for salvation without any precon-

---

not (1) improperly involve God in evil or (2) exclude moral responsibility, see Guillaume Bignon, *Excusing Sinners and Blaming God: A Calvinist Assessment of Determinism, Moral Responsibility, and Divine Involvement in Evil*, Princeton Theological Monograph Series 230 (Eugene, OR: Pickwick, 2018).

19. Rom. 3:4, 6, 31; 6:2, 15; 7:7, 13; 9:14; 11:1, 11; 1 Cor. 6:15; Gal. 2:17; 3:21.

ditions. Paul responds to that objection with *mē genoito* (9:14). He then argues that only God has the prerogative to extend mercy and compassion to whomever he wants. If your view of God's election doesn't lead to the objection in 9:14—"Is God unjust?" (NIV)—then your view of election is not Paul's view.[20]

Here is the principle: When you are explaining a passage in which Paul uses the phrase *mē genoito*, you are not accurately explaining Paul's argument unless it naturally leads to the objection that Paul raises. You are not saying what Paul is saying if your explanation doesn't lead to Paul's objection. You are not saying what Paul is saying if you explain Paul's argument in such a way that people think, "Oh, now I get it. It all clicks now. That makes sense." The questions in 9:14 and 9:19 presuppose unconditional election. An insurmountable problem of explaining Romans 9 with corporate election or conditional individual election is that those views do not lead to the two objections Paul refutes in 9:14 and 9:19. No one responds to the Arminian view of corporate election or conditional individual election by objecting, "But that's not fair."

4. God Foreknew People

The Living Bible (a paraphrase by Kenneth Taylor) renders Romans 8:29 consistent with the Arminian view of conditional election: "From the very beginning God decided that *those who came to him—and all along he knew who would*—should become like his Son" (emphasis added).

But note the following words in italics, which indicate that God foreknew *people*—not events:

---

20. Similarly, Paul says earlier in the same letter, "You are not under law but under grace" (Rom. 6:14). "But Paul," you might ask, "don't you realize the implications of that statement?" Yes, Paul knows. That's why he writes this next: "What then? Are we to sin because we are not under law but under grace? By no means!" (6:15). So if your view of grace isn't so radical that it leads to the question, "Are we to sin because we are not under law but under grace?," then your view of grace is not Paul's view.

"*Those whom* he foreknew he also predestined to be conformed to the image of his Son." (Rom. 8:29)

"God did not reject *his people, whom* he foreknew." (Rom. 11:2 NIV)

"To *those who are elect exiles* . . . according to the foreknowledge of God the Father." (1 Pet. 1:1–2)

"*He* [Christ] *was foreknown* before the foundation of the world." (1 Pet. 1:20)

Foreknowledge in these passages does not refer to God's *foreseeing choices* that people would make. Foreknowledge refers to God's *foreloving certain people*. It is God's intimately knowing and loving specific people beforehand. That is, foreknowledge means that God personally committed himself to specific individuals, and God did this for us before we even existed.[21]

That definition of foreknowledge may sound strange to you, but the Bible frequently speaks about *knowing* as more than intellectual information—like how "Adam *knew* Eve his wife, and she conceived" (Gen. 4:1). Instead of "knew" in Genesis 4:1, other translations say, "made love to" (NIV), "was intimate with" (CSB), "had marital relations with" (NET), and "had sexual relations with" (NLT). Knowing in this sense is not merely factual but relational. For example, I know about C. S. Lewis *factually*, but I don't know him *relationally*. God *knows* people in an intimate relational way—for example,

I *have chosen* [know (KJV)] him. (Gen. 18:19)

God saw the people of Israel—and God *knew* [was concerned about (NIV)] them. (Ex. 2:25)

21. See S. M. Baugh, "The Meaning of Foreknowledge," in *Still Sovereign: Contemporary Perspectives on Election, Foreknowledge, and Grace*, ed. Thomas R. Schreiner and Bruce A. Ware (Grand Rapids, MI: Baker, 2000), 183–200.

The LORD *knows* [watches over (NIV, CSB, NLT), guards (NET)] the way of the righteous. (Ps. 1:6)

Before I formed you in the womb I *knew* [chose (CSB, NET)] *you*. (Jer. 1:5)

It was I who *knew* [cared for (NASB, NIV, NET)] you in the wilderness. (Hos. 13:5)

You only have I *known* [chosen (NIV, NET)] of all the families of the earth. (Amos 3:2)

I never *knew* you; depart from me, you workers of lawlessness. (Matt. 7:23)

If anyone loves God, he *is known* by God. (1 Cor. 8:3)

You have come to know God, or rather to *be known* by God. (Gal. 4:9)

5. God's Sovereign Choice Removes All Grounds for Human Boasting

God chose certain people for a specific purpose:

For consider your calling, brothers: not many of you were *wise* according to worldly standards, not many were *powerful*, not many were *of noble birth*. But God *chose* what is *foolish* in the world to shame the wise; God *chose* what is *weak* in the world to shame the strong; God *chose* what is *low and despised* in the world, even things that are not, to bring to nothing things that are, *so that no human being might boast in the presence of God*. And because of him you are in Christ Jesus, who became to us wisdom from God, righteousness and sanctification and redemption, so that, as it is written, "*Let the one who boasts, boast in the Lord.*" (1 Cor. 1:26–31)

God called "not many" (which is not the same as "not any") who were wise, powerful, or of noble birth. In contrast, "God chose" the opposite of the wise, the strong, and the high and esteemed (cf. James 2:5). For what purpose? "So that no human being might boast in the presence of God" (1 Cor. 1:29). God's sovereign choice to save lowly individuals removes all grounds for human boasting. If you are going to boast, Christian, don't boast in yourself but "in the Lord" (1:31).

If the decisive factor of election is what a *human* chooses, then we would have grounds for boasting in ourselves.[22] But if the decisive factor is what *God* chooses, then we have no grounds for boasting in ourselves. And God explicitly says here that we have no grounds for boasting in ourselves. "God chose . . . God chose . . . God chose . . . so that no human being might boast in the presence of God" (1:27–29).

A person cannot rightly say, "I knew a good deal when I saw one because I am smarter than the average guy. That's why God chose me." Arminian theologians would not say that. They would (rightly) say that we are radically depraved and thus need God's special grace in order to repent and believe in Jesus. But they would also say that God gives that special prevenient grace to everyone (on prevenient grace, see chap. 5). The logical inference of that view is that the decisive factor in election is not God's choice but instead what a human freely chooses. That would entail that a believer decisively chose God and has a ground for boasting. And that directly contradicts 1 Corinthians 1:26–31.

God decisively chose us, and *God* gets all the glory. Jesus illustrates this principle when he tells his disciples, "You did not choose me, but I chose you" (John 15:16).[23] That hum-

---

22. Again, some Arminians protest describing their view with the word *decisive* like this. See my footnote on table 5.1 at the end of chap. 5 below.

23. Cf. D. A. Carson, *The Farewell Discourse and Final Prayer of Jesus: An Exposition of John 14–17* (Grand Rapids, MI: Baker Books, 1980), 107.

bling logic is similar to 1 John 4:19: "We love because he first loved us." As Leon Morris observes while explaining John 6:37, "People do not come to Christ because it seems a good idea to them. It never does seem a good idea to sinful people."[24]

6. Jesus's Sheep Are His Sheep Even before They Believe

Jesus refers to his people as his sheep:

> And I have *other sheep* that are not of this fold. I must bring them also, and they will listen to my voice. So there will be one flock, one shepherd. . . . But *you do not believe because you are not among my sheep.* My sheep hear my voice, and I know them, and they follow me. (John 10:16, 26–27)

In the immediate literary context, Jesus is using a Middle Eastern sheep-farming metaphor (10:1–5) and expands three features: the gate (10:7–10), the shepherd (10:11–18), and the shepherd's own sheep (10:26–30). In contrast to a hired hand who cares more about protecting himself than protecting the sheep (10:12–13), Jesus is "the good shepherd" (10:11, 14). Jesus and his sheep experientially know each other (10:3–4, 14, 16, 27). The "other sheep" Jesus has (10:16) are those outside the sheep pen of Judaism—that is, Samaritans and Gentiles (cf. John 11:51–52; Isa. 56:8; Rev. 5:9). The one people of God are part of "one flock" (John 10:16; cf. Eph. 2:11–22).

This remarkable sentence is jarring: "But you do not believe because you are not among my sheep" (John 10:26). Spurgeon remarks, "Some divines [theologians] would like to read that— 'Ye are not my sheep, because ye do not believe.' As if believing

---

24. Leon Morris, *The Gospel According to John*, 2nd ed., New International Commentary on the New Testament (Grand Rapids, MI: Eerdmans, 1995), 325.

made us the sheep of Christ; but the text puts it—'Ye believe not because ye are not of my sheep.'"[25]

The Father has given specific individuals to Jesus as his sheep. The rest are not his sheep. Every human is either among Jesus's sheep or not. The fundamental reason a human does not believe is that he is not one of Jesus's sheep: "You do not believe *because* you are not among my sheep" (10:26). In the sheep-farming metaphor, a human does not become a sheep in Jesus's flock by believing in Jesus. Rather, a human believes in Jesus *because* he is already a sheep from from God's perspective; that is why Jesus earlier says, "I have other sheep" (10:16)—sheep who have not yet believed in him.[26] When a human first believes in Jesus, he does not experience a transformational status change from *not Jesus's sheep* to *Jesus's sheep*. From God's perspective, every human is either among Jesus's sheep or not, and no human ever changes the status from *not Jesus's sheep* to *Jesus's sheep*. God considers a human to be Jesus's sheep even before he believes in Jesus. A human believes in Jesus *because* he is already a sheep—that is, someone whom the Father previously gave to the Son. Being among Jesus's sheep explains why a person believes in Jesus, and not being among Jesus's sheep explains why a person does not believe in Jesus (10:26). The fundamental reason a human does not believe in Jesus is that he is "not of God" (8:47).

Jesus gives each of his sheep "eternal life" (10:28)—that is, resurrection life of the age to come that believers experience in some measure now (cf. 17:3). Consequently, Jesus's sheep "will never perish" in eternal judgment (10:28). Jesus powerfully keeps his sheep from harm (10:28; cf. 10:11). Their security

---

25. C. H. Spurgeon, *Faith: What It Is, and What It Leads To* (London: Passmore and Alabaster, 1903), 21.

26. Cf. J. Ramsey Michaels, *The Gospel of John*, New International Commentary on the New Testament (Grand Rapids, MI: Eerdmans, 2010), 598.

rests with the good shepherd, who faithfully fulfills his mission to preserve everyone the Father has given to him (6:37–40). Therefore, no force or person can sever the relation between the true believer and Jesus (10:29). There is no greater security (cf. Col. 3:3).

7. Election Based on Foreseen Faith Is *Post*destination (Not *Pre*destination)

According to the view that election is based on foreseen faith, God's foreknowledge is his knowledge of what humans would freely choose. *After* God foresaw that specific individuals would freely choose to believe in him, he chose to save those individuals.

But why would God choose to save individuals who were already going to be saved anyway? What does his choice add? Those individuals would be saved even if God did not choose to save them. If election means that God foresaw that some humans would choose him, then God did not choose people in any meaningful sense. Turretin describes such a view as *post*-destination: "If election is from foreseen faith, God would not have elected man, but rather man would have elected God, and so predestination should rather be called postdestination."[27]

Responding with a Prayer

Father, it is *humbling* to know that you chose what is foolish in the world to shame the wise; you chose what is weak in the world to shame the strong; you chose what is low and despised in the world, even things that are not, to bring to nothing things that are, so that no human being might boast in your presence (1 Cor. 1:27–29). I have no grounds to boast. None. Thank you

---

27. Francis Turretin, *Institutes of Elenctic Theology*, ed. James T. Dennison Jr., trans. George Musgrave Giger, 3 vols. (Phillipsburg, NJ: P&R, 1992–1997), 1:361.

that you have chosen those who are poor in the world to be rich in faith and heirs of the kingdom, which you have promised to those who love you (James 2:5). Thank you that your sovereign choice is decisive.

> 'Tis not that I did choose Thee,
>   For, Lord! that could not be:
> This heart would still refuse Thee,
>   But Thou hast chosen me;—
> Hast, from the sin that stained me,
>   Washed me and set me free;
> Of old thou hast ordained me,
>   That I should live to Thee.
>
> 'Twas Sovereign Mercy called me,
>   And taught my opening mind;
> The world had else enthralled me,
>   To heavenly glories blind.
> Thy grace, my young heart guiding,
>   Infixed me in the Root,
> In which by faith abiding,
>   I bear my humble fruit.
>
> Truly I am Thy servant;
>   By birth, by ransom Thine.
> Oh, that with zeal more fervent,
>   I made Thy pleasure mine!
> My heart owns none before Thee;
>   For Thy rich grace I thirst;
> This knowing, if I love Thee,
>   Thou must have loved me first.[28]

---

28. Josiah Conder, *Hymns of Praise, Prayer, and Devout Meditation* (London: Snow, 1856), 84.

5

Is Unconditional Election Unfair?

A common objection to unconditional election is that it's unfair. Isn't God unfair to choose to save only some humans not based on any human condition but solely on his sovereign good pleasure? Isn't there injustice on God's part that some people are not elect?

Paul directly answers this objection in Romans 9:14–18, and Jesus indirectly answers it in Matthew 20:1–16.

God Is Fair When He Sovereignly Has Mercy on Whomever He Wants (Rom. 9:14–18)[1]

We're back in Romans 9 again (see the beginning of chap. 4). Paul anticipates that Romans 9:6–13 may provoke some to object that it would not be right for God to sovereignly and decisively choose to save only certain individuals and not others. So in 9:14–23, Paul argues that God has the right to do whatever he wants with his creatures.

---

1. This section updates Andrew David Naselli, *Romans: A Concise Guide to the Greatest Letter Ever Written* (Wheaton, IL: Crossway, 2022), 119–20.

In 9:14–18, Paul answers the objection that it's unfair for God to choose to save individuals unconditionally. It is wrong to infer from 9:6–13 that there is injustice on God's part (9:14). In the four sentences that follow (9:15–18), Paul supports that statement with two proofs and draws inferences from those proofs.

Sentence 1 (9:15) = proof 1 that there is no injustice on God's part. "For he says to Moses, 'I will have mercy on whom I have mercy, and I will have compassion on whom I have compassion'" (9:15). Paul quotes Exodus 33:19 to prove that God can have mercy on whomever he wants. God would be just if he did not show mercy to a single sinful human. None of us deserves God's mercy.

Sentence 2 (9:16) = inference of 9:15. "So then it depends not on human will or exertion, but on God, who has mercy" (9:16). The word "it" refers to God's showing mercy and compassion to save individuals (9:15). What is decisive in whether an individual receives mercy is not "human will or exertion." In other words, what is decisive is not your unfettered will or your vain effort to advance spiritually. What is decisive is "God, who has mercy."

Sentence 3 (9:17) = proof 2 that there is no injustice on God's part. "For the Scripture says to Pharaoh, 'For this very purpose I have raised you up, that I might show my power in you, and that my name might be proclaimed in all the earth'" (9:17). Paul quotes Exodus 9:16 to prove that God can harden whomever he wants in order to accomplish his purposes. God raised up Pharaoh to show his power in Pharaoh. The purpose (and result) was that others would proclaim God's name in all the earth.

Sentence 4 (9:18) = inference of 9:15–17. "So then he has mercy on whomever he wills, and he hardens whomever he wills" (9:18). God has mercy on whomever he wants, and he hardens whomever he wants. (On hardening, see chap. 12.)

So "Is there injustice on God's part?" (9:14). No, God is fair when he sovereignly has mercy on whomever he wants.

God Is Fair When He Is Undeservedly Kind to Some and Not Others (Matt. 20:1–16)

Some people reject unconditional election because they presuppose that God does not have the right to treat one person differently from another. Does God have the right to treat one person differently from another? God himself says that he does. And God—not our sense of justice—is the standard for what is right.

When God deals with people, the following two statements are true:

1. *God is always fair.* That is, God is always righteous or just. God is never unfair, unrighteous, or unjust.
2. *Sometimes God is undeservedly kind.* That is, sometimes God is merciful and gracious to people who are both undeserving (i.e., they don't deserve God's kindness) and ill-deserving (i.e., they deserve the opposite of God's kindness; they deserve God's wrath).

Does anyone *deserve* God's kindness? No. When God is *undeservedly kind* to some people but not others, he is still *fair* to all people without exception. God does not have to be undeservedly kind to everyone equally in order to be fair. To be fair, God needs only to give people what they deserve. God is always fair: "all his ways are justice" (Deut. 32:4).

A standard way to define *equity* is the quality of being fair and impartial. More recently some people have redefined *equity* to refer to equal outcomes. So some people think that God is unfair if there are unequal outcomes. But we must distinguish between impartiality and equal outcomes. God is impartial, but that does not mean everyone experiences equal outcomes because God has the freedom to show undeserved kindness to whomever he wants.

Jesus's parable of the laborers in the vineyard illustrates that God is always fair and that he is sometimes undeservedly kind:

> For the kingdom of heaven is like a master of a house who went out early in the morning to hire laborers for his vineyard. After agreeing with the laborers for a denarius a day, he sent them into his vineyard. And going out about the third hour he saw others standing idle in the marketplace, and to them he said, "You go into the vineyard too, and whatever is right I will give you." So they went. Going out again about the sixth hour and the ninth hour, he did the same. And about the eleventh hour he went out and found others standing. And he said to them, "Why do you stand here idle all day?" They said to him, "Because no one has hired us." He said to them, "You go into the vineyard too." And when evening came, the owner of the vineyard said to his foreman, "Call the laborers and pay them their wages, beginning with the last, up to the first." And when those hired about the eleventh hour came, each of them received a denarius. Now when those hired first came, they thought they would receive more, but each of them also received a denarius. And on receiving it they grumbled at the master of the house, saying, "These last worked only one hour, and you have made them equal to us who have borne the burden of the day and the scorching heat." But he replied to one of them, "Friend, I am doing you no wrong. Did you not agree with me for a denarius? Take what belongs to you and go. I choose to give to this last worker as I give to you. Am I not allowed to do what I choose with what belongs to me? Or do you begrudge my generosity?" So the last will be first, and the first last. (Matt. 20:1–16)

The master gives each laborer what he deserves, and he gives some laborers more than they deserve. It is not unfair to give extra to some, even when they are less deserving than others. Note the words I have emphasized: "*I choose to give to this last worker as I give to you. Am I not allowed to do what I choose with what belongs to me? Or do you begrudge my generosity?*" (Matt. 20:14–15). As long as God gives each person what he deserves, he is not unfair when he sovereignly chooses to be undeservedly kind to some and not others. And not one of us deserves God's kindness. It is reasonable to ask, "Why did God choose to save some *and not others*?" (See part 2 of this book.) But it is better to ask, "Why did God choose to save *any*?" (See chap. 1.) As John Bunyan says, "The least of mercies are not deserved by the best of sinners."[2] God is not unfair when he is undeservedly kind to some and not others.

Does the Arminian View of Prevenient Grace Accurately Explain How Election Is Fair?

In the hymn "Free Grace" (now known as "And Can It Be?"), Charles Wesley, arguably the greatest Arminian hymn writer, exults,

> Long my imprison'd spirit lay,
>> Fast bound in Sin and Nature's Night:
> Thine Eye diffus'd a quick'ning Ray;
>> I woke; the Dungeon flam'd with Light:

---

2. John Bunyan, "Reprobation Asserted: or, The Doctrine of Eternal Election and Reprobation Promiscuously Handled, in Eleven Chapters Wherein the Most Material Objections Made by the Opposers of This Doctrine, Are Fully Answered; Several Doubts Removed, and Sundry Cases of Conscience Resolved," in *The Whole Works of John Bunyan, Accurately Reprinted from the Author's Own Editions*, 3 vols. (London: Blackie and Son, 1862), 2:346.

My Chains fell off, my Heart was free,
    I rose, went forth, and follow'd Thee.[3]

Calvinists typically love to sing those lines because we believe that we cannot repent and believe in Christ until God's Spirit enables us by regenerating us. But when Wesley says, "Thine eye diffused a quickening ray," he is not referring to regeneration (i.e., God's imparting spiritual life to a spiritually dead person) but to the Arminian concept of prevenient grace.

Prevenient grace is special grace that comes before we can repent and believe. Arminians and Calvinists agree that we need God's special grace *before* we can repent and believe because we are radically depraved. But we disagree on five key issues regarding God's special grace (see table 5.1).

Table 5.1   Arminianism versus Calvinism on God's Special Grace

	Arminianism	Calvinism
1. Who receives God's special grace?	Everyone: God's special grace is universal.	Only some people—the elect: God's special grace is particular.
2. Is God's special grace ultimately resistible?	Yes, it is ultimately resistible.	No, it is ultimately irresistible. It is effective because it is invincible.
3. What is free will? (See chap. 6.)	We can choose differently—that is, we can make equally alternative choices in the same circumstances.	We always choose what we most want.

---

3. John Wesley and Charles Wesley, *Hymns and Sacred Poems*, 5th ed. (London: n.p., 1756), 78.

(Table 5.1 continued)

	Arminianism	Calvinism
4. How does the Spirit work? (See chap. 6.)	The Spirit gives prevenient grace to every individual and thus makes it possible for every individual to repent and believe. Prevenient grace enables every individual to freely choose or reject Christ. Thus, man's choice is decisive.[a]	The Spirit does not force a man to repent and believe against his will; the Spirit transforms a man's heart with the result that he wants to and is able to repent and believe. Thus, God's choice is decisive.
5. How do regeneration, repentance, and faith relate theologically?	Repentance and faith precede and cause regeneration.	Regeneration precedes and causes repentance and faith.

a. "Man's choice is decisive" is my way of summarizing what I think is necessarily true in the Arminian system. Contrast how two Arminian theologians summarize this issue: (1) Brian Shelton: "*Does prevenient grace put the burden of salvation on each person, so that individual choice becomes the determining factor for salvation, regardless of God?* No, Paul makes it clear in Ephesians 2:8–9 that even faith (the necessary prerequisite for salvation) finds its source in God alone. Those who would accuse Arminians of prioritizing free will above all else ignore the Arminian emphasis on Christ's atoning work and the absolute necessity of divine enabling grace." W. Brian Shelton, *Prevenient Grace: God's Provision for Fallen Humanity* (Wilmore, KY: Francis Asbury Press, 2014), 262; emphasis original. (2) Roger Olson: "Some Calvinist critics still maintain that Arminius made the free acceptance of the gift of salvation, including faith, the decisive factor in salvation. . . . For all classical Arminians, the decisive factor is the grace of God—from beginning to end." Olson, *Arminian Theology*, 165–66. Specifically, Arminians believe that God's grace is decisive with respect to the ability to make a free choice to repent and believe in Christ. So I still think it is logically accurate to summarize the Arminian view as making an individual's choice the determining factor for whether or not a person is elect. What else could the decisive factor be? It is not God because an individual can make equally alternative choices. Prevenient grace enables merely the *possibility* of making the right choice, but it does not *guarantee* it. It is necessary but not sufficient to save. Arminians say that we need God's grace (which all receive via prevenient grace) but that we must personally avail ourselves of that grace in order for it to be effective. Thus, the decisive factor is man's choice. (I concede that my reasoning here frustrates some Arminian theologians similar to how Calvinist theologians feel when Arminians describe Calvinism as necessarily making God the author of sin—something that Calvinists explicitly deny.)

In the book that most robustly defends prevenient grace, Arminian theologian Brian Shelton defines prevenient grace as "the belief that God enables all people to exercise saving faith in Christ by mitigating the effects of sinful depravity."[4] Prevenient grace is God's saving grace that is universal, empowering, and resistible (not particular and effective). This special grace enables every human to choose to repent and believe. This is the case, Arminians argue, because Jesus "gives light to everyone" (John 1:9); Jesus draws "all people" to himself (12:32); "the grace of God has appeared, bringing salvation for all people" (Titus 2:11); and the way God invites, warns, and commands everyone does not make sense unless everyone is able to obey.[5] Robert Picirilli describes prevenient grace as "pre-regenerating grace."[6] The effect of prevenient grace, explains Roger Olson, is "partial regeneration," which contrasts with "full regeneration" at conversion.[7]

Does the Arminian view of prevenient grace accurately explain how election is fair? No. The main reason is that proof texts for prevenient grace do not support the theory.[8] A devastating critique is that conditional election and prevenient grace

---

4. Shelton, *Prevenient Grace*, 259. Cf. H. Orton Wiley, *Christian Theology*, 3 vols. (Kansas City, MO: Beacon Hill, 1940–1943), 2:344–57.

5. In addition to Shelton's *Prevenient Grace*, see David T. Fry, "Grace Enough: An Exposition and Theological Defense of the Wesleyan Concept of Prevenient Grace" (Trinity Evangelical Divinity School, PhD diss., 2014); J. Matthew Pinson, *40 Questions about Arminianism*, 40 Questions (Grand Rapids, MI: Kregel Academic, 2022), 191–241.

6. Robert E. Picirilli, *Grace, Faith, Free Will: Contrasting Views of Salvation; Calvinism and Arminianism* (Nashville: Randall House, 2002), 153–60. See also Robert E. Picirilli, *Free Will Revisited: A Respectful Response to Luther, Calvin, and Edwards* (Eugene, OR: Wipf and Stock, 2017), 95–99.

7. Olson, *Arminian Theology*, 36. Olson clarifies that for Arminius, "There is an intermediate stage between being unregenerate and regenerate. The intermediate stage is when the human being is not so much free to respond to the gospel (as the semi-Pelagians claimed) but is *freed* to respond to the good news of redemption in Christ. Arminius thus believes not so much in free will but in a freed will, one which, though initially bound by sin, has been brought by the prevenient grace of the Spirit of Christ to a point where it can respond freely to the divine call. This intermediate stage is neither unregenerate nor regenerate, but perhaps post-unregenerate and pre-regenerate" (164–65; emphasis original). See also Roger Olson, *Against Calvinism* (Grand Rapids, MI: Zondervan, 2011), 171.

8. Cf. Thomas R. Schreiner, "Does Scripture Teach Prevenient Grace in the Wesleyan Sense?," in *Still Sovereign: Contemporary Perspectives on Election, Foreknowledge, and Grace*, ed. Thomas R. Schreiner and Bruce A. Ware (Grand Rapids, MI: Baker, 2000), 229–46; William W. Combs, "Does the Bible Teach Prevenient Grace?," *Detroit Baptist Seminary Journal* 10 (2005): 3–18.

do not logically lead to the objections in Romans 9:14 and 9:19; to the contrary, prevenient grace explains election in such a way that nobody would raise those objections (see chap. 4).

Responding with a Prayer

Thank you, Father, for your undeserved kindness to me. I deserve the opposite of your kindness. I deserve your wrath. And yet you sovereignly chose to save me. You sovereignly chose to be merciful and gracious to me. Thank you.

6

Do We Have Free Will?

In chapters 4–6, I am following what Paul argues in Romans 9:6–23:

Chapter 4: Did God choose to save individuals based on foreseen faith? (9:6–13)
Chapter 5: Is unconditional election unfair? (9:14–18)
Chapter 6: Do we have free will? (9:19–23)

As we consider free will, let's start with Romans 9:19–23 and branch out from there.[1] Paul anticipates that 9:6–13 may provoke some to object that it would not be right for God to sovereignly and decisively choose to save certain individuals and not others. So in 9:14–23, Paul argues that God has the right to do whatever he wants with his creatures. In 9:14–18, Paul answers the objection that it's not fair for God to choose to save individuals unconditionally: "So then *it depends not on human will* or exertion, *but on God*, who has mercy" (9:16). God is fair when he sovereignly has mercy on whomever he wants.

---

1. This introductory section updates Andrew David Naselli, *Romans: A Concise Guide to the Greatest Letter Ever Written* (Wheaton, IL: Crossway, 2022), 120–21.

In 9:19–23, Paul answers the objection that it's not fair for
God to blame people for doing what he ordained they would do.
This second objection is a wrong inference of 9:15–18. In other
words, the objection is that it's unfair for God to hold humans
morally responsible and guilty since no one resists his sovereign
will (9:19).[2] Paul answers this objection with two forceful re-
sponses: (1) Who do you think you are to backtalk our Creator?
(2) The Potter is free to mold the clay however he wants.

Response 1: Who Are You to Say That It's Unfair for God to Blame People? (Rom. 9:20a)

Instead of giving a philosophical answer to the apparent di-
lemma in Romans 9:19, Paul rebukes anyone who would dare
question God's right to "find fault." He asks rhetorically, "Who
are you, O man, to answer back to God?" (9:20a). Paul is not
committing the *ad hominem* fallacy. His point is that it is au-
daciously arrogant for mere humans to backtalk our Creator.
How dare a sinful and finite man disrespectfully mouth off to
the all-knowing, all-powerful, all-good Creator? If you don't
understand how it's fair for God to "find fault" when he sovereignly has mercy on whomever he wants, then put your hand
over your mouth. Don't call God's justice into question. Who
do you think you are to criticize God Almighty?[3]

Response 2: The Potter (God) Is Free to Mold the Clay (Us) However He Wants (Rom. 9:20b–23)

God relates to humans like a potter relates to clay (Rom. 9:20b–
23; cf. Job 10:9; Isa. 45:7–9; 64:8; Jer. 18:1–6). It would be
ridiculous for the thing molded to complain to its molder, "Why

---

2. See Andrew David Naselli, *From Typology to Doxology: Paul's Use of Isaiah and Job in Romans 11:34–35* (Eugene, OR: Pickwick, 2012), 15.

3. Qualification: It is okay to ask a question about God and his ways if we ask in good faith with the right attitude—such as "How long, O Lord?" (Pss. 13:1; 79:5; 89:46). But we deserve a rebuke if we ask a question in a way that condemns God.

have you made me like this?" (Rom. 9:20b; cf. Isa. 29:16, 45:9). The potter is free to mold clay however he wants. Doesn't the potter have the right to use a lump of clay to form vessels "for honorable [special] use" such as a fancy wine cup or a decorative flower vase? And doesn't the potter have the right to form from that same lump of clay vessels "for dishonorable [common] use" such as a chamber pot or trash can (Rom. 9:21)? Romans 9:21 is a rhetorical question, and the Greek syntax requires that the answer is yes. The idea is "The potter has this right, doesn't he?" or "Doesn't the potter have this right?" (cf. NASB, NIV, NLT).

Like a potter with his clay, God has the right to do whatever he wants with his creatures. God is free to prepare "vessels of wrath" and "vessels of mercy" (9:22–23). (On "vessels of wrath," see part 2 of this book.)

In What Sense Do We Have a Free Will?

When we try to make sense of God's sovereignty and human responsibility, we tend to be adamant that we have a free will. Fair enough—everything in our experience confirms that our choices are genuine choices. For example, for lunch today I chose to eat salmon, white rice, and steamed broccoli. I could have chosen grilled chicken or sweet potatoes or salad or purple grapes, but I chose that particular lunch. *I* chose it, and my choice was *free*, not coerced.

But here's the problem: Many of us presuppose that because our choices are genuine choices, God therefore cannot ordain our free choices. Otherwise, we may (wrongly) conclude, God would be guilty of forcing us to sin, and God would be unjust for condemning certain individuals for doing what he ordained they would do. So some people argue that God does not ordain who will believe in Christ and who will reject Christ because he wants a genuine, loving relationship—not a mechanical, preprogrammed, robotic outcome.

Why is that view wrong? Because it contradicts what God has revealed in the Bible. It assumes a definition of "free will" that is not in the Bible and then explains away what the Bible explicitly teaches about God's meticulous sovereignty, which includes the eternal destiny of every human.[4] I'll attempt to explain this in seven steps.[5]

1. A Foundational Truth: God the Creator Is Distinct from His Creation

The Creator-creature distinction is fundamental to rightly understanding reality. God created the universe (Gen. 1:1; Pss. 19:1; 33:8–9; Isa. 44:24; Jer. 10:12; John 1:3; 1 Cor. 8:6; 11:12; Col. 1:16; Heb. 1:2). As the Creator, God is distinct from his creation. God is not part of creation. The universe is everything that is not God, and the eternal God existed before he created the universe. God's aseity means that he is eternally self-existent; he is not dependent on anyone or anything else (Acts 17:24–29; Rom. 11:35–36).

There is no one like God; he is unlike everyone and everything else (Ex. 8:10; 9:14; Deut. 33:26; 2 Sam. 7:22; 1 Chron. 17:20; Ps. 86:8; Isa. 46:9; Jer. 10:6–7). There was a time when my phone did not exist. There was a time when I did not exist. There was a time when the United States of America did not exist. There was a time when the earth did not exist. There was a time when the entire universe did not exist. But there was never a time when God did not exist.

---

4. For a robust argument that "free will" (in the sense that God cannot ordain our choices) is not only not required for authentic love but actually undermines authentic love, see Thaddeus J. Williams, *God Reforms Hearts: Rethinking Free Will and the Problem of Evil* (Bellingham, WA: Lexham Academic, 2021). Williams argues that we can love most authentically when God reforms our hearts; that is true freedom.

5. I'm starting with a foundational truth, considering some analogies, and then describing in what sense we have a free will. This basic approach (which I've conveyed in my own words) is similar to an insightful eighteen-minute video by Douglas Wilson: "The Sovereignty of God – Douglas Wilson | Reformed Basics #1," Christ Church, September 14, 2020, YouTube video, https://www.youtube.com/.

And it's not as if God is like a gigantic elephant while we are like gnats. No, God is not the biggest, most powerful, most knowledgeable creature within creation. God is not a creature. He is not contained within creation at all. He eternally exists outside of creation. He is transcendent. He is not part of creation. He is the Almighty Creator, not a created being.

The Creator-creature distinction is a foundational truth. The difference between God and "not God" is the bedrock for making sense of how God's sovereignty and human responsibility are compatible.

2. A Terrible Analogy: A Girl and Her Doll

Some object that God's ordaining everything makes God unjust—something like this scenario of a girl playing with her doll. Imagine a girl who sternly commands her doll to stay on her bed. But then while playing with her doll, she intentionally pushes the doll from the bed to the floor. Then she scolds and spanks the doll.

That is a terrible analogy for at least two reasons: (1) the doll lacks self-consciousness and thus is not morally responsible, and (2) God does not exercise authority over his creation by coercing or manipulating.[6] If God were within creation, then his meticulous sovereignty really would displace and remove our freedom, and that would make him a cosmic tyrant. That kind of sovereignty is repugnant.

---

6. Cf. Guillaume Bignon, *Excusing Sinners and Blaming God: A Calvinist Assessment of Determinism, Moral Responsibility, and Divine Involvement in Evil*, Princeton Theological Monograph Series 230 (Eugene, OR: Pickwick, 2018), 15–48. Bignon explains, "In usual cases of human free choices, God does not determine the actions of humans *against* their wills, but *through* their wills. God usually employs neither threats nor physical force, but rather, he providentially influences human hearts to willingly accomplish his purposes in all things" (23; emphasis original).

3. A Useful Analogy: A Novelist and the Characters in His Story

A much better analogy for God's sovereignty is a novelist and the characters in his story.[7] In C. S. Lewis's *The Lion, the Witch, and the Wardrobe*, the character Edmund betrays his three siblings and Aslan. Who is responsible for that betrayal—Edmund or C. S. Lewis? Do they share responsibility—50 percent Edmund and 50 percent Lewis? Or maybe 75 percent Edmund and 25 percent Lewis? No, Edmund is fully responsible, and Lewis is fully responsible. But they are responsible in different senses. Edmund is fully responsible as a creature, a character in a fictional story; and Lewis is fully responsible as the creator, the author of the fictional story. Lewis (the author) *ordained* what Edmund (the character) *freely chose* to do. Edmund has moral responsibility for his choices, and Lewis does not. That's something like what we mean when we say that God (the Creator) ordained what humans (the creatures) freely choose to do. The Creator has authority over his creation like a novelist has authority over his story.

You might say to me then, "But that analogy fails because it compares cardboard characters in a fictional story to complex human beings in the real world. It's much more complicated than that." I concede that it is much more complicated than that. So, yes, the analogy has limitations—but not mainly for that reason.

---

7. Cf. Wayne Grudem, *Systematic Theology: An Introduction to Biblical Doctrine*, 2nd ed. (Grand Rapids, MI: Zondervan, 2020), 427–28; John M. Frame, *The Doctrine of God*, A Theology of Lordship (Phillipsburg, NJ: P&R, 2002), 156–59; Joe Rigney, *The Things of Earth: Treasuring God by Enjoying His Gifts* (Wheaton, IL: Crossway, 2015), 51–54; Scott Christensen, *What about Evil? A Defense of God's Sovereign Glory* (Phillipsburg, NJ: P&R, 2020), 202–5; Peter Sammons, *Reprobation and God's Sovereignty: Recovering a Biblical Doctrine* (Grand Rapids, MI: Kregel Academic, 2022), 195–98.

It is telling that the main way people object to the analogy is like this: "But humans in the real world are much greater than people in a fictional story." I have never heard someone object like this: "But God is far more powerful and knowledgeable and benevolent than a human author." In other words, God is much greater than C. S. Lewis! God can do way better than write a fictional story. He can design the universe with complex characters who freely and responsibly choose precisely what he ordains.

The Bible uses this analogy that God writes our story. David says in Psalm 139:16,

> In your book were written, every one of them,
>> the days that were formed for me,
>> when as yet there was none of them.

Jim Hamilton comments, "God had every day of David's life written in his book before any of them came to be. This reference to a 'book' is again an accommodated, anthropomorphic way of describing the preordained plan of God, and David says that God's plan extends to every day of his whole life."[8]

If it offends you to be compared to a character in a fictional story, then what do you think of God repeatedly comparing you to a clay pot? (See Job 10:9; Isa. 29:16; 45:7, 9; 64:8; Jer. 18:1–6; Rom. 9:20b–23.)

4. Defining Key Terms: *Incompatibilism* versus *Compatibilism*

The Bible does not define the term *free will*. It is complicated to define *free will* because it involves historical and systematic

---

8. James M. Hamilton Jr., *Psalms*, 2 vols., Evangelical Biblical Theology Commentary (Bellingham, WA: Lexham Academic, 2021), 2:461.

theology.[9] I don't want to use confusing philosophical jargon, but it will be helpful to define some terms before we consider the question, In what sense do we have a free will?

> *Will* is the ability to choose. My will enables me to either sit or stand, speak or be silent.
>
> A *constraining cause* forces a person to act against his will. I occasionally acted as a constraining cause when one of my daughters was having a tantrum as a toddler; I would pick her up *against her will* and carry her away to discipline her.
>
> A *nonconstraining cause* does not force a person to act against his will, but it is sufficient to cause an action. Here is a *negative example*: I would like to dead-lift five hundred pounds, but I can't because I'm not strong enough. My physical weakness is a nonconstraining cause; it causes me to deadlift less than five hundred pounds. If I have the desire to do something but lack the ability to do it, then that lack of ability is a (restraining) nonconstraining cause. Here is a *positive example*: While I am in the zone researching and writing, I suddenly smell bacon sizzling in the kitchen. The smell does not force me to eat bacon against my will, but it is sufficient to cause me to want to eat bacon.
>
> *Determined* means that prior conditions determine (i.e., cause or ensure) that something must occur. A Calvinist would say, "God determined (as a nonconstraining cause) that I would believe in Christ."

---

9. The overall best accessible book on free will that I am aware of is Scott Christensen, *What about Free Will? Reconciling Our Choices with God's Sovereignty* (Phillipsburg, NJ: P&R, 2016). For historical theology, see R. C. Sproul, *Willing to Believe: The Controversy over Free Will* (Grand Rapids, MI: Baker, 1997). For systematic theology, see John S. Feinberg, *No One Like Him: The Doctrine of God*, Foundations of Evangelical Theology, ed. John S. Feinberg (Wheaton, IL: Crossway, 2001), 625–796, 843–55.

Indeterminism means that genuinely free acts are not decisively determined by forces outside my own power of choosing. An Arminian would say, "If God determined that I would believe in Christ, then my belief in Christ would not be genuinely free. God would be forcing me to act against my will (as a constraining cause)."

Determinism means that everything in the universe is determined. As a Calvinist, I believe that God determined (i.e., ordained) and thus ensures everything that occurs in the universe—including what humans freely choose. God interacts with humans as a non-constraining cause. That is, God ultimately determines what humans choose, while at the same time humans freely choose what we want; God decisively ensures what humans choose, but he does not constrain us (i.e., coerce us against our wills).

Still with me? Now for the most controversial question: What does *free* mean? There are two (mutually exclusive) ways to answer that question: *incompatibilism* and *compatibilism* (see table 6.1).[10]

---

10. Another view is Molinism. For a defense, see John D. Laing, *Middle Knowledge: Human Freedom in Divine Sovereignty* (Grand Rapids, MI: Kregel Academic, 2018). Like Arminianism, Molinism affirms libertarian freedom, but unlike Arminianism, it attempts to affirm meticulous sovereignty via middle knowledge. Molinism is "the viewpoint that the future choices of people are not *directly* determined by God, but God knows them anyway, because he knows *how each free creature would respond* in any set of circumstances that might occur, and then he creates a world in which those circumstances will occur." Grudem, *Systematic Theology*, 1515–16; emphasis original (see also 456–62). Cf. Paul Helm, *The Providence of God*, Contours of Christian Theology (Downers Grove, IL: InterVarsity Press, 1993), 55–68; Paul Helm and Terrance L. Tiessen, "Does Calvinism Have Room for Middle Knowledge? A Conversation," *Westminster Theological Journal* 71 (2009): 437–54; Steven B. Cowan, "Molinism, Meticulous Providence, and Luck," *Philosophia Christi* 11, no. 1 (2009): 156–69; Matthew A. Postiff, "God and Counterfactuals," *Detroit Baptist Seminary Journal* 15 (2010): 23–73; Greg Welty, "Molinist Gunslingers: God and the Authorship of Sin," in *Calvinism and the Problem of Evil*, ed. David E. Alexander and Daniel M. Johnson (Eugene, OR: Pickwick, 2016), 56–77; Henri Blocher, "'Middle Knowledge': Solution or Seduction?," *Unio Cum Christo: International Journal of Reformed Theology and Life* 4, no. 1 (2018): 29–46.

Table 6.1 Incompatibilism versus Compatibilism

	Incompatibilism (as Typically Held by Arminians)	Compatibilism (as Typically Held by Calvinists)
Definition	Determinism and human freedom are incompatible.	Determinism and human freedom are compatible.
God's Sovereignty	In philosophical terms, God did not determine (i.e., ordain) what we freely choose (indeterminism).[a]	In philosophical terms, God determined (i.e., ordained) everything in the universe—including what we freely choose (determinism).
	In theological terms, God's sovereignty is general. God is in charge of everything, but he does not ordain everything. Specifically, God did not ordain the eternal destiny of each individual.	In theological terms, God's sovereignty is meticulous. God is in charge of everything, and he ordains everything. Specifically, God ordained the eternal destiny of each individual.
God's Sovereignty	We have a free will in the sense that we are morally responsible for what we choose. (Both views agree.)	
	We have a free will in the sense that we can choose differently. That is, we can make equally alternative choices in the same circumstances.	We have a free will in the sense that we always choose what we most want. That is, we voluntarily choose what we most want in any given circumstance as long as our choices are not constrained.
	I am just as able to choose Christ as I am able not to choose Christ. As a radically depraved sinner, I am able to choose Christ because prevenient grace enables me to freely do so if I decide.	I am unable to choose Christ until God changes my heart. I choose whatever my heart desires. I always choose what I choose because I want what I want because I am who I am (see figure 6.1 below). I always choose according to my nature. A tomato plant cannot produce apples, and I cannot choose Christ unless God changes my "wanter" (i.e., my nature or my heart).

Incompatibilism (as Typically Held by Arminians)	Compatibilism (as Typically Held by Calvinists)
Labels for this view include *libertarian freedom* (I have liberty to choose something or not), *contra-causal free will* (my choices are not ultimately or decisively caused or determined by anything outside myself), *the power of contrary choice* (even if various causes incline me to make a particular choice, I have the power to make a contrary choice), *the liberty of indifference* (I have liberty to choose this or that for no decisive or sufficient reason), and *self-determining choice* (I alone am the decisive cause for what I choose).[b]	Labels for this view include *compatibilist freedom* (I freely choose in a way compatible with some form of determinism), *free agency* (I am genuinely free to do what I most want without restraint), *the freedom of inclination* (I freely choose what I am most inclined to choose, which is always what I think is in my best interest), and *the liberty of spontaneity* (I have liberty to choose what I most desire to choose).
God did not determine that specific individuals would believe in Christ. Otherwise, their choices would not be free but constrained.	God determined that specific individuals would believe in Christ and that they would do so freely (i.e., without constraint). God decisively and effectively changes your heart with the result that you want to believe in Christ.

(Table 6.1 continued)

Incompatibilism (as Typically Held by Arminians)	Compatibilism (as Typically Held by Calvinists)
A God-ordained choice is not a real choice.	A God-ordained choice is a real choice.
Moral responsibility requires this kind of freedom to choose differently—that is, to make equally alternative choices in the same circumstances. And this freedom is incompatible with God's meticulous sovereignty.	This freedom to choose what we most want is compatible with moral responsibility. We cannot fully understand how God's meticulous sovereignty is compatible with human freedom, but such a mystery is not surprising because we are talking about the ways of the infinite God.

a. "Hard determinists" are also incompatibilists because they believe that determinism and human freedom are incompatible. But unlike indeterminists, they reject human freedom rather than determinism. Compatibilism is a "soft determinism" because it affirms both determinism and human freedom. Both incompatibilism and compatibilism reject fatalism. Fatalism is a mechanical system in which the impersonal force "fate" (not the personal God) has determined everything; consequently, it is futile for humans to make an effort to improve or influence or change things because that would make no difference since everything is inevitable.

b. Piper labels the incompatibilist view of human freedom as *ultimate self-determination*: "By *ultimate*, I simply mean the control that finally decides the outcome. . . . When we pause to define *free will*, I think people simply mean, at one level, something like this: 'I do something of my own free will when my choice is not coerced, say, by someone putting a gun at my head (or my child's head).' But at a deeper level, if you ask people about who finally or ultimately controls their choices, they would, I think, ordinarily say something like, 'If I don't have the final control, then I don't have free will.' Then they would probably add: 'And if I don't have free will, then I am not responsible. I'm a robot.'" John Piper, *Providence* (Wheaton, IL: Crossway, 2021), 213–14; emphasis original.

So in what sense do we have a free will? We have a free will in the sense that we always choose what we most want (without constraint). And that is compatible with God's meticulous sovereignty.[11]

5. A Clarifying Distinction: Natural Freedom to Choose What I Want (Natural Ability) versus Moral Freedom to Choose What God Wants (Moral Ability)

It is helpful to distinguish two kinds of freedom:[12]

1. *Natural freedom to choose what I want.* This is the *natural* or *general* ability to choose one thing or another. (1) These choices do not require God's special, saving grace. We can choose to sit down or stand up, to wear a red shirt or a blue shirt, to read a book or listen to a podcast, to drink water or coffee. (2) We choose within our creaturely limitations. We don't have the natural ability to fly like a bird or to breathe underwater like a fish or to deadlift seven thousand pounds.

2. *Moral freedom to choose what God wants.* This is the *moral* or *spiritual* ability to glorify God by enjoying

---

11. Arminian theologian Tom McCall argues that what D. A. Carson calls "compatibilism" (which is what I am calling compatibilism) is actually not compatibilism according to metaphysics. Thomas H. McCall, *An Invitation to Analytic Christian Theology* (Downers Grove, IL: InterVarsity Press, 2015), 56–81. Carson responds that he (like some evangelical philosophers) is intentionally using categories from the Bible (i.e., God's sovereignty and human responsibility) instead of analytic philosophy (i.e., determinism and freedom). D. A. Carson, "Biblical-Theological Pillars Needed to Support Faithful Christian Reflection on Suffering and Evil," *Trinity Journal* 38 (2017): 69–71.

12. See Jonathan Edwards, *Freedom of the Will*, ed. Paul Ramsey, vol. 1 of *The Works of Jonathan Edwards* (New Haven, CT: Yale University Press, 2009), 159–60. The view of free will that I am defending is basically paraphrasing Jonathan Edwards's *Freedom of the Will*. Cf. C. Samuel Storms, "Jonathan Edwards on the Freedom of the Will," *Trinity Journal* 3 (1982): 131–69; Sam Storms, "The Will: Fettered Yet Free (*Freedom of the Will*)," in *A God-Entranced Vision of All Things: The Legacy of Jonathan Edwards*, ed. John Piper and Justin Taylor (Wheaton, IL: Crossway, 2004), 201–20. I am simplifying Edwards's more complex descriptions. Edwards argues that we have a natural ability to love God but not a moral ability to love God; we have a moral inability because of our depravity and cannot love God unless he regenerates us.

him. This is the freedom to obey God, which includes the
moral ability to repent of your sins and believe in Jesus.

In both kinds of freedom, you are free to choose according
to your nature. All humans have natural freedom (except when
there is a constraining cause like a gun pointing at your head),
but only regenerate humans have moral freedom. We usually
have the natural freedom to choose what we want, but not all
of us have the moral freedom to choose what God wants.

Augustine articulates four possibilities for whether humans
are morally free to choose what God wants.[13] Thomas Boston
labels those four states as innocence (or primitive integrity),
entire deprivation, grace (or begun recovery), and the eternal
state (or the state of consummate happiness).[14] I reword those
four possibilities in table 6.2.

Table 6.2   Four Possibilities for Whether Humans Are Morally Free to
Choose What God Wants

Moral Ability	Ability to Sin	Explanation
1. Unconfirmed moral ability: Adam and Eve were free to choose what God wants and free not to choose what God wants.	Able to sin and able not to sin	Before Adam and Eve fell, there was a testing period in which they were able not to sin but also able to sin. Ever since Adam and Eve fell, every human (other than Christ) has inherited a sinful nature. We retain our natural freedom, but three possibilities remain for whether we have moral freedom.

13. See Augustine, "Admonition and Grace," in *Saint Augustine: Christian Instruction; Admonition and Grace; The Christian Combat; Faith, Hope and Charity*, ed. Joseph Deferrari, trans. John Courtney Murray, 2nd ed., Fathers of the Church 2 (Washington, DC: Catholic University of America Press, 1950), 33 (285–86); Augustine, "Faith, Hope and Charity," in Defarrari, *Saint Augustine*, 30 (394–95).

14. Thomas Boston, *Human Nature in Its Fourfold State, of Primitive Integrity, Entire Depravation, Begun Recovery, and Consummate Happiness or Misery, Subsisting in the Parents of Mankind in Paradise, the Unregenerate, the Regenerate, All Mankind in the Future State; in Several Practical Discourses*, 23rd ed. (Perth: Book-Sellers, 1776).

(Table 6.2 continued)

Moral Ability	Ability to Sin	Explanation
2. No moral ability: Unregenerate sinners are not free to choose what God wants.	Able to sin and not able not to sin	We all are born with a radically corrupt nature. We do not have moral freedom to choose what God wants because we are spiritually dead and in bondage to sin's enslaving power. An unbeliever is morally unable to choose to follow Christ and has no desire to do so (Rom. 8:7). An unbeliever chooses what he wants, and he will never want to follow Christ as his master unless God first changes his "wanter." "You refuse [are unwilling (NASB), are not willing (CSB, NET)] to come to me that you may have life" (John 5:40). "Everyone who practices sin is a slave to sin. . . . You are of your father the devil, and your will is to do your father's desires" (John 8:34, 44).
3. Partial moral ability: Regenerate sinners are partially free to choose what God wants.	Able to sin and able not to sin	We receive this new nature when God regenerates us and gives us spiritual life (Eph. 2:1–10). God first enables us to repent and believe in Christ, and he continues to give us moral freedom to choose what he wants. But this is a partial freedom because we are in an already-not-yet state—we are already free from sin but not yet fully free from sin. We are no longer in bondage to sin's enslaving power, but we are still sinful and continually fight our sins (Rom. 6–7; Gal. 5:16–26; Col. 3; 1 Pet. 2:11).
4. Total moral ability: God's glorified people are fully free to choose what God wants.	Able not to sin and not able to sin	This is our final nature when God glorifies us. Never again will we even want to be glory thieves who steal from the supremely glorious God. Never again will we put ourselves in the place of God. Never again will we trust our own senses, our own experience, and our own reasoning such that we think we know better than God. Never again will we disregard God, disbelieve God, disobey God, and belittle God. We will be fully free to glorify God by enjoying him forever!

All of us—unregenerate and regenerate—have the natural freedom to choose what we want. That natural freedom is a gracious gift from God, who made us in his image.

But we do not all have the moral freedom to choose what God wants.[15] As Augustine argues, the will's "choice is truly free only when it is not a slave to sin and vice."[16] And as Martin Luther argues, the nature of our will is like a beast in bondage either to Satan or to God (cf. Matt. 6:24; Luke 16:13).[17] Moral freedom—*true* freedom—is a gracious gift from God. Jesus explains, "No one can come to me unless it is granted him by the Father" (John 6:65). God is so merciful and kind that he planned to save certain individuals from bondage to sin's enslaving power. The Father chose to save the elect in eternity past; Christ died in our place and paid the penalty we deserve to pay; and the Spirit gives spiritual life to the spiritually dead so that we are morally free to choose what God wants. God sovereignly grants us the freedom to do what he commands.

Incompatibilists and compatibilists agree on natural ability but not on moral ability. The core issue of moral ability is our heart or nature (see figure 6.1).

---

15. This is contrary to the Arminian view of prevenient grace (see the end of chap. 5). Wesley asserts, "There is a measure of free-will supernaturally restored to every man, together with that supernatural light which 'enlightens every man that cometh into the world.'" John Wesley, "Predestination Calmly Considered," in *The Works of John Wesley*, 3rd ed. (London: Wesleyan Methodist Book Room, 1872), 229–30.

16. Augustine, *The City of God: Books VIII–XVI*, trans. Gerald G. Walsh and Grace Monahan, Fathers of the Church 14 (Washington, DC: Catholic University of America Press, 1952), 376.

17. See Martin Luther, "The Bondage of the Will," in *Career of the Reformer III*, ed. and trans. Philip S. Watson, vol. 33 of *Luther's Works* (Philadelphia: Fortress, 1972), 3–295. Luther argues, "Free choice without the grace of God is not free at all, but immutably the captive and slave of evil, since it cannot of itself turn to the good. . . . In relation to God, or in matters pertaining to salvation or damnation, a man has no free choice, but is a captive, subject and slave either of the will of God or the will of Satan" (67, 70).

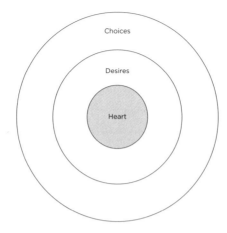

Figure 6.1   How Our Choices, Desires, and Heart Relate[18]

Choices:	I always	choose	what I choose
Desires:	because I	want	what I want
Heart:	because I	am	who I am.

The heart is the core:

1. "I always choose what I choose." Choices are the outer-most, superficial level.

2. "Because I want what I want." I choose according to my strongest desires—what I think is most to my advantage. As Jonathan Edwards puts it, "The will is always determined by the strongest motive."[19] In other words, I always do what I most want to do. Ronald Nash explains, "Everyone has a scale of values by which his needs, wants, and goals are ranked in order of the importance and urgency he attaches to them."[20]

---

18. This figure is inspired by and builds on that in Christensen, *What about Free Will?*, 177.

19. Edwards, *Freedom of the Will*, 148.

20. Ronald H. Nash, *Life's Ultimate Questions: An Introduction to Philosophy* (Grand Rapids, MI: Zondervan, 1999), 333; cf. 326–41.

3. "Because I am who I am." My heart is the core or essence of who I am—my "innermost being."[21] And I have a heart problem: "The LORD saw that the wickedness of man was great in the earth, and that every intention of the thoughts of his heart was only evil continually" (Gen. 6:5). Another way to refer to my heart is my *nature*, which is a complex of attributes.[22] My heart or my nature determines what I want. My nature is either unregenerate or regenerate, and that is the core reason I either do not or do have the moral ability to glorify God. By using the phrase "because I am who I am," I do not intend to minimize moral responsibility. I might dismiss one of my vices by saying, "It's just who I am"— as if that absolves me of moral responsibility. It doesn't. I cannot blame my sinful desires and choices on my sinful nature. *I* am responsible for my desires and choices because *I* am responsible for my sinful heart (see 1 Sam. 24:13; Jer. 13:23; Matt. 12:33–37; 15:18–19).

In contrast to what I am arguing, the tract in figure 6.2 assumes incompatibilism. It assumes that what is ultimately decisive for whether you are a believer or an unbeliever is your ability to choose differently.

6. Ten Reasons for Compatibilism

Here are ten reasons for compatibilism—that God's meticulous sovereignty (particularly regarding predestination) is compatible with human freedom (particularly the God-enabled freedom to believe in Christ and the moral responsibility for not believing in Christ).

---

21. Moisés Silva, ed., *New International Dictionary of New Testament Theology and Exegesis*, 2nd ed., 5 vols. (Grand Rapids, MI: Zondervan, 2014), 2:626 (καρδία).
22. William W. Combs, "Does the Believer Have One Nature or Two?," *Detroit Baptist Seminary Journal* 2 (1997): 84.

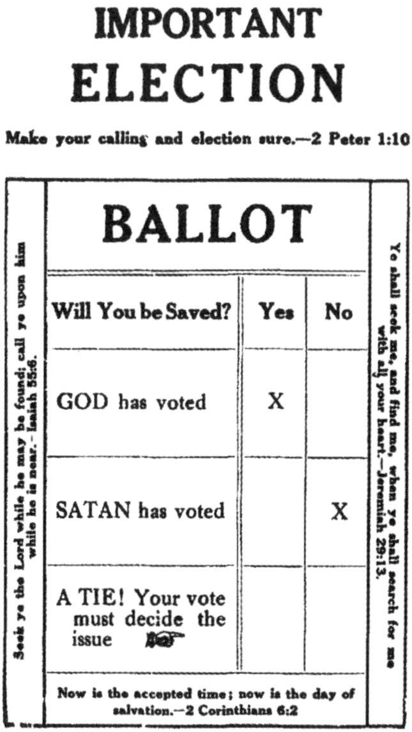

IMPORTANT
ELECTION

Make your calling and election sure.—2 Peter 1:10

BALLOT		
Will You be Saved?	Yes	No
GOD has voted	X	
SATAN has voted		X
A TIE! Your vote must decide the issue ☞		

Seek ye the Lord while he may be found; call ye upon him while he is near.—Isaiah 55:6.

Ye shall seek me, and find me, when ye shall search for me with all your heart.—Jeremiah 29:13.

Now is the accepted time; now is the day of salvation.—2 Corinthians 6:2

Figure 6.2   Evangelism That Assumes Incompatibilism[23]

1. The Bible teaches that God is meticulously sovereign. "Our God is in the heavens; / he does all that he pleases" (Ps. 115:3). The Most High

> does according to his will among the host of heaven
> and among the inhabitants of the earth;
> and none can stay his hand
> or say to him, "What have you done?" (Dan. 4:35)

God is the supreme King (1 Chron. 16:31; Pss. 47:8; 97:1; 99:1; Dan. 4:25). God "works all things according to the counsel of

---

23. This tract from the Bible Institute Colportage Association appeared in *The Christian Workers Magazine*, March 1919: 493.

his will" (Eph. 1:11; cf. Job 42:2; Isa. 46:9–10; Matt. 10:29). He ordains everything, including through secondary causes the evil that humans freely choose to commit. Joseph explained to his brothers, "You meant evil against me, but God meant it for good" (Gen. 50:20). The Lord proclaims,

> I form light and create darkness;
>> I make well-being and create calamity;
>> I am the LORD, who does all these things. (Isa. 45:7)

Amos proclaimed,

> Does disaster come to a city,
>> unless the LORD has done it?" (Amos 3:6)

God ordained all things. That includes:

- every water droplet, every snowflake, every fire ember, every gust of wind
- every single respiratory droplet and airborne particle that transmits viruses
- every moon and planet and star in the Milky Way galaxy
- every nation and human ruler
- every natural evil
- every moral evil—including every human decision to reject Christ
- every human decision to turn from sin and embrace Christ

God ordained not only what every human would do but also that every human would do so *freely*.[24]

---

24. On God's meticulous sovereignty, see John S. Feinberg, "God Ordains All Things," in *Predestination and Free Will: Four Views of Divine Sovereignty and Human Freedom*, ed. David Basinger and Randall Basinger (Downers Grove, IL: InterVarsity Press, 1986), 19–43 (also 85–88, 125–29, 163–68); Paul Helm, "The Augustinian-Calvinist View," in *Divine Foreknowledge: Four Views*, ed. James K. Beilby and Paul R. Eddy, Spectrum Multiview Books (Downers Grove, IL: InterVarsity Press, 2001), 161–89 (also 61–64, 114–18, 155–59);

2. The Bible teaches that we have a free will in the sense that we choose what we most want and that we are morally accountable to God, but nowhere does it teach that we have a free will in the sense that we can make equally alternative choices. When God commands you to love your neighbor as yourself (Lev. 19:18; Matt. 19:19; 22:39; Rom. 13:9; Gal. 5:14; James 2:8), he assumes that you always act according to what you think is in your best interest (cf. Matt. 7:12; Eph. 5:29; Phil. 2:4). You choose *what you most want.* That is different from saying that you have *moral freedom to make equally alternative choices.* The incompatibilist view of human freedom (see table 6.1 above) is what many people assume. But the Bible does not teach it. To the contrary, the Bible teaches that the deciding, decisive, ultimate reason a man comes to God is God and not man (see chap. 4).

3. The Bible never says that God gives up even a sliver of his sovereignty in order to make room for our free will to make equally alternative choices, and the Bible never says that we are free in the sense that God does not ultimately or decisively determine what we freely choose. The Bible does not teach that we have a free will in the sense that we can make equally alternative choices. Arminians assume this view because it seems self-evident in light of experience, intuition, and common sense. For example, Jerry Walls and Joseph Dongell hold to libertarian freedom for three reasons:

> First, the common experience of deliberation assumes that our choices are undetermined. . . . All of this assumes that it really is up to us how we will decide.
>
> Second, it seems intuitively and immediately evident that many of our actions are up to us in the sense that when faced with a decision, both (or more) options are within our power to choose. . . .

D. A. Carson, *How Long, O Lord? Reflections on Suffering and Evil*, 2nd ed. (Grand Rapids, MI: Baker Academic, 2006), 177–203; Paul Kjoss Helseth, "God Causes All Things," in *Four Views on Divine Providence*, ed. Dennis W. Jowers, Counterpoints (Grand Rapids, MI: Zondervan, 2011), 25–52 (also 101–13, 165–69, 209–23); Piper, *Providence*.

Third, libertarians take very seriously the widespread judgment that we are morally responsible for our actions and that
moral responsibility requires freedom.

. . . A person cannot be held morally responsible for an act
unless he or she was free to perform that act and free to refrain
from it. This is a basic moral intuition.

. . . The common-sense view of freedom is libertarian
freedom.[25]

These Arminian professors appeal not to the Bible here but to
"common experience" and to what "seems intuitively and immediately evident" and to "basic moral intuition."

4. The Bible teaches as a proverbial truth that God's meticulous sovereignty and human freedom are simultaneously true.
"The heart of man plans his way, / but the LORD establishes his
steps" (Prov. 16:9).

5. The Bible teaches that God's meticulous sovereignty and
human freedom are simultaneously true in the crucifixion of
Christ. This is the most remarkable example of compatibilism.
Peter preached on Pentecost, "This Jesus, delivered up according to the definite plan and foreknowledge of God, you crucified and killed by the hands of lawless men" (Acts 2:23). The
early church prayed in Jerusalem, "For truly in this city there
were gathered together against your holy servant Jesus, whom
you anointed, both Herod and Pontius Pilate, along with the
Gentiles and the peoples of Israel, to do whatever your hand
and your plan had predestined to take place" (Acts 4:27–28).
In the crucifixion of Jesus, God was meticulously sovereign,
and those who crucified Jesus are morally culpable before God.

6. The Bible teaches that God's meticulous sovereignty and
human freedom are simultaneously true in the writing of Scripture.
Who wrote the Bible: God or humans? The answer is yes. God

---

25. Jerry L. Walls and Joseph R. Dongell, *Why I Am Not a Calvinist* (Downers Grove,
IL: InterVarsity Press, 2004), 103–6. Cf. Jack Cottrell, *What the Bible Says about God
the Ruler* (Joplin, MO: College Press, 1984), 161–228.

sovereignly authored the Bible: "All Scripture is breathed out by God [God-breathed (NIV)]" (2 Tim. 3:16). And humans freely authored the Bible—but without the freedom to write independently or differently from what God intended: "No prophecy of Scripture comes from someone's own interpretation. For no prophecy was ever produced by the will of man, but men spoke from God as they were carried along by the Holy Spirit" (2 Pet. 1:20–21).[26]

7. The Bible teaches that God's meticulous sovereignty and human freedom are simultaneously true in the perseverance of believers. If we have a free will in the sense that we can make equally alternative choices, then a genuine believer can choose to reject Christ and no longer be saved from his sins. Arminians concede this point and think that a genuine Christian can apostatize, but I am convinced that the Bible teaches that a genuine Christian cannot irreversibly abandon and renounce orthodox Christianity because *God* preserves every genuine believer (John 10:28–29). God enables all genuine Christians to persevere—that is, all genuine Christians work because God works (Phil. 2:12–13).[27]

8. The Bible teaches that God knows what we will freely choose. God's knowledge or omniscience means that "God fully knows himself and all things actual and possible in one simple and eternal act."[28] God's knowledge includes what humans freely choose to do in the future (see Isa. 44:6–7; 46:9–10). If

26. See Stephen J. Wellum, "The Importance of the Nature of Divine Sovereignty for Our View of Scripture," *Southern Baptist Journal of Theology* 4, no. 2 (2000): 76–90. Cf. Andrew David Naselli, "Scripture: How the Bible Is a Book like No Other," in *Don't Call It a Comeback: The Old Faith for a New Day*, ed. Kevin DeYoung (Wheaton, IL: Crossway, 2011), 59–69; D. A. Carson, ed., *The Enduring Authority of the Christian Scriptures* (Grand Rapids, MI: Eerdmans, 2016); John S. Feinberg, *Light in a Dark Place: The Doctrine of Scripture*, Foundations of Evangelical Theology (Wheaton, IL: Crossway, 2018).

27. Cf. John Murray, *Redemption: Accomplished and Applied* (Grand Rapids, MI: Eerdmans, 1955), 148–50; Robert A. Peterson, *Our Secure Salvation: Preservation and Apostasy*, Explorations in Biblical Theology (Phillipsburg, NJ: P&R, 2009); Andrew David Naselli, "What Is Apostasy? Can a Christian Become Apostate?," The Gospel Coalition, 2020, https://www.thegospelcoalition.org/.

28. Grudem, *Systematic Theology*, 1513.

God knows precisely what we will freely choose (not merely what we might choose), then God has in some sense determined what we will freely choose, and we do not have a free will in the sense that we can make equally alternative choices.[29]

A case in point is prophecy in the Bible. God cannot infallibly predict what will happen if we have a free will in the sense that we can make equally alternative choices. For example, the Bible condemns Judas for betraying Jesus when Judas could not have chosen differently. Jesus knew from the beginning that Judas would betray him, and one reason Judas betrayed Jesus was to fulfill Scripture:

> *Jesus knew from the beginning* who those were who did not believe, and *who it was who would betray him.* (John 6:64)

> Jesus answered them, "Did I not choose you, the twelve? And yet one of you is a devil." He spoke of Judas the son of Simon Iscariot, for *he,* one of the twelve, *was going to betray him.* (John 6:70–71; cf. 13:11)

> I am not speaking of all of you; I know whom I have chosen. But *the Scripture will be fulfilled,* "He who ate my bread has lifted his heel against me." I am telling you this now, before it takes place, that when it does take place you may believe that I am he. (John 13:18–19)

> While I was with them, I kept them in your name, which you have given me. I have guarded them, and not one of them has been lost except the son of destruction, *that the Scripture might be fulfilled.* (John 17:12; cf. Acts 1:16–17)

> This ministry and apostleship from which Judas [freely] turned aside to go to his own place. (Acts 1:15)

There's a good reason parents don't name their sons *Judas.* If you look up *Judas* in a thesaurus, you'll see words like *traitor,*

---

29. Cf. Feinberg, "God Ordains All Things," 33–34.

betrayer, back-stabber, double-crosser, false friend, turncoat,
and *renegade.* That is what Judas epitomizes. God ordained
Judas's wicked betrayal, and God holds Judas morally responsible for his wickedness (Matt. 26:23–24).[30]

9. The Bible teaches that God himself does not have a free
will in the sense that he can make equally alternative choices. If
we define "free will" as the ability to make equally alternative
choices, then God himself does not have a free will. God is om-
nipotent in the sense that he can do whatever he wants; he can
do all his holy will; he can do anything consistent with his holy
nature. That means that there are some things that God cannot
do—things that are not consistent with his nature. For example,

- "It is impossible for God to lie" (Heb. 6:18; cf. Titus 1:2).
- God "cannot deny himself" (2 Tim. 2:13).
- "God cannot be tempted with evil" (James 1:13).

If God has a free will in the sense that he can make equally alternative choices, then God could lie, God could deny himself,
and God could be tempted with evil. But the Bible explicitly
says that God cannot do those things.

10. The Bible teaches that God's glorified people in the eternal state will not have a free will in the sense that we can make
equally alternative choices. If we define "free will" as the ability
to make equally alternative choices, then we will not have a free
will in the eternal state. The reason is that in the new heavens

---

30. Carson observes, "Divine ultimacy even behind evil actions is presupposed. But
divine ultimacy operates in some mysterious way so that human responsibility is in
no way mitigated, while the divine being is in no way tarnished. In particular, Judas
is responsible even when Satan is using him [John 13:2, 27]; but over both stands the
sovereignty of God." D. A. Carson, *Divine Sovereignty and Human Responsibility: Biblical Perspectives in Tension*, 2nd ed. (Grand Rapids, MI: Baker Books, 1994), 132. Cf.
John Piper, *Spectacular Sins: And Their Global Purpose in the Glory of Christ*, in *The
Collected Works of John Piper*, ed. David Mathis and Justin Taylor, 14 vols. (Wheaton,
IL: Crossway, 2017), 7:319–26; Richard M. Blaylock, *Vessels of Wrath*, 2 vols. (Eugene,
OR: Pickwick, 2023), 2:141–52.

and new earth God will reverse the effects of the fall (see Rev. 22:3) with the result that God's people will not be able to sin. Death is the payment for sin (Rom. 6:23), and in the new heaven and new earth, "death shall be no more" (Rev. 21:4). We eagerly anticipate "new heavens and a new earth in which righteousness dwells" (2 Pet. 3:13). "True freedom consists in knowing the best and right choices, in being unhindered in making them, and in experiencing the greatest joy when we do make them."[31]

7. How? It's a Mystery[32]

Some Bible doctrines like the Trinity and Christ's person involve tensions. For each doctrine, there are at least three propositions that the Bible teaches, and we feel that the propositions are in tension. It makes sense that any two could be true, but it becomes hard to understand when you add the third. Since it is difficult to explain how all three can be true at the same time, people tend to accept two and deny or explain away the third (see table 6.3).

Table 6.3   Doctrinal Tensions

Doctrine	Tension	Explanations to Resolve the Tension
The Trinity	A. There is one God.	Tritheists deny A.
	B. Three persons are called God.	Arians (e.g., Jehovah's Witnesses) deny B.
	C. Those three persons are distinct.	Modalists and Sabellians deny C.

---

31. Christensen, *What about Free Will?*, 225.
32. Parts of this section update Andrew David Naselli, *How to Understand and Apply the New Testament: Twelve Steps from Exegesis to Theology* (Phillipsburg, NJ: P&R, 2017), 288–90, and Naselli, "Chosen, Born Again, and Believing: How Election, Regeneration, and Faith Relate to Each Other in the Gospel According to John," *Master's Seminary Journal* 32, no. 2 (2021): 283–84.

(Table 6.3 continued)

Doctrine	Tension	Explanations to Resolve the Tension
The person of Christ	A. Christ is fully God.	Ebionites and Arians deny A.
	B. Christ is fully human.	Gnostics/Docetists and Apollinarians deny B.
	C. Christ is one person.	Nestorians deny C.
The problem of evil	A. God is all-good.	Some Calvinists (e.g., Gordon Clark) qualify A.
	B. God is all-powerful and all-wise.	Finitists (e.g., Edgar S. Brightman) deny B, and open theists qualify B.
	C. Evil exists.	Pantheists (e.g., Benedict Spinoza) and adherents of Mary Baker Eddy's Christian Science deny C.
Providence	A. God is meticulously sovereign. B. Humans are morally responsible.	Arminians deny A; they believe that A is incompatible with B and C.[a] Calvinists believe that A, B, and C are compatible.
	C. God is holy, all-good, and never blameworthy.	Arminians claim that C is incompatible with A. Calvinists qualify that God ordains evil but in a way that he is not guilty of sin; he stands behind good and evil asymmetrically. God is the ultimate cause who orchestrates, ordains, or ensures all things through proximate and efficient causes such as human agents and natural laws (see the end of chap. 12).

a. Arminian theologian Roger Olson embraces libertarian free will for two reasons: "[1] It is necessary to preserve human responsibility for sin and evil, and [2] it is necessary to preserve God from being responsible for sin and evil. . . . God allows his perfect will [i.e., what he truly wishes to happen] to be thwarted by his human creatures whom he loves and respects enough not to control them." Olson, *Against Calvinism*, 23, 100. Olson asserts, "God limits himself to allow for human free agency (for the sake of genuine relationships that are not manipulated or controlled). . . . The real reason Arminians reject divine control of every human choice and action is that this would make God the author of sin and evil. For Arminians this makes God at least morally ambiguous and at worst the *only* sinner. . . . Arminianism is all about protecting the reputation of God by protecting his character. . . . Love and justice are necessary to goodness, and both exclude willing determination of sin, evil or eternal suffering." Roger E. Olson, *Arminian Theology: Myths and Realities* (Downers Grove, IL: IVP Academic, 2006), 39, 99–100; emphasis original.

We feel tension when a doctrine involves *mystery*. R. C. Sproul helpfully distinguishes three terms:

1. *Contradiction*: "a thing cannot be what it is and not be what it is at the same time and in the same relationship."[33]
2. *Paradox*: "an apparent contradiction that upon closer scrutiny can be resolved."[34]
3. *Mystery*: "that which is true but which we do not understand."[35]

Sproul continues,

> No one understands a contradiction because contradictions are intrinsically unintelligible.
>
> . . . Mysteries are capable of being understood. The New Testament reveals to us things that were concealed and not understood in Old Testament times. There are things that once were mysterious to us that are now understood. This does not mean that everything that is presently a mystery to us will one day be made clear, but that many current mysteries will be unraveled for us.
>
> . . . Christianity has plenty of room for mysteries. It has no room for contradictions.[36]

God is so amazing that he ordained both (1) what we choose and (2) that we freely choose what we most want. How exactly does God do that in a way that he is blameless and we are morally responsible for what we choose? I don't fully know because he doesn't tell us.[37] It's a mystery; there is a tension here that we do not fully understand.[38]

---

33. R. C. Sproul, *Chosen by God* (Wheaton, IL: Tyndale House, 1986), 43.
34. Sproul, *Chosen by God*, 44.
35. Sproul, *Chosen by God*, 46.
36. Sproul, *Chosen by God*, 47.
37. See the end of chap. 12 for an attempt to answer this question more specifically.
38. Cf. K. Scott Oliphint, *The Majesty of Mystery: Celebrating the Glory of an Incomprehensible God* (Bellingham, WA: Lexham, 2016), 155; Joel D. Arnold, *Theologi-*

Acts 2:23 and 4:27–28 (quoted above) powerfully illustrate why we must affirm that God's meticulous sovereignty is compatible with human moral responsibility. Carson explains,

> Christians who may deny compatibilism on front after front become compatibilists (knowingly or otherwise) when they think about the cross. There is no alternative, except to deny the faith. . . . One of the common ingredients in most of the attempts to overthrow compatibilism is the sacrifice of mystery. The problem looks neater when, say, God is not behind evil in any sense. But quite apart from the fact that the biblical texts will not allow so easy an escape, the result is a totally nonmysterious God. And somehow the god of this picture is domesticated, completely unpuzzling.[39]

We feel this tension between God's sovereignty and our responsibility in the Gospel according to John. Jesus explains, "You do not believe because you are not among my sheep" (John 10:26). On the one hand, being a sheep depends solely on God's sovereign choice. On the other hand, you are responsible to believe, so you are culpable if you do not believe. Jesus demands, "You must be born again" (3:7). On the one hand, being born again is solely a work of God. On the other hand, you are responsible to be born again, so you are culpable if you are not born again. So on the one hand, God's sovereignty regarding election and regeneration is absolute; it is not contingent on our faith. On the other hand, humans are morally responsible to believe in Jesus; we are culpable if we do not believe in Jesus.

God is absolutely sovereign to choose to save individuals and regenerate them, and humans are morally responsible and

---

cal Antinomy: A Biblical Theology of Paradox, Paternoster Theological Monographs (Milton Keynes, UK: Paternoster, 2020), 79–84, 146–48.
39. Carson, *How Long, O Lord?*, 188, 200.

thus culpable without being puppets or robots. Both of those statements are true at the same time without contradicting each other. God's sovereignty and human responsibility are compatible; they exist together without conflicting. They do not break the law of noncontradiction.

Bible passages that emphasize human responsibility do not cancel out or contradict passages that emphasize God's meticulous sovereignty. The Bible forthrightly proclaims both God's meticulous sovereignty and human responsibility without embarrassment and without attempting to philosophically harmonize them. Both are gloriously true (as my colleague Tom Steller often says), and we dare not tweak what the Bible teaches in order to remove an element of mystery. If we sense a problem, then the problem is not with the God-breathed text but with our finite and fallen minds. We cannot put all the puzzle pieces together partly because we do not have all the puzzle pieces.[40]

Calvin warns and exhorts us, "To seek any other knowledge of predestination than what the Word of God discloses is not less insane than if one should purpose to walk in a pathless waste, or to see in darkness. And let us not be ashamed to be ignorant of something in this matter, wherein there is a certain learned ignorance."[41] We do not fully understand how God's meticulous sovereignty is compatible with human freedom and responsibility. But that does not mean that such harmony is illogical or impossible for the infinite God. Instead of leading us to question God and his ways, this should lead us to worship the infinite God.

---

40. Cf. D. A. Carson, "Unity and Diversity in the New Testament: The Possibility of Systematic Theology," in *Scripture and Truth*, ed. D. A. Carson and John D. Woodbridge (Grand Rapids, MI: Zondervan, 1983), 81–82.

41. John Calvin, *Institutes of the Christian Religion*, ed. John T. McNeill, trans. Ford Lewis Battles, 2 vols., Library of Christian Classics (Philadelphia: Westminster, 1960), 3.21.2 (923).

Responding with a Prayer

Father, thank you for choosing to save me. Thank you, God, for saving me from my radical corruption. Thank you for resurrecting my spiritual corpse and for freeing me from the bondage to sin's enslaving power. Thank you for changing my heart so that I now want to trust and obey you. Amen.

Does Election Contradict God's Desire That All Humans Be Saved?

Explaining a human's will can be complicated. There's a scene in book five of the Harry Potter series that makes me laugh. Hermione (my favorite character) is explaining to her friends Harry and Ron how a girl named Cho is feeling:

> "Well, obviously, [1] she's feeling very sad, because of Cedric dying. [2] Then I expect she's feeling confused because she liked Cedric and now she likes Harry, and she can't work out who she likes best. [3] Then she'll be feeling guilty, thinking it's an insult to Cedric's memory to be kissing Harry at all, and [4] she'll be worrying about what everyone else might say about her if she starts going out with Harry. [5] And she probably can't work out what her feelings toward Harry are anyway, because he was the one who was with Cedric when Cedric died, so that's all very mixed up and painful. [6] Oh, and she's afraid she's going

to be thrown off the Ravenclaw Quidditch team because she's been flying so badly."

A slightly stunned silence greeted the end of this speech, then Ron said, "One person can't feel all that at once, they'd explode."

"Just because you've got the emotional range of a teaspoon doesn't mean we all have," said Hermione nastily.[1]

That humorous exchange illustrates that a human's will is complex. Do you even completely understand your own will—let alone the will of someone else you think you know well? Since it is difficult to fully understand the will of a finite human, it should not surprise us that it is difficult to fully understand the will of the incomprehensible and infinite God. ("Difficult" is an understatement!)

We Must Distinguish Two Aspects of God's Will

God has one will, but it appears to us to have two aspects.[2] Calvin explains, "Even though his will is one and simple in him, it appears manifold to us because, on account of our mental incapacity, we do not grasp how in divers ways it wills and does not will something to take place."[3] In order for us finite creatures to make sense of specific statements in Scripture, we must distinguish two aspects of God's will—two ways that God wills: (1) what God would like to see happen and (2) what God actually wills to happen. That helpful wording is from I. Howard

---

1. J. K. Rowling, *Harry Potter and the Order of the Phoenix* (New York: Levine, 2003), 459.

2. John Piper's fingerprints are all over this chapter. The resource that has most influenced my thinking on the two aspects of God's complex will is this sixty-two-page book: John Piper, *Does God Desire All to Be Saved?* (Wheaton, IL: Crossway, 2013).

3. John Calvin, *Institutes of the Christian Religion*, ed. John T. McNeill, trans. Ford Lewis Battles, 2 vols., Library of Christian Classics (Philadelphia: Westminster, 1960), 1.18.3 (234).

Marshall, an eminent Arminian scholar.[4] Table 7.1 illustrates with biblical examples those two ways that God wills.

Table 7.1 Biblical Examples That Distinguish Two Ways That God Wills[a]

What God Would Like to See Happen	What God Actually Wills to Happen
"Thus says the LORD, the God of Israel, 'Let my people go'" (Ex. 5:1; cf. 7:16; 8:1, 20; 9:1, 13; 10:3).	"I will harden his heart" (Ex. 4:21; cf. 7:3). "The LORD hardened the heart of Pharaoh" (9:12; cf. 10:1, 20, 27; 11:10; 14:8).
"Honor your father and your mother" (Ex. 20:12; Matt. 15:4; Eph. 6:2). "*I have no pleasure* [Heb. *haphez*] in the death of the wicked, but that the wicked turn from his way and live" (Ezek. 33:11; cf. Ezek. 18:23, 32; Lam. 3:32–33).	"Now Eli was very old, and he kept hearing all that his sons were doing to all Israel, and how they lay with the women who were serving at the entrance to the tent of meeting. And he said to them, 'Why do you do such things? For I hear of your evil dealings from all these people. No, my sons; it is no good report that I hear the people of the LORD spreading abroad. If someone sins against a man, God will mediate for him, but if someone sins against the LORD, who can intercede for him?' But they would not listen to the voice of their father, for *it was the will* [Heb. *haphez*] of the LORD to put them to death" (1 Sam. 2:22–25). "As the LORD took delight in doing you good and multiplying you, so the LORD will take delight in bringing ruin upon you and destroying you" (Deut. 28:63).

---

4. "The fact that God wishes or wills that all people should be saved does not necessarily imply that all will respond to the gospel and be saved. We must certainly distinguish between *what God would like to see happen* and *what he actually does will to happen*, and both of these things can be spoken of as God's will." I. Howard Marshall, "Universal Grace and Atonement in the Pastoral Epistles," in *The Grace of God, the Will of Man: A Case for Arminianism*, ed. Clark H. Pinnock (Grand Rapids, MI: Zondervan, 1989), 56; emphasis added.

(Table 7.1 continued)

What God Would Like to See Happen	What God Actually Wills to Happen
"You shall not murder" (Ex. 20:13; Matt. 5:21; Rom. 13:9). Thus, those who contributed to the murder of Jesus are responsible for their sin: "You crucified and killed [Jesus] by the hands of lawless men" (Acts 2:23b). "Truly in this city there were gathered together against your holy servant Jesus, whom you anointed, both Herod and Pontius Pilate, along with the Gentiles and the peoples of Israel" (Acts 4:27).	"We esteemed him stricken, / smitten by God, and afflicted. . . . It was the will of the LORD to crush him" (Isa. 53:4, 10). "Jesus [was] delivered up according to the definite plan and foreknowledge of God" (Acts 2:23a). ". . . to do whatever your hand and your plan had predestined to take place" (Acts 4:28).
God genuinely desires all people to be saved. "It is not the will of my Father who is in heaven that one of these little ones should perish" (Matt. 18:14; see also Matt. 11:28; 23:37; John 3:16; 7:37; 1 Tim. 2:4; 2 Pet. 3:9).	**God sovereignly chose to save only some people.** "I thank you, Father, Lord of heaven and earth, that you have hidden these things from the wise and understanding and revealed them to little children; yes, Father, for such was your gracious will" (Matt. 11:25–26; Luke 10:21; see the rest of this book).

a. Cf. Piper, *Does God Desire All to Be Saved?*, 19–30.

The final row of table 7.1 includes 1 Timothy 2:4 and 2 Peter 3:9 because those are the most common proof texts that God wants all people to be saved. But I am not convinced they are good proof texts. When Paul says that God "desires all people to be saved and to come to the knowledge of the truth" (1 Tim. 2:4), I think he means *all kinds of people*—Jew and Gentile, rich and poor, and so on. And when Peter says that the Lord "is patient toward you, not wishing that any should perish, but that all should reach repentance" (2 Pet. 3:9), I think he means that the Lord is patient toward *you believers* and that he does not wish that *any of you believers* should perish but that *all of you believers* should reach repentance (cf. "beloved" in 3:1, 8, 14, 17).[5]

But even if 1 Timothy 2:4 and 2 Peter 3:9 teach that God genuinely desires that all people without exception be saved (which many Calvinists believe), that would do nothing to overturn God's sovereign election of individuals. It would simply be another example that God can desire something in one sense (column 1 in table 7.1) and not desire it in another sense (column 2 in table 7.1). Theologians distinguish these two ways that God wills with various terms (see table 7.2).

Table 7.2   Terms That Distinguish Two Ways That God Wills

What God Would Like to See Happen	What God Actually Wills to Happen
Commanded will: This is what God commands. It does not always happen.	Decreed will: This is what God decrees. It always happens.
Moral will: We should obey this. God tells us what is right and wrong, but we often do not obey God.	Sovereign will: This is what God ordains, and it always happens. God's moral will includes that we submit to his sovereign will—for example, by not complaining about it, worrying about it, or questioning God's power, goodness, and wisdom.
Revealed will: God tells us what we must do.	Secret or hidden will: God normally does not reveal his detailed plan to us ahead of time. (An exception is predictive prophecy such as Daniel 10.)

5. See Michael Riccardi, *To Save Sinners: A Critical Evaluation of the Multiple Intentions View of the Atonement* (Eugene, OR: Wipf and Stock, 2023), 188–96, 302n7.

(Table 7.2 continued)

What God Would Like to See Happen	What God Actually Wills to Happen
Antecedent will: God generally values some things as good.	Consequent will: God specifically chooses "among those good things (in view of the overall nature of the world he intends to make)."[a]
Looking at a painful or wicked event through a narrow lens: God "sees the tragedy or the sin for what it is in itself, and he is angered and grieved."[b]	Looking at a painful or wicked event through a wide-angle lens: God "sees the tragedy or the sin in relation to everything leading up to it and everything flowing out from it. He sees it in all the connections and effects that form a pattern or mosaic stretching into eternity. This mosaic, with all its (good and evil) parts, he does delight in."[c]

a. John M. Frame, *The Doctrine of God*, A Theology of Lordship (Phillipsburg, NJ: P&R, 2002), 530.
b. Piper, *Does God Desire All to Be Saved?*, 45.
c. Piper, *Does God Desire All to Be Saved?*, 45.

So does God desire all people to be saved? Yes, in the sense that he would like to see that happen. No, in the sense that God did not actually will for that to happen. Otherwise all would be saved; but the Bible rejects universalism.[6] "Many are called, but few are chosen" (Matt. 22:14).

What God Values More Highly Than Saving All Humans

Arminians and Calvinists agree that (1) not all humans without exception will be saved, (2) in some sense God wills in two distinct ways, and (3) God does not save all humans without exception because God values something else more highly. Arminians and Calvinists disagree on what that "something else" is that God values more highly (see table 7.3).

6. See J. I. Packer, "Universalism: Will Everyone Ultimately Be Saved?," in *Hell under Fire: Modern Scholarship Reinvents Eternal Punishment*, ed. Christopher W. Morgan and Robert A. Peterson (Grand Rapids, MI: Zondervan, 2004), 169–94.

Table 7.3   What Does God Value More Highly Than Saving All Humans without Exception?[a]

According to Arminianism	According to Calvinism
God more highly values a genuinely loving relationship, which requires us to have a free will in the sense that we can make equally alternative choices (see chap. 6).	God more highly values displaying his glory in mercy and wrath (Rom. 9:22–23) and receiving all the glory for sovereignly saving individuals (see chap. 1).
Our choice is decisive or ultimate.[b]	God's choice is decisive or ultimate.

a. Cf. Piper, *Does God Desire All to Be Saved?*, 39–40.

b. Again, some Arminians protest describing their view with the word *decisive* like this. See my footnote on table 5.1 at the end of chap. 5.

God's choice—not our choice—is the deciding factor. That is why Paul writes, "*God may perhaps grant them repentance* leading to a knowledge of the truth, and they may come to their senses and escape from the snare of the devil, after being captured by him to do his will" (2 Tim. 2:25–26).

How Can God's Desire to Save People Be Genuine If He Has Decreed Not to Save Them?

Some examples might help illustrate that distinguishing two ways that God wills is reasonable and not doublespeak. (I concede up front that analogies about a human's will break down because they cannot flawlessly illustrate God's will. For example, humans may have confused and mutually inconsistent feelings, but God is not conflicted like humans can be.) Here are five examples.

1. On the one hand, I desire to eat sweets—glazed donuts, apple cake with cream cheese frosting, vanilla ice cream, brownies, chocolate-covered pretzels, chocolate chip cookies, caramel and cheese popcorn. On the other hand, I desire to become healthier, stronger, and leaner. My desire to eat sweets is

genuine, but most of the time I choose not to eat sweets because I more highly value becoming healthier, stronger, and leaner.

2. While Miguel Menendez was head coach of a high school baseball team in Tampa, Florida, he had to make a difficult decision—what he called "probably the hardest thing I've had to do in my life."[7] On the one hand, he wanted his oldest child, Miguel Jr., to play on his baseball team. On the other hand, he wanted to be a successful and fair head coach of a program that had just won the state championship in 2019 and that Collegiate Baseball had ranked as the number one high school team in America. The father decided to cut his son from the team during baseball tryouts in his son's junior year. (The son worked hard to make the team in his senior year.) The father's desire for his son to play on his team was genuine, but he more highly valued being a successful and fair coach.

3. One of my friends is a school president. When his school had a faculty opening, one of the applicants was a close friend of the president and was about to lose his current job. On the one hand, the president wanted to add his friend to the faculty. He thought it would be good for the school and would also meet his friend's need to have a job. On the other hand, it was clear to the president that another applicant was a better fit for the position. He decided to hire the other person instead of his friend. But that decision did not mean that his desire to hire his friend was fake.

4. One of my friends is the president of his company. One of his senior employees was a Christian brother who worked with diligence. But it became increasingly clear to my friend that this employee was a bad fit for his particular role and that it would be better for him, the other employees, and the clients if he

---

7. Ralph Morrow, "Key West's Miguel Menendez Finds Success at Tampa Jesuit," *Keys Weekly*, December 9, 2021, https://keysweekly.com/.

resigned. My friend decided to have some hard conversations with his employee and to encourage him to move on. My friend genuinely desired to avoid these difficult conversations and possible relational conflict, but he more highly valued doing what he deemed was best for his company and for this employee.

5. During the American Revolution, Benedict Arnold (a disaffected American general) and John André (a British major) conspired for the British to capture West Point. Americans discovered the plot and captured the spy André, but the traitor Arnold defected to the British. On the one hand, General George Washington did not want to execute André. He offered to exchange André for Arnold, but the British refused. On the other hand, Washington desired to uphold justice, so he ordered that André be hanged for espionage. Washington genuinely desired to avoid executing André, but he more highly valued doing what he deemed was just.[8]

Those examples illustrate that it is possible for a person to genuinely have two competing or conflicting desires and to act in accord with one desire without in any way making the other desire fake or false. Jesus is not pretending to feel compassion when he laments, "O Jerusalem, Jerusalem, the city that kills the prophets and stones those who are sent to it! How often would I have gathered your children together as a hen gathers her brood under her wings, and you were not willing!" (Matt. 23:37; cf. Luke 13:34). God genuinely "so loved the world, that he gave his only Son, that whoever believes in him should not perish but have eternal life" (John 3:16). But it does not necessarily follow that our free choice must be decisive or ultimate in order for Jesus's compassion to be genuine or for God's love to be genuine. It is sensible to distinguish two ways that God wills.

---

8. See Ron Chernow, *Washington: A Life* (New York: Penguin, 2010), 380–87; Piper, *Does God Desire All to Be Saved?*, 47–53.

God's sovereign choice to save only some humans is compatible with God's desire that all humans be saved.

Responding with a Prayer

Our Father in heaven, may your name be honored. May your kingdom come, and may your will be done (both what you command and what you decree), on earth as it is in heaven (Matt. 6:10; cf. 26:42).

8

How Does God Accomplish His Plan to Save Individuals?

Three actions summarize how the triune God saves his people from their sins: *plan*, *accomplish*, and *apply*.[1]

1. God *planned* to save individuals when he chose them before he created the world.
2. God *accomplishes* his plan through Christ's saving work.
3. God initially *applies* his plan by effectively calling and regenerating individuals.

The triune God planned, accomplishes, and applies our salvation. In particular, the *Father* planned, the *Son* accomplishes, and the *Spirit* applies our salvation. The Father, Son, and Spirit inseparably work together—never against each other.[2] As Shai Linne puts it,

---

1. Cf. John Murray, *Redemption: Accomplished and Applied* (Grand Rapids, MI: Eerdmans, 1955).

2. We must not infer that one member of the Trinity ever acts independently of the other two. God has an indivisible essence, so all three persons harmoniously work together in everything the triune God does. All three persons always operate inseparably. Cf. Stephen J. Wellum, *God the Son Incarnate: The Doctrine of Christ*, Foundations of Evangelical Theology (Wheaton, IL: Crossway, 2016), 289–90n14; Adonis Vidu, *The Same God Who Works*

Father, Son, and Spirit, three and yet one,
working as a unit to get things done.[3]

So how does the triune God execute his sovereign plan to save individuals? Three ways: (1) Christ's saving work, (2) the Holy Spirit's regenerating work, and (3) God-ordained means—through hearing God's word and through prayer.

God Accomplishes His Sovereign Plan to Save Individuals through Christ's Saving Work

Robert Peterson specifies nine saving events that constitute Christ's one saving work (see figure 8.1):

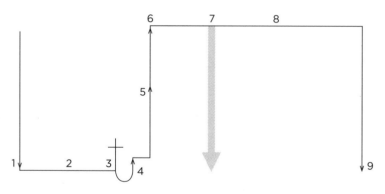

1. Incarnation	4. Resurrection	7. Pentecost
2. Sinless Life	5. Ascension	8. Intercession
3. Death	6. Session	9. Second Coming

Figure 8.1   Christ's Nine Saving Events[4]

God accomplishes his sovereign plan to save individuals through Christ's saving work. That is why God "chose us in him [in Christ]"

All Things: Inseparable Operations in Trinitarian Theology (Grand Rapids, MI: Eerdmans, 2021); Mike Riccardi, "Triune Particularism: Why Unity in the Trinity Demands a Particular Redemption," *Master's Seminary Journal* 33 (2022): 159–83.

3. Shai Linne, "Triune Praise," *The Atonement* (Lamp Mode, 2008).

4. Robert A. Peterson, *Salvation Accomplished by the Son: The Work of Christ* (Wheaton, IL: Crossway, 2012), 551. Peterson unpacks these nine events in the first part of his book (21–269).

(Eph. 1:4) and "predestined us . . . through Jesus Christ" (Eph. 1:5). God chose us *in Christ* in the sense that he chose us *by means of Christ*.[5] Christ accomplishes the salvation that our election entails.

God Initially Applies His Sovereign Plan to Save Individuals through the Holy Spirit's Regenerating Work[6]

The Father planned to save us, the Son accomplishes our salvation, and the Spirit applies our salvation by regenerating us. Regeneration is an act of God in which he graciously gives spiritual life to a spiritually dead person. Those who believe in Jesus "were born, not of blood nor of the will of the flesh nor of the will of man, but of God" (John 1:13). Only God's Spirit can produce spiritual life (3:3–8; 6:63). When God causes a human to be born again (cf. 1 Pet. 1:3), he changes that person's nature so that he or she willingly comes to Christ; the Father effectively persuades or "draws" each person he has given to the Son (John 6:39–40, 44, 65).[7] "It is the Spirit who gives life; the flesh is no help at all" (6:63).

God alone causes a human to be born again (i.e., monergism). Being born again is not a joint effort between God and a human (i.e., synergism). From God's perspective (logically or *theo*logically), regeneration precedes and enables faith. From our perspective, regeneration and faith seem to be chronologically simultaneous. In other words, we do not discern a time

---

5. Constantine R. Campbell, *Paul and Union with Christ: An Exegetical and Theological Study* (Grand Rapids, MI: Zondervan, 2012), 177. This instrumental use of "in him" (*en autō*) in the sense of "by him" is similar to how God created the world in Christ: "by him [Gk. *en autō*]" (Col. 1:16). On election and union with Christ, see Robert Letham, *Union with Christ: In Scripture, History, and Theology* (Phillipsburg, NJ: P&R, 2011), 65–72.

6. This section updates Naselli, "Chosen, Born Again, and Believing: How Election, Regeneration, and Faith Relate to Each Other in the Gospel According to John," *Master's Seminary Journal* 32, no. 2 (2021): 281–83.

7. The effectual call is the means of regeneration. Cf. Jonathan Hoglund, *Called by Triune Grace: Divine Rhetoric and the Effectual Call*, Studies in Christian Doctrine and Scripture (Downers Grove, IL: IVP Academic, 2016), 6, 124–25.

gap between the moment that (1) God instantaneously imparts spiritual life to a spiritually dead human and (2) a human first believes in Jesus. Though we perceive that we experience regeneration and faith simultaneously, that does not mean that regeneration and faith must be simultaneous from God's perspective. There is a logical order in which one enables and causes the other (see table 8.1).

Table 8.1   Analogies for How Regeneration Enables and Causes Faith

Regeneration: God Regenerates a Human	Faith: A Human First Believes in Jesus
Turn on a water faucet.	Water runs out of the faucet.[a]
Flip a toggle switch in a dark room.	Light fills the room (cf. 2 Cor. 4:6; 1 Pet. 2:9).
Jesus commands, "Lazarus, come out" (John 11:43).	"The man who had died came out" (John 11:44).
A mother gives birth to an infant.	The infant breathes.[b]

a. Anthony A. Hoekema, *Saved by Grace* (Grand Rapids, MI: Eerdmans, 1989), 107.
b. Piper clarifies, "We will not make any significant distinction between the imagery of conception and the imagery of birth. Even pre-scientific, first-century people knew that children were alive and kicking before birth. But the biblical writers did not press the details of gestation in discussing the new birth. In general, when they (and we) speak of the new birth, we are speaking more broadly of new life coming into being whether one thinks of the point of conception or the point of birth." John Piper, *Finally Alive: What Happens When We Are Born Again*, in *The Collected Works of John Piper*, ed. David Mathis and Justin Taylor, 14 vols (Wheaton, IL: Crossway, 2017), 7:354n1.

All the analogies in table 8.1 illustrate that regeneration is both passive and instantaneous. The actions are passive in that the first action happens to another item or agent; the item or agent does not perform the first action—that is, water does not turn on the faucet; light does not flip the toggle switch; Lazarus does not command his corpse to come out of the tomb; and an infant does not decide to be conceived and born. Piper explains that we act (i.e., we exercise faith) only because God acts (i.e., he enables us to believe):

Repentance and faith are our work. But we will not repent and believe unless God does his work to overcome our hard and rebellious hearts. This divine work is called *regeneration*. Our work is called *conversion* [repentance and faith].

Conversion does indeed include an act of will by which we renounce sin and submit ourselves to the authority of Christ and put our hope and trust in him. We are responsible to do this and will be condemned if we don't. But just as clearly, the Bible teaches that, owing to our hard heart and willful blindness and spiritual insensitivity, we cannot do this.[8]

Regeneration is what God does to us; it is not something we do. Regeneration and initial faith are instantaneous in that they appear to occur simultaneously. There is not a noticeable time delay between flipping a toggle switch and light filling a room.

I concede the analogies in table 8.1 are imperfect because they do not exactly parallel how regeneration and faith relate. For example, a water faucet and toggle switch are impersonal items, not personal agents. The most helpful aspect of the analogies is how they illustrate that one action enables and causes another. The first action is logically prior to the second action.

When God regenerates a human, he creates a believer. Most of us become aware of this reality later. Charles Spurgeon recounts in his autobiography, "When I was coming to Christ, I thought I was doing it all myself."[9] But as Sproul says, "God intervenes in the hearts of the elect and changes the disposition of their soul. He creates faith in faithless hearts."[10] Regeneration

---

8. John Piper, *Desiring God: Meditations of a Christian Hedonist*, in *The Collected Works of John Piper*, ed. David Mathis and Justin Taylor, 14 vols (Wheaton, IL: Crossway, 2017), 2:67.

9. C. H. Spurgeon, *C. H. Spurgeon Autobiography*, vol. 1, *The Early Years, 1834–1859*, ed. Susannah Spurgeon, Joseph Harrald, and Banner of Truth Trust, rev. ed. (1898; repr., Carlisle, PA: Banner of Truth, 1962), 164.

10. R. C. Sproul, *Everyone's a Theologian: An Introduction to Systematic Theology* (Orlando, FL: Reformation Trust, 2014), 228.

is the means through which God initially applies his sovereign plan to save individuals.

God Ordained That Individuals Would Repent and Believe through Hearing God's Word and through Prayer

If God ordains that you will live for the next hour, then he also ordains the means to that end—your heart will keep pumping, and you will keep breathing. When God ordains an end, he also ordains the means to that end. So when God ordains that an individual will repent and believe, he also ordains the means to that end. The Bible specifies two means for conversion:

1. *Hearing God's word:* An unbeliever *hears* God's word— whether the gospel is preached in a sermon or proclaimed through some other medium such as a book, talk, or personal conversation.
2. *Prayer:* Someone *asks* God to save an unbeliever.

Paul explains, "It pleased God through the folly of what we preach to save those who believe" (1 Cor. 1:21). Hearing God's words is a God-ordained means for unbelievers to exercise a God-enabled repentance and faith. When Paul and Barnabas preached in Antioch in Pisidia, they first preached to Jews and then preached to Gentiles: "When the Gentiles heard this, they began rejoicing and glorifying the word of the Lord, and as many as were appointed to eternal life believed" (Acts 13:48; cf. 1 Thess. 1:2–10). The text does not say that after the preaching "as many as believed were appointed to eternal life." No, "as many as were appointed to eternal life believed."

In a letter that exhorts Timothy to faithfully "preach the word" (2 Tim. 4:2), Paul writes, "Remember Jesus Christ, risen from the dead, the offspring of David, *as preached in my gospel*, for which I am suffering, bound with chains as a criminal. But *the word of God is not bound!* Therefore *I endure everything for the sake of the elect, that they also may obtain the salvation that is in Christ Jesus with eternal glory*" (2 Tim. 2:8–10). The means that God has ordained (i.e., preaching God's word) is so important that Paul suffers in prison for it. Paul is chained, but God's word is not chained. Paul's suffering is worth it because it is "for the sake of the elect"—God will save the individuals he chose to save.

God sovereignly chose to give us spiritual birth through the message of truth: "*Of his own will* [In the exercise of His will (NASB), By his own choice (CSB), By his sovereign plan (NET)] he brought us forth [gave us birth (NASB, CSB, NET)] *by the word of truth*, that we should be a kind of firstfruits of his creatures" (James 1:18).

Hearing God's word is not the only God-ordained means. Another is prayer. Note how Paul connects election, faith, preaching, and prayer:

> We ought always to give thanks to God for you, brothers beloved by the Lord, because *God chose you* as the firstfruits to be saved, through sanctification by the Spirit and *belief in the truth. To this he called you through our gospel,* so that you may obtain the glory of our Lord Jesus Christ. . . . Finally, brothers, *pray for us, that the word of the Lord may speed ahead* [spread rapidly (NASB, NIV, CSB, NLT)] *and be honored, as happened among you.* (2 Thess. 2:13–14; 3:1)

We get to pray that God's word would *run* and transform idolaters into God worshipers. Prayer is a God-ordained means for God to grant repentance and faith to the elect in response to hearing the gospel.[11] That is why elsewhere Paul exhorts,

---

11. See G. K. Beale, *1–2 Thessalonians*, IVP New Testament Commentary 13 (Downers Grove, IL: InterVarsity Press, 2003), 235–43.

"Devote yourselves to prayer, . . . praying at the same time for us as well, *that God will open up to us a door for the word*, so that we may proclaim the mystery of Christ, for which I have also been imprisoned" (Col. 4:2–3 NASB; cf. Eph. 5:18–20; 2 Cor. 1:11).

Application: Proclaim God's Word to Unbelievers, Support Others Who Do That, and Ask God to Save Unbelievers

We get to evangelize, to support those who evangelize, and to ask God to save specific individuals. We get to proclaim the gospel nonselectively to all people without distinction. We get to proclaim "the unsearchable riches of Christ" to anyone and everyone (Eph. 3:8; cf. Gal. 1:16).

Do not try to discern which unbelievers are elect. Only God knows who the elect are. Your responsibility and privilege is to proclaim the gospel indiscriminately—not to discriminate between people you think are elect and people you think are not elect. God "commands *all people everywhere* to repent" (Acts 17:30). "Repentance for the forgiveness of sins should be proclaimed in his name *to all nations*" (Luke 24:47; cf. Matt. 28:19–20).

Obey God—Even If You Don't Have All Your Questions Answered

How does this work? If you fail to proclaim God's word and to support missionaries and to pray, does that mean that God will not save an individual he chose to save before the foundation of the world? No. So why should you bother proclaiming God's word and praying? Because God tells you to, and whatever God commands you is for your good. He ordained both the end and the means. You are responsible to obey God—even if you don't have answers to all your philosophical questions. (See the end of chap. 6 on mystery.)

You probably don't struggle with God-ordained ends and means in other areas. For example, if God decreed that you would go on a three-mile walk, then what is the use of picking up one leg at a time to take steps?

God has ordained both the end *and the means to that end.* It would be foolish to conclude, "Since God ordained that I will live for ten more years, I don't need to breathe or sleep or eat or drink at all." God ordained the exact length of your life, but you don't know whether God ordained for you to live for ten more years or just ten more seconds. You are responsible to keep breathing and sleeping and eating and drinking. That responsibility is perfectly compatible with God's meticulous sovereignty about how long you will live.

Similarly, God ordained which individuals he will save, but you don't know who they are. You are responsible to proclaim the gospel to unbelievers and to pray for them. That responsibility is perfectly compatible with God's meticulous sovereignty about whom he chose to save.

It is not our job to try to discern who the elect are before we proclaim God's word to unbelievers and pray for them. It is our job to proclaim God's word and to pray. God ordains both the end and the means. He does not always tell us exactly what the end is, but he does tell us what the means are. And we please God when we obey him.[12] "How beautiful are the feet of those who preach the good news!" (Rom. 10:15).

On your own you cannot possibly proclaim the gospel to every unbeliever on the planet. But you can testify on behalf of King Jesus to your family and friends and neighbors and

---

12. Wayne Grudem, "Pleasing God by Our Obedience: A Neglected New Testament Teaching," in *For the Fame of God's Name: Essays in Honor of John Piper*, ed. Sam Storms and Justin Taylor (Wheaton, IL: Crossway, 2010), 272–92.

coworkers. You can pray for them and for the nations. And you can support others who are devoting their lives to proclaiming the gospel—regionally, nationally, and internationally. As John writes, "We ought to support people like these, that we may be fellow workers for the truth" (3 John 8).

Evangelize and Support Missionaries

> The Lord said to Paul one night in a vision, "Do not be afraid, but go on speaking and do not be silent, for I am with you, and no one will attack you to harm you, *for I have many in this city who are my people.*" And he stayed a year and six months, teaching the word of God among them. (Acts 18:9–11)

This passage does not promise you that wherever you are God has many people there. But be encouraged that wherever you are there may be people whom God chose before the foundation of the world (cf. 2 Tim. 2:10; Titus 1:1). The elect are Jesus's sheep, and his sheep hear his voice (John 10:16, 26–28). Proclaiming the gospel to unregenerate people is like going from tombstone to tombstone in a cemetery; only God can raise the spiritually dead, so we do not help the situation by shouting more loudly or by using manipulative methods.[13] God's sovereignty should encourage you to faithfully evangelize and to support missionaries.[14]

---

13. Cf. David Bennett, *The Altar Call: Its Origin and Present Usage* (New York: University Press of America, 2000).

14. On evangelism, see Mark Dever, *The Gospel and Personal Evangelism* (Wheaton, IL: Crossway, 2007); J. Mack Stiles, *Evangelism: How the Whole Church Speaks of Jesus*, 9Marks: Building Healthy Churches (Wheaton, IL: Crossway, 2014). On missions, see John Piper, *Let the Nations Be Glad! The Supremacy of God in Missions*, 3rd ed. (Grand Rapids, MI: Baker Academic, 2010); David M. Doran, *For the Sake of His Name* (Allen Park, MI: Detroit Baptist Theological Seminary, 2018); Daniel L. Akin, Benjamin L. Merkle, and George G. Robinson, *40 Questions about the Great Commission*, 40 Questions (Grand Rapids, MI: Kregel Academic, 2020).

Pray for Unbelievers

In C. S. Lewis's *The Magician's Nephew*, Polly and Digory are terribly hungry while the winged horse Fledge is happily eating grass:

> "Well, I *do* think someone might have arranged about our meals," said Digory.
>
> "I'm sure Aslan would have, if you'd asked him," said Fledge.
>
> "Wouldn't he know without being asked?" said Polly.
>
> "I've no doubt he would," said the Horse (still with his mouth full). "But I've a sort of idea he likes to be asked."[15]

Like Aslan, God likes to be asked (cf. Matt. 7:11).

Christians (including both Calvinists and Arminians) seem to universally affirm God's sovereignty in salvation in (1) how we thank God for our own conversion and (2) how we ask God to save specific unbelievers.

First, when you think about how God saved you, do you ever think something like this? "My decision to choose Christ is the decisive reason I am a Christian. I am so glad that I sized up my situation before God with a cost-benefit analysis and then decided to choose Christ. So many people are foolishly rejecting Christ, but it makes perfect sense to choose Christ." You would never put it that way, right? You know that *God* saves sinners. You know that *God* is the ultimate reason you are a Christian. That's why you thank *God* for saving you.[16]

Second, J. I. Packer explains another way that Christians seem to universally affirm that God is sovereign in salvation:

---

15. C. S. Lewis, *The Magician's Nephew*, The Chronicles of Narnia (New York: HarperCollins, 1955), 163.
16. See J. I. Packer, *Evangelism and the Sovereignty of God* (Downers Grove, IL: InterVarsity Press, 1961), 12–13.

You pray for the conversion of others. In what terms, now, do you intercede for them? Do you limit yourself to asking that God will bring them to a point where they can save themselves, independently of Him? I do not think you do. I think that what you do is pray in categorical terms that God will, quite simply and decisively, save them: that He will open the eyes of their understanding, soften their hard hearts, renew their natures, and move their wills to receive the Saviour. You ask God to work in them everything necessary for their salvation. You would not dream of making it a point in your prayer that you are not asking God actually to bring them to faith, because you recognize that that is something He cannot do. Nothing of the sort! When you pray for unconverted people, you do so on the assumption that it is in God's power to bring them to faith. You entreat Him to do that very thing, and your confidence in asking rests upon the certainty that He is able to do what you ask. And so indeed He is: this conviction, which animates your intercessions, is God's own truth, written on your heart by the Holy Spirit.[17]

God's sovereignty should encourage you to pray for unbelievers.[18]

Calvinists Are Zealous to Evangelize and Pray

Some people think that Calvinists are so coldhearted and logic driven that they rarely if ever evangelize. That is sadly true about some Calvinists but only because of sin—not because

---

17. Packer, *Evangelism and the Sovereignty of God*, 15. Cf. A. A. Hodge, *Outlines of Theology*, 2nd ed. (New York: Hodder and Stoughton, 1878), 220–21.

18. See Sam Storms, "Prayer and Evangelism under God's Sovereignty," in *Still Sovereign: Contemporary Perspectives on Election, Foreknowledge, and Grace*, ed. Thomas R. Schreiner and Bruce A. Ware (Grand Rapids, MI: Baker, 2000), 307–23. Cf. Layton Talbert, *Not by Chance: Learning to Trust a Sovereign God* (Greenville, SC: Bob Jones University Press, 2001), 213–34.

of Calvinism.[19] It is mistaken to equate Calvinism with hyper-Calvinism. Phil Johnson explains,

> A hyper-Calvinist is someone who either:
> [1] Denies that the Gospel call applies to all who hear, OR
> [2] Denies that faith is the duty of every sinner, OR
> [3] Denies that the Gospel makes any "offer" of Christ, salvation, or mercy to the non-elect (or denies that the offer of divine mercy is free and universal), OR
> [4] Denies that there is such a thing as "common grace," OR
> [5] Denies that God has any sort of love for the nonelect.
> All five varieties of hyper-Calvinism undermine evangelism or twist the Gospel message.[20]

Calvinists are not the frozen chosen. We are zealous to evangelize locally and globally and to pray fervently.[21] We enthusiastically support international missions.[22]

When William Carey (1761–1834) was about twenty-five years old, the Calvinist proposed a question at a meeting for Baptist pastors: "Have the churches of Christ done all they ought to have done for heathen nations?" One of Carey's biographers records that the venerable John Ryland Sr. "sprang on his feet, and with eyes flashing like lightning, and in tones resembling thunder, cried out, 'Young man, sit down; when God pleases to convert the heathen world, he will do it without

---

19. See David M. Doran, "God's Sovereignty and the Spread of the Gospel," *Detroit Baptist Seminary Journal* 9 (2004): 183–214; Greg Dutcher, *Killing Calvinism: How to Destroy a Perfectly Good Theology from the Inside* (Adelphi, MD: Cruciform, 2012), 47–58.

20. Phillip R. Johnson, "A Primer on Hyper-Calvinism," *Sword and Trowel* 1 (2002): 11; also available at http://www.romans45.org/articles/hypercal.htm.

21. Cf. Iain H. Murray, *Spurgeon v. Hyper-Calvinism: The Battle for Gospel Preaching* (Carlisle, PA: Banner of Truth, 1995).

22. Cf. Kenneth J. Stewart, *Ten Myths about Calvinism: Recovering the Breadth of the Reformed Tradition* (Downers Grove, IL: IVP Academic, 2011), 123–48; Michael Horton, *For Calvinism* (Grand Rapids, MI: Zondervan, 2011), 151–69; Jason Helopoulos, "Does Calvinism Kill Missions?," *DeYoung, Restless, and Reformed* (blog), The Gospel Coalition, July 3, 2013, https://www.thegospelcoalition.org/.

your help or mine either.'"[23] That rebuke is infamous now because God used Carey as a catalyst for the modern missions movement.[24] About six years later in 1792, Carey finished his seminal eighty-seven page book: *An Enquiry into the Obligations of Christians to Use Means for the Conversion of the Heathens.*[25] Note especially the words *obligations* and *means*. He begins his book by arguing that Jesus's Great Commission is an *obligation* not just for the apostles but for all of Jesus's disciples, and he ends it by arguing that believers must do so using *means*—particularly by fervently praying, wisely strategizing, and generously giving. Later in 1792, Carey exhorted believers, "Expect great things [from God]. Attempt great things [for God]."[26]

Responding with a Prayer

Thank you, God, for planning, accomplishing, and applying my salvation. What a gift! Would you please help me to be a faithful steward of all that you have graciously given me? In particular, would you please help me faithfully and fruitfully proclaim your word to unbelievers—to my family, friends, neighbors, and others whom you providentially appoint for me to interact with? Please strengthen your servants all over this world by giving them words to open their mouths boldly to proclaim the gospel (Eph. 6:19). And

---

23. Joseph Belcher, *William Carey: A Biography* (Philadelphia: American Baptist Publication Society, 1853), 19.

24. John Rylands Sr. apparently was not a hyper-Calvinist but thought Christians should wait to invest heavily in foreign missions until God made it unmistakably clear that he was sending a remarkable revival—a kind of second Pentecost. See Iain H. Murray, "William Carey: Climbing the Rainbow," *Evangelical Review of Theology* 17 (1993): 359–60.

25. William Carey, *An Enquiry into the Obligations of Christians to Use Means for the Conversion of the Heathens: In Which the Religious State of the Different Nations of the World, the Success of Former Undertakings, and the Practicability of Further Undertakings, Are Considered* (Leicester: Ann Ireland, 1792).

26. Justin Matthew James, "William Carey: Fullerite Pastor, Pioneer Missionary" (PhD diss., Southeastern Baptist Theological Seminary, 2019), 199.

I ask particularly for these individuals who are not trusting and loving you: _____.
Would you please give them spiritual life? Would you please grant them repentance and faith? Please transform them from glory thieves to worshipers. Let the peoples praise you, O God; let all the peoples praise you! Let the nations be glad and sing for joy (Ps. 67:4)! I ask all this for the sake of your name. Amen.

9

How Do I Know If God
Has Elected Me?

Election is terrifying for some people. "Am *I* chosen by God? How can I know for sure? And what about _____ [my spouse, my child, my parent, my neighbor, or my friend]?" Election may be alarming because it means that God *the Creator* is supremely sovereign and that we *the creatures* are not. We prefer to be in control. But what God has revealed about election should be encouraging, comforting, humbling, exhilarating, and motivating (see chap. 1).

If you follow Christ and are struggling with whether you are elect, you are at war. You are fighting a scheme of the devil (Eph. 6:11–12). That is why Martin Luther asserts, "When man is assailed by thoughts regarding his election, he is being assailed by hell."[1] So how do we know if God has elected an individual? Cornelis Venema explains, "The warrant for the assurance of election is the same as the warrant for the assurance of salvation."[2]

1. Martin Luther, "A Sermon on Preparing to Die," in *Devotional Writings I*, ed. Martin O. Dietrich, vol. 42 of *Luther's Works* (Philadelphia: Fortress, 1969), 103. Cf. R. C. Sproul, ed., *Doubt and Assurance* (Grand Rapids, MI: Baker, 1993).
2. Cornelis Venema, *Chosen in Christ: Revisiting the Contours of Predestination*, Reformed, Exegetical and Doctrinal Studies (Fearn, Ross-shire, Scotland: Mentor, 2019),

Calling and Justification Are Evidence of Election

"We know that for those who love God all things work together for good, for those who are called according to his purpose" (Rom. 8:28). Paul supports those comforting words with four proofs (8:29–30):

1. God predestined (or elected) those whom he foreknew.
2. God called those whom he predestined.
3. God justified those whom he called.
4. God glorified those whom he justified.

This five-link chain of God's actions is unbreakable: foreknowledge, predestination (or election), calling, justification, and glorification. Every human is either the object of all five of those actions or none of them. If God has called you, then he has enabled you to believe the gospel and thus has judicially declared you to be righteous. Faith is the means of justification, and faith is also an evidence of election. Jesus says, "All that the Father gives me will come to [i.e., believe in] me" (John 6:37).

If you are the object of God's calling and justification, then you are also the object of God's predestination. In other words, if God has effectively called you (which means that God has regenerated you and enabled you to repent and believe), then you are elect. If you are justified (which is a result of God-enabled faith), then you are elect. Your calling and justification are evidence of your election.

---

360. This short chapter highlights passages that directly connect election and assurance; for more comprehensive studies on assurance, see D. A. Carson, "Johannine Perspectives on the Doctrine of Assurance," *Explorations* 10 (1996): 59–97; Carson, "Reflections on Assurance," in *Still Sovereign: Contemporary Perspectives on Election, Foreknowledge, and Grace*, ed. Thomas R. Schreiner and Bruce A. Ware (Grand Rapids, MI: Baker, 2000), 383–412; Joel R. Beeke, *Knowing and Growing in Assurance of Faith* (Fearn, Ross-shire, Scotland: Christian Focus, 2017), 89–105; Greg Gilbert, *Assured: Discover Grace, Let Go of Guilt, and Rest in Your Salvation* (Grand Rapids, MI: Baker, 2019), 93–107; Robert A. Peterson, *The Assurance of Salvation: Biblical Hope for Our Struggles* (Grand Rapids, MI: Zondervan, 2019), 137–75; Donald S. Whitney, *How Can I Be Sure I'm a Christian? The Satisfying Certainty of Eternal Life*, 2nd ed. (Colorado Springs, CO: NavPress, 2019).

Following Jesus the Shepherd Is Evidence of Election

Jesus's sheep are the elect. Jesus says, "My sheep hear my voice, and I know them, and they follow me" (John 10:27). Do you listen to Jesus and follow him? Then what Jesus says next is a precious assurance for you: "I give them eternal life, and they will never perish, and no one will snatch them out of my hand. My Father, who has given them to me, is greater than all, and no one is able to snatch them out of the Father's hand" (10:28–29; cf. 6:37–40).

A Transformed Life Is Evidence of Election

> We give thanks to God always for all of you, constantly mentioning you in our prayers, remembering before our God and Father your work of faith and labor of love and steadfastness of hope in our Lord Jesus Christ. For *we know*, brothers loved by God, *that he has chosen you* [your election (KJV)], because our gospel came to you not only in word, but also in power and in the Holy Spirit and with full conviction. You know what kind of men we proved to be among you for your sake. And you became imitators of us and of the Lord, for you received the word in much affliction, with the joy of the Holy Spirit, so that you became an example to all the believers in Macedonia and in Achaia. For not only has the word of the Lord sounded forth from you in Macedonia and Achaia, but your faith in God has gone forth everywhere, so that we need not say anything. For they themselves report concerning us the kind of reception we had among you, and how you turned to God from idols to serve the living and true God, and to wait for his Son from heaven, whom he raised from the dead, Jesus who delivers us from the wrath to come. (1 Thess. 1:2–10)

Paul thanks God (not the Thessalonian believers) because he knows that God has elected them. The evidence for their election is their transformed lives after they responded to the gospel (1:3, 5; cf. 2:13–14). They did not receive the gospel "merely in words" (1:5 NET). The gospel transformed them because the Holy Spirit powerfully convicted them and enabled them to produce the fruit of genuine repentance and faith. They received the word "in much affliction, with the joy of the Holy Spirit" (1:6). They "turned to God" (i.e., faith) "from idols" (i.e., repentance); they no longer were serving sin but "the living and true God" and eagerly awaiting Jesus's return (1:9–10). A transformed life is evidence of election. "We love because he first loved us" (1 John 4:19).

Application: Confirm Your Election

It is encouraging to know that a transformed life is evidence of election, yet we must not twist that truth by morbidly introspecting. Jonathan Edwards explains, "Although self-examination be a duty of great use and importance, and by no means to be neglected; yet it is not the principal means, by which the saints do get satisfaction of their good estate. Assurance is not to be obtained so much by self-examination, as by action."[3]

Yes, "Examine yourselves, to see whether you are in the faith. Test yourselves" (2 Cor. 13:5). But do not despair about election; instead, *confirm* your election. Peter tells us how:

> Make every effort to supplement your faith with virtue, and virtue with knowledge, and knowledge with self-control, and self-control with steadfastness, and steadfastness with godliness, and godliness with brotherly affection, and brotherly affection with love. For if these qualities are yours and are increasing, they keep you from being ineffective or unfruitful in the knowledge of our Lord Jesus Christ.

---

3. Jonathan Edwards, *Religious Affections*, ed. John E. Smith, vol. 2 of *The Works of Jonathan Edwards* (New Haven, CT: Yale University Press, 2009), 195.

For whoever lacks these qualities is so nearsighted that he is blind, having forgotten that he was cleansed from his former sins. Therefore, brothers, *be all the more diligent to confirm* [make certain about (NASB), be sure of (NET)] *your calling and election*, for if you practice these qualities you will never fall. For in this way there will be richly provided for you an entrance into the eternal kingdom of our Lord and Savior Jesus Christ. (2 Pet. 1:5–11)

We confirm that God called and elected us by cultivating the virtues listed in 1:5–7. We must be continually growing in those virtues. We must persevere in faith and good works until the end. Consequently, God will richly welcome us into his eternal kingdom (1:11)—like how the King richly welcomes Christian into the Celestial City at the end of John Bunyan's *The Pilgrim's Progress.*[4]

Election is not an excuse for lawlessness or laziness. We must put off sin and put on virtues (see Col. 3:1–4:1). That is what God's chosen people do: "Put on then, *as God's chosen ones* [as the elect of God (NET)], holy and beloved, compassionate hearts, kindness, humility, meekness, and patience" (Col. 3:12). The logic is similar to Philippians 2:12–13: "Work out your own salvation with fear and trembling, *for* it is God who works in you, both to will and to work for his good pleasure." We work *because* God works. Be diligent to confirm your election.

Responding with a Prayer

Father, please help me confirm my election by continually growing in faith, virtue, knowledge, self-control, steadfastness, godliness, brotherly affection, and love. Help me put on

---

4. John Bunyan, *The Pilgrim's Progress: From This World to That Which Is to Come,* ed. C. J. Lovik (Wheaton, IL: Crossway, 2009), 218–19.

a compassionate heart, kindness, humility, meekness, patience, forbearance, forgiveness, love, and thankfulness.

Thank you, Father, that since you are for me, no one (and nothing) can successfully be against me! No one can successfully bring any charge against your elect (Rom. 8:33a). No one can take me to court before you on judgment day and win a case against me because you are the one who has declared me to be righteous through Christ (Rom. 8:33b). Thank you.

10

Did God Elect Babies
Who Die?

When my wife, Jenni, was pregnant for the fourth time, she miscarried. It was heartbreaking. We learned that miscarriages are far more common than we realized. About one in four pregnancies ends in a miscarriage. Will those babies live forever in the new heaven and new earth? What about aborted babies, stillborn babies, and babies who die within a few years of birth? Did God elect those babies? The Bible does not directly answer this difficult question, but it is natural and good for us to consider it. I'll attempt to answer it by briefly unpacking eight statements.

1. Babies Who Die Are Sinners by Nature, Not Sinners by Choice

The Bible (especially Rom. 5:12–21) teaches both original guilt and original sin.[1] Original guilt means that we are guilty before

---

1. See Andrew David Naselli, *Romans: A Concise Guide to the Greatest Letter Ever Written* (Wheaton, IL: Crossway, 2022), 72–82.

God because all humans are originally guilty in Adam. Original sin means that we inherit a sinful nature. From the moment we are conceived, we are sinners *by nature*. At some point early in our lives as we develop, we become sinners *by choice*. We sin because we are sinners—that is, we sin by choice because we are sinners by nature. Babies who die are sinners by nature but not sinners by choice.

2. God Condemns People Who Consciously Rebel against Him

> For the wrath of God is revealed from heaven against all ungodliness and unrighteousness of men, *who by their unrighteousness suppress the truth*. For what can be known about God is plain to them, because God has shown it to them. For his invisible attributes, namely, his eternal power and divine nature, have been clearly perceived, ever since the creation of the world, in the things that have been made. *So they are without excuse*. (Rom. 1:18–20)

> We must all appear before the judgment seat of Christ, so that each one may receive what is due *for what he has done in the body*, whether good or evil. (2 Cor. 5:10)

God's wrath is against people who unrighteously suppress the truth about God. God has revealed this truth to them through creation and their conscience. Consequently, "they are without excuse" (Rom. 1:20). In Romans 1, Paul is not directly addressing the destiny of babies (and the severely mentally disabled), but I think this passage applies. God condemns people who consciously rebel against him. That implies that God does not condemn people who do not consciously rebel against him—who have not consciously committed any evil in their bodies (2 Cor. 5:10; Rev. 20:12–13). As John MacArthur puts it, "We are saved by grace, but 'damned' by works."[2] So God may be merciful to babies (and those with severe mental disabilities) because they have not consciously rebelled against him. They have an "excuse" (Rom. 1:20; cf. John 9:41). For example, God judged Israelites in the wilderness by forbidding them from seeing the Promised Land, but he exempted children because they had an excuse: "*The little ones* that you said would be taken captive, *your children who do not yet know good from bad*—they will enter the land" (Deut. 1:39 NIV; cf. 30:15–20). Infants are not guilty of consciously rebelling against God (cf. Ps. 106:37–38; Isa. 7:15–16; Jer. 19:4–5; Jonah 4:11).[3]

3. God Judges Some People More Severely Than Others

Jesus warns Capernaum, "It will be more tolerable on the day of judgment for the land of Sodom than for you" (Matt. 11:24). God judges some people more severely than others. God will judge some people less severely based on the degree to which God revealed himself to them. That may imply that God is merciful to infants who die (and to those with severe mental disabilities) since they could not understand any of God's revelation.

4. No Human Is Saved apart from Christ

"There is salvation in no one else, for there is no other name under heaven given among men by which we must be saved" (Acts 4:12; cf. John 14:6). Jesus is the exclusive Savior; no human is saved apart from Christ.[4]

---

2. John MacArthur, *Safe in the Arms of God: Truth from Heaven about the Death of a Child* (Nashville: Nelson, 2003), 79. Cf. John Piper, *Providence* (Wheaton, IL: Crossway, 2021), 507–8.

3. Does "Jacob I loved, but Esau I hated" in Romans 9:13 prove that God does not save some babies who die? No, when God says, "Esau I hated," he contemplates Esau in the totality of his existence, not simply Esau as an unborn baby. God ordained that Esau would grow up to be an adult man.

4. Cf. Christopher W. Morgan and Robert A. Peterson, eds., *Faith Comes by Hearing: A Response to Inclusivism* (Downers Grove, IL: IVP Academic, 2008).

If God mercifully saves babies who die (and those with severe mental disabilities), he somehow saves them by faith alone in Christ alone. I say "somehow" because the Bible does not specify how or when. The concept of a regenerate infant is conceivable since God had a special relationship with Jeremiah and John the Baptist while they were still in their mother's wombs (Jer. 1:5; Luke 1:15).[5]

5. King David Implies That God Mercifully Saves Babies Who Die

"The LORD afflicted the child that Uriah's wife bore to David, and he became sick" (2 Sam. 12:15). King David fasted and earnestly asked God to save the baby.

> On the seventh day the child died. And the servants of David were afraid to tell him that the child was dead, for they said, "Behold, while the child was yet alive, we spoke to him, and he did not listen to us. How then can we say to him the child is dead? He may do himself some harm." But when David saw that his servants were whispering together, David understood that the child was dead. And David said to his servants, "Is the child dead?" They said, "He is dead." Then David arose from the earth and washed and anointed himself and changed his clothes. And he went into the house of the LORD and worshiped. He then went to his own house. And when he asked, they set food before him, and he ate. Then his servants said to him, "What is this thing that you have done? You fasted and wept for the child while he was alive; but when the child died, you arose and ate food." He said, "While the child was still alive, I fasted and

---

5. Cf. Ronald H. Nash, *When a Baby Dies: Answers to Comfort Grieving Parents* (Grand Rapids, MI: Zondervan, 1999), 64–65.

wept, for I said, 'Who knows whether the LORD will be gracious to me, that the child may live?' But now he is dead. Why should I fast? Can I bring him back again? I shall go to him, but he will not return to me." (2 Sam. 12:18–23)

By saying, "I shall go to him," David possibly meant that he would join his son in the grave (not heaven). But I think David implies that God mercifully saves babies for at least two reasons: (1) David changes from dour mourning that he will lose his son to confident optimism that he will personally be with his son again, and (2) David responds much differently when his rebellious adult son Absalom dies: "The king was deeply moved and went up to the chamber over the gate and wept. And as he went, he said, 'O my son Absalom, my son, my son Absalom! Would I had died instead of you, O Absalom, my son, my son!'" (2 Sam. 18:33).

6. Conclusion: The Bible Implies That God Mercifully Saves Babies Who Die

This conclusion is most persuasive when we attempt to correlate what God has revealed. We cannot prove this conclusion with 100 percent certainty, but my sense of the cumulative weight of the arguments is that this conclusion is *almost certainly* true. It seems so probable that I think it is pastorally responsible to comfort grieving parents with these truths.

These truths have comforted my family. My wife and I have four daughters. We also have another child we have not yet met. Jenni miscarried in 2014 before we learned whether the baby was a boy or a girl. We named the child Anastasis Hope. *Anastasis* is the Greek word for resurrection, and my family *confidently expects* (that's what *hope* means) to meet Anastasis Hope in bodily form at the resurrection. There are sound reasons for believing this, even though the Bible does not answer all our questions about it.

7. Application: Trust God, Who Is Always Just and Good

"Shall not the Judge of all the earth do what is just?" asks Abraham (Gen. 18:25). Yes, the Judge of the whole earth always does what is right. So we should not be anxious that God may do something unjust. Will you pray with the psalmist, "You are good and do good" (Ps. 119:68)? Will you trust God to be just and do what is just? Will you trust him to be good and do good?[6]

8. Speculation: God's Sufficient Word Is Intentionally Not Explicitly Clear on the Destiny of Babies Who Die

God has reasons for what he does, and he does not reveal all those reasons to us. Why isn't the Bible clearer on this issue? I don't know. But I have a guess. I suspect one reason is that people would be more inclined to do horrible things if the Bible explicitly said that all babies will go to heaven and not hell.[7] Some people—including parents—would be more inclined to murder babies to ensure that those babies would go to heaven. Some would care less about helping infants who die of sickness. Some would be less inclined to help unborn children in the wombs of their mothers. Some would reason, "Better to murder babies than risk letting those babies grow up and go to hell." To that Paul would respond, "God forbid!"

---

6. Cf. Jessalyn Hutto, *Inheritance of Tears: Trusting the Lord of Life When Death Visits the Womb* (Minneapolis: Cruciform, 2015); Jonathan Gibson, *The Moon Is Always Round* (Greensboro, NC: New Growth, 2019).

7. Similarly, I suspect that one reason God has not preserved the original Hebrew, Aramaic, and Greek manuscripts of Scripture is that some people would worship those manuscripts if they existed (cf. 2 Kings 18:4).

Responding with a Prayer

I praise you, Father, that your work is perfect because all your ways are just. I don't understand all the reasons that babies die. But I know that you are just and that you do what is right. You are good, and you do good. I trust you. Please increase my trust. Amen.

PART 2

Vessels of Wrath

What Does the Bible Teach about Reprobation?

Election means that *God sovereignly and graciously chose to save individual sinners.* But what about the other people—the ones God did not plan to save? If God elected only *some* individuals, then did he plan to damn the rest? Answering that question requires great care because this is a difficult issue to process theologically and emotionally. The Bible teaches what theologians call *reprobation.*

Reprobation means that *God sovereignly and justly chose to pass over nonelect sinners and punish them.* Choosing some and passing over the rest accords with our experience of reality. If there are ten purple grapes in a bowl and I eat seven of them, then three grapes remain in the container. I chose seven grapes and passed over the remaining three. That reality is part of our ordinary experience.

So it is with election and reprobation: If God sovereignly and graciously chose to save certain individual sinners, then he chose *not* to save the rest. When I chose to ask my wife-to-be to marry me, I passed over all other women; I chose Jenni *and not the rest*. The concepts of *elect* and *election* necessarily imply the concepts of *nonelect* and *passing over*. But reprobation is not simply a doctrine that election logically implies; the Bible explicitly teaches it.[1]

---

1. Part 2 updates and expands Andrew David Naselli, *Romans: A Concise Guide to the Greatest Letter Ever Written* (Wheaton, IL: Crossway, 2022), 121–25.

11

Who Ultimately Causes Reprobation?

A handful of New Testament passages explicitly or implicitly specify who the ultimate cause of reprobation is. The primary passage in the Bible on reprobation is Romans 9:6–29, so we begin there.

God the Potter Prepared Vessels of Wrath for Destruction

God is the one who passes over individuals he has not chosen (Rom. 9:6–29). God chose Jacob and rejected Esau (Rom. 9:13)—"though they were not yet born and had done nothing either good or bad" (9:11). God sovereignly chose whether (1) to have mercy and compassion on a person or (2) to harden a person. What is decisive is not what a human desires or does: "it [i.e., God's choosing to have mercy or compassion on a person] depends not on human will or exertion, but on God, who has mercy" (9:16).

God is the potter, and humans are the clay (9:20–23). God has the right to form "one vessel for honorable use" (i.e., he has the right to choose to save a sinner) and "another for dishonorable use" (i.e., he has the right to choose to pass over and condemn a sinner) (9:21). Compare Proverbs 16:4: "The LORD has made everything for its purpose, / even the wicked for the day of trouble."

Humans fit in one of two groups: (1) "vessels of wrath prepared for destruction" or (2) "vessels of mercy, which he has prepared beforehand for glory" (Rom. 9:22–23). That's either reprobation or election. Some people object that the passive "prepared" does not explicitly identify God as the one who prepared the "vessels of wrath" for destruction. But "prepared" is what theologians call *a divine passive* because the unstated actor in the literary context is God (cf. 9:17–18).

It may help to illustrate what a *passive* is. What's the difference between these two statements?

1. I made mistakes.
2. Mistakes were made.

Which statement would a politician be more likely to say? "Mistakes were made." Why? The first statement is active (i.e., the subject, "I," does the acting) and explicitly identifies who made mistakes ("I"). The second is passive (i.e., the subject, "mistakes," receives the action) and thus does not identify who acted.

The phrase "vessels of wrath prepared for destruction" implies that God did the preparing, but it does not *emphasize* that God is the actor. (For more on this, see the below section "Double Predestination.")

God Destined Certain People to Disobey the Word and Stumble

After Peter emphasizes that God will judge unbelievers for rejecting Christ the cornerstone (1 Pet. 2:7–8a), he explains, "They stumble because they disobey the word, *as they were destined to do*" (2:8b). Who destined them to stumble? God did. This is a divine passive.[1] God destined or appointed that certain people would disobey the word and thus stumble.

Some argue that what is ultimately decisive for whether a person is a believer or an unbeliever is a person's free will (see chap. 6). So they argue that in 1 Peter 2:8, God does not appoint people to disobey the word (which is another way of referring to rejecting Christ or not believing in Christ—see 2:7). Rather, they argue, God appoints that people who disobey the word will stumble and thus be punished in hell. In other words, God appoints the *result* of disobeying the word (i.e., stumbling and punishment), but God does not appoint that "they disobey the word" (1 Pet. 2:8).[2]

The problem with that view is that it is not what the text says. Here is a more form-based translation of what the text says: "They stumble, disobeying the word, unto which also they were appointed." The phrase "unto which they were appointed" refers to both the stumbling and the disobeying. God destined both. The phrase "disobeying the word" is the *reason* they stumble—hence the ESV translation: "They stumble *because* they disobey the word." This corresponds to 2:7b–8a: "for those who do not believe . . . a stone of stumbling / and a rock of offense." Stumbling and being offended are parallel—to stumble is to take offense and thus not believe. The text says that God appointed or destined that those who do not believe stumble because they disobey the word.

Peter heard Jesus teach this about himself:

Have you never read in the Scriptures:

"The stone that the builders rejected
    has become the cornerstone;

---

1. Mark Dubis, *1 Peter: A Handbook on the Greek Text*, Baylor Handbook on the Greek New Testament (Waco, TX: Baylor University Press, 2010), 55.

2. E.g., John H. Elliott, *1 Peter: A New Translation with Introduction and Commentary*, Anchor Bible (New Haven: Yale University Press, 2001), 433–34; Jack W. Cottrell, "The Classical Arminian View of Election," in *Perspectives on Election: Five Views*, ed. Chad Owen Brand (Nashville: Broadman and Holman, 2006), 78.

> *this was the Lord's* doing,
>   and it is marvelous in our eyes"? (Matt. 21:42)

Jesus quotes Psalm 118:22–23 and emphasizes, "This was the Lord's doing." God destined that certain people would reject Jesus the cornerstone. God appointed it. God planned it without being guilty of sin himself (cf. Acts 2:23; 4:27–28). And "it is marvelous in our eyes" (Matt. 21:42). First Peter 2:8 teaches that God destined certain people to disobey and thus stumble—that is, he destined them to rebel against him and thus take offense at and reject Christ the cornerstone.[3]

This destining for disobedience and stumbling may be what 1 Thessalonians 5:9 implies: "For *God has not destined us for wrath*, but to obtain salvation through our Lord Jesus Christ." That gives the reason for the previous sentence: "Since we belong to the day, let us [brothers and sisters in Christ] be sober, having put on the breastplate of faith and love, and for a helmet the hope of salvation" (5:8). God has not destined *believers* for wrath; instead God saves us through Jesus. That hints that God has destined *unbelievers* for wrath; God does not save them.[4]

God Designated Certain People for Condemnation

For certain people have crept in unnoticed *who long ago were designated for this condemnation*, ungodly people,

---

3. See Wayne Grudem, *1 Peter: An Introduction and Commentary*, Tyndale New Testament Commentaries 17 (Downers Grove, IL: InterVarsity Press, 1988), 112–17; Thomas R. Schreiner, *1 and 2 Peter and Jude*, 2nd ed., Christian Standard Commentary (Nashville: Holman, 2020), 117–20; Richard M. Blaylock, *Vessels of Wrath*, 2 vols. (Eugene, OR: Pickwick, 2023), 2:111–19. Piper explains how this is an encouraging word in the context of 1 Peter: "So he is saying to these embattled exiles who are so rejected and shamed and insulted and persecuted, 'Take heart, none of your adversaries will thwart God's plans.' I think that's why Peter says here, 'They stumble because they disobey.' All these people that surround you—[they] are stumbling and making your life miserable—they were destined to do this, which means they are not obstructing, thwarting, [or] denying God's plan. They are fulfilling it. Take heart, just as Jesus was rejected and rose, you too will be honored." John Piper, "They Were Destined to Disobey God: 1 Peter 2:4–8, Part 2," Desiring God, November 24, 2015, https://www.desiringgod.org/.

4. See G. K. Beale, *1–2 Thessalonians*, IVP New Testament Commentary 13 (Downers Grove, IL: InterVarsity Press, 2003), 153.

who pervert the grace of our God into sensuality and deny
our only Master and Lord, Jesus Christ. (Jude 4)

"Were designated" translates a verb that means "to write
in advance or before, *write before(hand)*."[5] It is another divine
passive: *God* is ultimately the one who designated certain people for condemnation. Interpreters handle "were designated"
in three main ways:

1. Jude refers to earlier New Testament writings (e.g., Acts
20:29–30; 1 Tim. 4:1–3; 2 Tim. 3:13; 2 Pet. 2—if Peter wrote
2 Peter before Jude wrote his letter). But this view is unlikely since
Jude modifies "were designated" with the adverb "long ago."

2. Jude refers to the opposite of the book of life (Rev. 13:8;
17:8). This would be an ancient heavenly book in which God
wrote down the names of unrepentant sinners.[6] This view is
possible but unlikely since this would be the only passage in the
Bible that alludes to such a book.[7]

3. Jude refers to Old Testament judgment prophecies—the
type Jude refers to in verses 5–7 and 11. D. A. Carson holds
this view: "Taken together, they [ancient OT prophecies] dem-
onstrate that, at least typologically, the judgment that befell
certain people in ancient times points to similar judgment fall-
ing on those with similar failings in Jude's own day."[8] This
view is most likely, and it further supports that God ultimately
causes reprobation because God is the one who breathed out
the Old Testament judgment prophecies and thus foreordained

5. BDAG 867 (πρόγονος).

6. J. Daryl Charles, "Jude," in *Hebrews–Revelation*, ed. Tremper Longman III and
David E. Garland, 2nd ed., Expositor's Bible Commentary 13 (Grand Rapids, MI:
Zondervan, 2006), 551.

7. See Richard J. Bauckham, *2 Peter, Jude*, World Biblical Commentary 50 (Dallas:
Word, 1983), 35–36.

8. D. A. Carson, "Jude," in *Commentary on the New Testament Use of the Old Testament*, ed. G. K. Beale and D. A. Carson (Grand Rapids, MI: Baker Academic, 2007),
1070. Cf. Douglas J. Moo, *2 Peter, Jude*, NIV Application Commentary (Grand Rapids,
MI: Zondervan, 1996), 229–30; Schreiner, *1 and 2 Peter and Jude*, 525–47.

the condemnation he pronounced. "Their condemnation pronounced long ago is not sitting idly by" (2 Pet. 2:3 NET).

God Did Not Write the Names of Certain Individuals in the Book of Life

And all who dwell on earth will worship it, everyone *whose name has not been written* before the foundation of the world in the book of life of the Lamb who was slain. (Rev. 13:8)

And the dwellers on earth *whose names have not been written* in the book of life from the foundation of the world will marvel to see the beast, because it was and is not and is to come. (Rev. 17:8)

Both passages use the passive voice for not writing names in the book of life. These are divine passives: *God* wrote certain names and not others in this book before he created the world. The book of life records the names of those who will enjoy eternal life with God (cf. Rev. 3:5; 20:12, 15; 21:27; Ex. 32:32–33; Ps. 69:28; Dan. 12:1; Luke 10:20; Phil. 4:3).

The Greek word order in Revelation 13:8 is "the Lamb who was slain before the foundation of the world." But the ESV is likely correct for at least three reasons: (1) Greek word order does not settle the issue; (2) 17:8 unambiguously refers to writing names in the book of life before the foundation of the world; (3) the Lamb was slain during history—not before God created the world (though God foreordained it—Acts 2:23; 4:28; 1 Pet. 1:19–20).[9] So according to Revelation 17:8 and probably 13:8 as well, God intentionally did not write the names of certain individuals in the book of life before he created the world.

---

9. Cf. Richard Bauckham, "Revelation," in *The Oxford Bible Commentary*, ed. John Barton and John Muddiman (Oxford: Oxford University Press, 2001), 1297; Thomas R. Schreiner, "Revelation," in *Hebrews–Revelation*, vol. 12 of *ESV Expository Commentary*, ed. Iain M. Duguid, James M. Hamilton Jr., and Jay Skla (Wheaton, IL: Crossway, 2018), 670.

God Hid Jesus's Message from the Wise and Understanding

> Jesus declared, "I thank you, Father, Lord of heaven and earth, that *you have hidden these things from the wise and understanding* and revealed them to little children; yes, Father, for such was your gracious will." (Matt. 11:25–26; Luke 10:21)

What does "these things" refer to? D. A. Carson explains that "these things" refers to "the significance of Jesus' miracles (cf. vv. 20–24 [in Matt. 11]), the messianic age unfolding largely unnoticed, the content of Jesus' teaching."[10] In other words, God hid *Jesus's message* from certain people and revealed it to others. Jesus's prayer is striking because he praises God not merely for *revealing* his message to little children (i.e., "those who are dependent and love to be taught"); he praises God for *hiding* his message from the wise and understanding (i.e., "those who are self-sufficient and deem themselves wise").[11] Why did Jesus praise God for that? Because that was the Father's "gracious will" (Matt. 11:26) or "good pleasure" (CSB). "It pleased you to do it this way!" (NLT). If something pleases the Father, it also pleases the Son. And if something pleases God the Creator, it should also please us creatures.

Carson warns us not to draw the wrong conclusion from God's concealing and revealing in Matthew 11:25–26:

> We must not think that God's concealing and revealing are symmetrical activities arbitrarily exercised toward neutral human beings who are both innocent and helpless in the face of the divine decree. God is dealing with a race of sinners (cf. 1:21; 7:11) whom he owes nothing. Thus to

---

10. D. A. Carson, "Matthew," in *Matthew–Mark*, ed. Tremper Longman III and David E. Garland, 2nd ed., Expositor's Bible Commentary 9 (Grand Rapids, MI: Zondervan, 2010), 318.

11. Carson, "Matthew," 318.

conceal "these things" is not an act of injustice but of judgment. . . . The astonishing thing about God's activity is not that God acts in both mercy and judgment but who the recipients of that mercy and judgment are: those who pride themselves in understanding divine things are judged; those who understand nothing are taught. The predestination pattern is the counterpoint of grace.[12]

The next section further considers whether God reveals and conceals in the same way (i.e., symmetrically).

Double Predestination: Are Election and Reprobation Symmetrical?

Double predestination refers to election (positive predestination) and reprobation (negative predestination). But there are two different views on double predestination: (1) equal or symmetrical and (2) unequal or nonsymmetrical. See table 11.1.

Table 11.1   Two Views on Double Predestination[a]

Equal or Symmetrical Double Predestination	Unequal or Nonsymmetrical Double Predestination
God elects and reprobates people in the same way.	God elects and reprobates people in different ways.
Election and reprobation are equally active decrees.	Election and reprobation are not equally active decrees.
In reprobation, God sovereignly chose to work unbelief in certain unfallen individuals and condemn them.	In reprobation, God sovereignly and justly chose to pass over nonelect sinners and withhold his regenerating grace.

a. Cf. R. C. Sproul, *Chosen by God* (Wheaton, IL: Tyndale House, 1986), 141–60; Sproul, *Grace Unknown: The Heart of Reformed Theology* (Grand Rapids, MI: Baker, 1997), 157–61. See also Carson, *Divine Sovereignty and Human Responsibility: Biblical Perspectives in Tension*, 2nd ed. (Grand Rapids, MI: Baker Books, 1994), 195–97.

12. Carson, "Matthew," 318.

Consider again my example of ten purple grapes in a bowl. If I choose to eat seven of the grapes, then I pass over the three remaining grapes. But according to the equal or symmetrical view, I would choose to eat seven grapes *and also choose to throw the three remaining grapes into the trash.* The two choices are equally active.

Both views on double predestination agree that God is absolutely sovereign over reprobation. When God chose to save certain individuals and to pass by others, his choices were deliberate. But the two views differ in how God thought about individuals when he chose them or passed over them. In the equal view, God thought about individuals as unfallen and morally neutral. In the unequal view, God thought about individuals as fallen and sinful.

At least five reasons support unequal or nonsymmetrical predestination:

1. God chose to save individuals "in love" (Eph. 1:4) and with delight,[13] but reprobation brings God great sorrow (see Ezek. 33:11; Rom. 9:1–4).

2. Elect sinners are in no way responsible for election, but nonelect sinners are responsible for condemnation (see chap. 15). No sinner deserves election; every sinner deserves condemnation. Reprobation does not mean that God decreed to transform innocent humans into wicked ones and then damn them. God does not harden or condemn *innocent* humans: "None is righteous, no, not one" (Rom. 3:10). Michael Horton explains,

> The "whole lump" [in Rom. 9:21] is guilty and corrupt. It is not a neutral lump of clay, but a condemned mass. God is

---

13. See John Piper, *The Pleasures of God: Meditations on God's Delight in Being God*, in *The Collected Works of John Piper*, ed. David Mathis and Justin Taylor, 14 vols (Wheaton, IL: Crossway, 2017), 2:469–99.

not arbitrarily choosing some and rejecting others. Rather, he is choosing some of his enemies for salvation and leaving the rest to the destiny that all of us would have chosen for ourselves.[14]

3. Election highlights that God is gracious, and reprobation highlights that God is just. As Moo concludes, "God's bestowing of mercy and his hardening are not equivalent acts. God's mercy is given to those who do not deserve it; his hardening affects those who have already by their sin deserved condemnation."[15]

Eternal life and death are not symmetrical in the sense that God dispenses them differently. Consider the principle in Romans 6:23: "The wages [payoff (NET)] of sin is death, but the free [gracious (NASB)] gift of God is eternal life in Christ Jesus our Lord." Paul is not directly addressing reprobation in Romans 6, but the principle he states is not merely about physical death but *eternal* death.[16] See table 11.2.

Table 11.2   Eternal Death and Eternal Life in Romans 6:23

Eternal Death	Eternal Life
The payment for sin (a deserved paycheck)	A gracious gift from God (an undeserved present)
Not a gracious gift from God	Not a payment for righteousness
Highlights that God is just	Highlights that God is gracious

Eternal death is a paycheck; it's what sinners deserve. Eternal life is a gracious gift from God; it's not what sinners deserve.

---

14. Michael Horton, *For Calvinism* (Grand Rapids, MI: Zondervan, 2011), 57.

15. Douglas J. Moo, *The Letter to the Romans*, 2nd ed., New International Commentary on the New Testament (Grand Rapids, MI: Eerdmans, 2018), 619.

16. Cf. Moo, *Letter to the Romans*, 433–34; Thomas R. Schreiner, *Romans*, 2nd ed., Baker Exegetical Commentary on the New Testament (Grand Rapids, MI: Baker Academic, 2018), 339.

Eternal death is not a gift, and eternal life is not a payment. God sovereignly dispenses both eternal death and eternal life, but he dispenses them in different ways. He dispenses eternal death as a payment, and he dispenses eternal life as a gracious gift.

4. On the one hand, Romans 9:18 parallels God's actions that flow from election and reprobation: "he has mercy on whomever he wills, and he hardens whomever he wills." But on the other hand, Romans 9:22–23 uses an *active* voice for election and a divine *passive* for reprobation:

> active: "vessels of mercy, which *he has prepared beforehand for glory*"
> passive: "vessels of wrath *prepared for destruction*"

Paul's use of the active and passive here suggests that we should not treat election and reprobation as symmetrical.

5. According to equal double predestination, God thought about individuals as unfallen and morally neutral when he chose to save them. But the Bible depicts God as thinking about us before the foundation of the world as guilty sinners and thus needing to be saved.[17] One goal of election is "that we should be holy and blameless" (Eph. 1:4; see chap. 1). That presupposes that when God chose to save individuals "before the foundation of the world" (1:4), he thought about us as *unholy* and *blameworthy* (cf. 2 Tim. 1:9). The ultimate goal of election is to praise God's glorious grace (Eph. 1:4–6), which presupposes that when God elected individuals, he thought about us as sinful because we needed his grace. God "lavished upon us" that grace by redeeming us through Christ's death—namely, "the forgiveness of our trespasses" (1:7–8).

---

17. Cf. Francis Turretin, *Institutes of Elenctic Theology*, ed. James T. Dennison Jr., trans. George Musgrave Giger, 3 vols. (Phillipsburg, NJ: P&R, 1992–1997), 1:341–50.

You don't plan to show mercy to someone unless that person is in need; God planned to show mercy to us because he thought about us as sinners who need to be rescued. We need God's *mercy* (Rom. 9:15–16, 18) because we are sinful.

How Does Predestination Relate to Supralapsarianism and Infralapsarianism?

Your eyes may glaze over when you read those strange *lapsarian* words. I mention them because the symmetrical and non-symmetrical views on predestination relate to an arcane debate about the logical order of different aspects of God's decree.[18] See table 11.3.

Table 11.3 Two Views on the Logical Order of Different Aspects of God's Decree

Supralapsarianism (May Affirm Equal or Unequal Double Predestination)	Infralapsarianism (Affirms Unequal Double Predestination)
1. Decree to elect some and pass over the rest	1. Decree to create humans
2. Decree to create humans	**2. Decree to permit all humans to fall**
3. Decree that all humans would fall	**3. Decree to elect some and pass over the rest**
4. Decree to send Christ to provide and accomplish salvation for the elect	4. Decree to send Christ to provide and accomplish salvation for the elect
5. Decree to send the Spirit to effectively call the elect	5. Decree to send the Spirit to effectively call the elect

18. I say *decree* instead of *decrees* because God's timeless, eternal, all-encompassing decree is singular: "the definite plan" (Acts 2:23; cf. 4:28), "his will" (Rom. 9:19), "the purpose of his will" (Eph. 1:5), "the counsel of his will" (Eph. 1:11), "the eternal purpose" (Eph. 3:11; cf. Rom. 8:28).

These two "lapsarian" positions have distinguishing pre-fixes—*supra* (above, before) and *infra* or *sub* (below)—to in-dicate the timing of God's decree of election and reprobation with reference to his decree of mankind's fall (*lapsum*). Supra-lapsarianism places God's decree of election and reprobation *before* (*supra*) God's decree of the fall, and infralapsarianism (or sublapsarianism) places God's decree of election and repro-bation *after* (*infra*) God's decree of the fall.

Some supralapsarians are Calvinists who affirm unequal double predestination, but some are hyper-Calvinists. Hyper-Calvinism affirms equal double predestination and overem-phasizes God's sovereignty in a way that removes human responsibility.[19] All hyper-Calvinists are supralapsarians; a mi-nority of Calvinists are supralapsarians; the majority of Calvin-ists are infralapsarians.

I am wary of discussing the order of different aspects of God's eternal decree because it is speculative. It involves a great deal of conjecture—conclusions based on incomplete information. It debates what God has not revealed to us. It seems presumptuous for us to speculate about the logi-cal order in which God—in eternity past—planned what he would do.[20]

Supralapsarianism rightly emphasizes that God's ultimate purpose is his glory (which is why he sovereignly ordained evil as part of his wise plan). Infralapsarianism rightly em-phasizes that God is working out his plan in history in a way that magnifies his mercy and justice (God does not directly

---

19. Cf. Phillip R. Johnson, "A Primer on Hyper-Calvinism," *Sword and Trowel* 1 (2002): 10–14; also available at http://www.romans45.org/articles/hypercal.htm.

20. For an argument that "we should not take any position on the debate between infralapsarians and supralapsarians," see John M. Frame, *Doctrine of God*, A Theology of Lordship (Phillipsburg, NJ: P&R, 2002), 334–39. For an argument that the supra- and infra- categories are inadequate, see Herman Bavinck, *Reformed Dogmatics*, vol. 2, *God and Creation*, ed. John Bolt, trans. John Vriend (Grand Rapids, MI: Baker Academic, 2004), 383–92 (cf. 361–70).

work unbelief into innocent humans). Rather than debate the *logical order* of different aspects of God's eternal decree, it is more profitable to focus on the *purpose* of God's eternal decree. Scott Christensen does this by summarizing how God deemed it best to glorify himself to humans and angels:

1. "God freely decided to supremely magnify his glory to his intelligent creatures."
2. "In order to do this, God decided to create the universe, and our world in particular, as a theater for his extrinsic glory and placed his creatures within it to enjoy that glory."
3. "God determined, however, that his glory be supremely magnified in the redemption of his creation and his particular image-bearing creatures—human beings. Thus, election finds its grounding in the broader scriptural motif of redemption."
4. "Redemption is not necessary unless God has decreed humanity's fall and that of creation as a whole. . . . God's glory is best magnified in the juxtaposition of creation, fall, and redemption. Note that the accent never rests on evil (the fall), but always on redemption's triumph over it."
5. "God could have chosen to redeem all his image-bearing creatures, but he determined that redemption magnifies his glory more greatly when some are damned (reprobated) and others redeemed (elected)."
6. "This merciful and gracious work of redemption is accomplished only through the incarnated Son of God so that he exists as the center of God's glory."[21]

---

21. Scott Christensen, *What about Evil? A Defense of God's Sovereign Glory* (Phillipsburg, NJ: P&R, 2020), 467–70.

Responding with a Prayer

Thank you, Father, Lord of heaven and earth, that you have hidden Jesus's message from those who are self-sufficient and think they are wise. Thank you that you have revealed Jesus's message to those who depend on you and who love for you to teach them. You, the Potter, prepared vessels of wrath for destruction. You destined certain people to disobey the word and thus stumble. You designated certain people for condemnation. You intentionally did not write the names of certain individuals in the book of life before you created the world. I don't fully understand you and your ways, but I acknowledge that you are the all-powerful, all-good, all-knowing, all-wise Creator. And I put my hand over my mouth in reverential awe.

12

How Does God Accomplish Reprobation?

When you have two options and you choose one of them, that means that you do not choose the other option. The early church chose Matthias *and not Barsabbas* to be an apostle (Acts 1:23–25), and Paul chose Silas *and not Mark* to travel with him (15:39–40).

If you select a certain number of individuals for something, that means that you are not selecting the remaining individuals. The early church chose seven men *and not other men* to serve tables (6:1–6), and they chose to send certain men *and not other men* to Antioch (15:22–27). After Jesus rose from the dead, God ordained for Jesus to appear "not to all the people" but specifically to those "who had been chosen by God as witnesses" (10:39–41).

That is how choosing works in everyday life. If you pick an apple from a bowl full of apples, you are choosing only one apple *and not choosing the rest of the apples*. In a similar way, if God chose to save certain individuals, *then he chose not to save the others*.

But the Bible says more than simply that God did not choose some. The Bible says that God accomplishes reprobation through means. *How* does God carry out his decree of reprobation? God accomplishes reprobation by hardening hearts, blinding eyes, and deafening ears.[1]

God Hardens Hearts, Blinds Eyes, and Deafens Ears

The primary means of reprobation is hardening. Several passages combine two more metaphors to hardening: blinding and deafening.

God Hardened Pharaoh, and He Hardens Whomever He Wills

> For the Scripture says to Pharaoh, "For this very purpose *I have raised you up*, that I might show my power in you, and that my name might be proclaimed in all the earth." So then he has mercy on whomever he wills, and *he hardens whomever he wills*. (Rom. 9:17–18)

When God hardens an individual, he "renders a person insensitive to God and his word," explains Moo, and "if not reversed, culminates in eternal damnation."[2] When God hardens individuals, he is not merely *reacting* to how they previously decided to harden their hearts for themselves. God uncondition-

---

1. Sometimes God hardens, blinds, or deafens individuals in a particular situation but not necessarily for eternal death. For example, God hardened King Sihon specifically that he would not let the Israelites pass through his land (Deut. 2:30), which illustrates Proverbs 21:1: "The king's heart is a stream of water in the hand of the LORD; / *he turns it wherever he will*" (cf. Ezra 6:22; 7:27; Prov. 16:1, 9; 19:21; Isa. 10:5–7). In this chapter I am focusing on instances in which God hardens, blinds, and deafens with reference to eternal death. For lists of passages that distinguish God's divine reprobating activity as either eternal or noneternal, see Richard M. Blaylock, *Vessels of Wrath*, 2 vols. (Eugene, OR: Pickwick, 2023), 1:177–78, 2:185–86.

2. Douglas J. Moo, *The Letter to the Romans*, 2nd ed., New International Commentary on the New Testament (Grand Rapids, MI: Eerdmans, 2018), 617. Schreiner agrees: "The 'hardening' word group in Paul (σκληρότης, *sklērotēs*, hardness; πωροῦν, *pōroun*, to harden; πώρωσις, *pōrōsis*, hardness) denotes an inflexibility and insensibility to the gospel that hinders people from being saved (Rom. 2:5; 11:7, 25; 2 Cor. 3:14; Eph. 4:18)." Thomas R. Schreiner, *Romans*, 2nd ed., Baker Exegetical Commentary on the New Testament (Grand Rapids, MI: Baker Academic, 2018), 500.

ally hardened Pharaoh's heart (see Ex. 4:21; 7:3; 9:12; 10:1, 20, 27; 11:10; 14:4, 8) and the hearts of the Egyptians (14:17).[3] God freely chose to have mercy on whomever he wanted, and he freely chose to harden whomever he wanted. That is his right (Rom. 9:19–23), and his choice is decisive.

God Hardened, Blinded, and Deafened Nonelect Israelites

What then? Israel failed to obtain what it was seeking. The elect obtained it, but *the rest were hardened*, as it is written,

> "*God gave them a spirit of stupor*,
>   *eyes that would not see*
>   and *ears that would not hear*,
> down to this very day."

And David says,

> "Let their table become a snare and a trap,
>   a stumbling block and a retribution for them;
> *let* their *eyes be darkened so that they cannot see*,
>   and bend their backs forever." (Rom. 11:7–10)

The people Paul speaks about are either "the elect" or "the rest" (Rom. 11:7). In this context, "the rest" are nonelect Israelites, and God hardened, blinded, and deafened them (cf. Deut. 29:4; Pss. 69:22–23; 115:3–8; Isa. 29:10; 44:18).[4]

God Hardens, Deafens, and Blinds Certain Sinners

Go, and say to this people:

---

3. See G. K. Beale, "An Exegetical and Theological Consideration of the Hardening of Pharaoh's Heart in Exodus 4–14 and Romans 9," *Trinity Journal* 5 (1984): 129–54; Robert V. McCabe, "An Old Testament Sanctifying Influence: The Sovereignty of God," *Detroit Baptist Seminary Journal* 15 (2010): 9–15; John Piper, *Providence* (Wheaton, IL: Crossway, 2021), 434–44; Blaylock, *Vessels of Wrath*, 1:24–39, 2:77–91; Phil Gons, "Why Did God Harden Pharaoh's Heart? A Case for Divine Ultimacy," *Phil Gons* (blog), January 3, 2021, https://philgons.com/.

4. Cf. Blaylock, *Vessels of Wrath*, 2:98–103.

"Keep on hearing, but *do not understand*;
keep on seeing, but *do not perceive*."
Make the heart of this people dull,
    and *their ears heavy*,
    and *blind their eyes*;
lest they see with their eyes,
    and hear with their ears,
and understand with their hearts,
    and turn and be healed. (Isa. 6:9–10)

How would you feel if God commanded you to announce that message? That is how God commissioned Isaiah. The New Testament quotes this passage at least five times (Matt. 13:14–15; Mark 4:12; Luke 8:10; John 12:39–40; Acts 28:26–27; cf. John 9:39; Rom. 11:8). Isaiah 6:9–10 does not specify that eternal punishment is in view, but that is what the New Testament passages imply in their literary contexts.[5] These passages presuppose that God sovereignly hardens, deafens, and blinds certain sinners. Remarkably, the gospel message that can soften hearts and open ears and unveil eyes can also harden hearts and deafen ears and blind eyes. The sun melts ice and hardens clay.

How Does God Harden?

Peter Sammons thoughtfully organizes the means of reprobation into four categories: abandonment, hardening, personal agency, and nonpersonal agency.[6] I think it is simpler to say that the primary means is hardening and that the other categories are ways that God hardens.

---

5. See Blaylock, *Vessels of Wrath*, 1:94–105, 2:33–42, 44–51, 122–33.
6. See Peter Sammons, *Reprobation and God's Sovereignty: Recovering a Biblical Doctrine* (Grand Rapids, MI: Kregel Academic, 2022), 227–81.

God Hardens by Withholding Grace

Our sinful hearts are worse than we think. It should not surprise us when a horde loots a store when no police are present or available. God has kindly given God-hating rebels all kinds of restraining grace so that people do not behave as wickedly as they possibly could (e.g., Gen. 20:6; 1 Sam. 25:34, 39). One way that God hardens individuals is simply by withholding grace. God withholds grace when he hides Jesus's message from people (Matt. 11:25–26; Luke 10:21; cf. Matt. 15:14). God withholds grace when he removes moral restraints and gives people up to what their sinful hearts desire (Rom. 1:24, 26, 28).

This is why A. A. Hodge describes hardening as "doubtless a judicial act wherein God withdraws from sinful men, whom he has not elected to life, for the just punishment of their sins, all gracious influences, and leaves them to the unrestrained tendencies of their own hearts, and to the uncounteracted influences of the world and the devil."[7] R. C. Sproul explains,

> All that God has to do to harden people's hearts is to remove the restraints. He gives them a longer leash. Rather than restricting their human freedom, he increases it. He lets them have their own way. In a sense he gives them enough rope to hang themselves. It is not that God puts his hand on them to create fresh evil in their hearts; he merely removes his holy hand of restraint from them and lets them do their own will.[8]

God Hardens through Sinful People

God uses wicked people to accomplish his purposes. This includes humans such as Joseph's brothers (Gen. 50:20), the

---

7. A. A. Hodge, *Outlines of Theology*, 2nd ed. (New York: Hodder and Stoughton, 1878), 223.
8. R. C. Sproul, *Chosen by God* (Wheaton, IL: Tyndale, 1986), 145.

Sabeans who murdered Job's servants and plundered his live-stock (Job 1:15), the Babylonians (Hab. 1), and Judas (John 17:12). This also includes Satan and demons (1 Chron. 21:1; Job 1:7–12). God can accomplish his decree of reprobation by hardening hearts and blinding eyes through wicked people (see 2 Thess. 2:8–10; Rev. 13:5, 8; 17:8, 12–18).

God Hardens with the Truth

God hardens people with the truth (e.g., Isa. 6:9–10; Matt. 13:14–15). This reminds me of the treacherous Dwarfs at the end of C. S. Lewis's *The Last Battle*. The Dwarfs sense that they are confined in a pitch-black stable, and when Lucy picks some fresh flowers and asks Diggle the Dwarf if he can smell them, he angrily shouts, "How dare you! What do you mean by shoving a lot of filthy stable-litter in my face?"[9] For those being saved, the truth is "the aroma of Christ . . . a fragrance from life to life," but to others the very same message is "a fragrance from death to death" (2 Cor. 2:15–16). Believers consider Jesus the cornerstone as "precious," but "those who do not believe" reject the cornerstone; unbelievers "stumble because they disobey the word, as they were destined to do" (1 Pet. 2:6–8).

Is That Fair?

Roger Olson, an Arminian theologian, says that if reprobation is true, it is difficult for him to distinguish God from Satan:

> Taken to their logical conclusion, that even hell and all who will suffer there eternally are foreordained by God, God is thereby rendered morally ambiguous at best and a moral monster at worst. I have gone so far as to say that this kind of Calvinism, which attributes everything to God's will and

9. C. S. Lewis, *The Last Battle*, The Chronicles of Narnia (New York: HarperCollins, 1956), 166.

control, makes it difficult (at least for me) to see the difference between God and the devil.[10]

In chapter 5, we addressed the question "Is Unconditional Election Unfair?" But is it fair for God to harden, blind, and deafen sinners? Is it fair that God accomplishes reprobation by *withholding* grace and by *hardening* hearts, *blinding* eyes, and *deafening* ears? It is crucial to remember two truths:

1. God is the supreme Creator, and we are his creatures. Paul anticipated the "unfair" objection:

> You will say to me then, "Why does he still find fault? For who can resist his will?" But who are you, O man, to answer back to God? Will what is molded say to its molder, "Why have you made me like this?" Has the potter no right over the clay, to make out of the same lump one vessel for honorable use and another for dishonorable use? (Rom. 9:19–21)

God is all-powerful, all-good, all-knowing, and all-wise, and we are not. So it should not surprise us that we don't fully understand him and his ways.

2. When God hardens, blinds, and deafens an individual by withholding grace, that person is not innocent but already guilty (see "Is That Fair?" in chap. 15). God shows mercy to certain *sinners*, and he hardens certain *sinners*.

We are not innocent, neutral people whom God chose to save or pass over. Each of us is a rebel against the King, an idolator, a wicked traitor. And God sovereignly and graciously chose to rescue some sinners and to condemn the rest.

God ultimately causes reprobation *but not in the same way that he sovereignly chose to save individuals*. God hardens, blinds, and deafens sinners *but not in the same way that he*

---

10. Roger Olson, *Against Calvinism* (Grand Rapids, MI: Zondervan, 2011), 23; see also 84–85, 104, 110, 180, 190.

softens the hearts, opens the *eyes, and opens the ears of sin-ners.* (On nonsymmetrical double predestination, see chap. 11.) Michael Horton contrasts how God hardens and softens hearts:

> God is not active in hardening hearts in the same way that he is active in softening hearts. Scripture does speak of God hardening hearts, not only in Exodus 7:3 and Romans 9:18 but also in Joshua 11:20; John 12:40; Romans 11:7; 2 Corinthians 3:14. Yet it also speaks of sinners hardening their own hearts (Ex. 8:15; Ps. 95:8; Isa. 63:17; Matt. 19:8; Heb. 3:8, 13). However, no passage speaks of sinners softening their own hearts and regenerating themselves. Human beings are alone responsible for their hardness of heart, but God alone softens and in fact re-creates the hearts of his elect (1 Kings 8:58; Ps. 51:10; Isa. 57:15; Jer. 31:31–34; Ezek. 11:19; 36:26; 2 Cor. 3:3; 4:6; Heb. 10:16). In short, God only has to leave us to our own devices in the case of reprobation, but it requires the greatest works of the triune God to save the elect, including the death of the Father's only begotten Son.[11]

We must not conclude that God's hardening, blinding, and deafening contradicts his goodness. God gives common (non-saving) grace to all humans. He often gives more temporal material blessings to unbelievers than he does to believers. But unbelievers are sinners who despise God's goodness and deserve condemnation (Rom. 2:4–5). "Everyone who does wicked things hates the light and does not come to the light" (John 3:20; cf. 6:44, 65); "no one seeks for God" (Rom. 3:11; on free will, see chap. 6). Unbelievers are responsible moral agents who willfully reject what God has revealed about himself. God is just and good, and God always does what is just and good (Gen. 18:25; Ps. 119:68).

---

11. Michael Horton, *For Calvinism* (Grand Rapids, MI: Zondervan, 2011), 57–58.

How Can God Ordain Sin but Not Be Guilty of Sin?

How is it possible that God ordained both (1) what we choose and (2) that we freely and responsibly choose what we most want? I don't know precisely how. It's a mystery. (See the end of chap. 6.) But God has revealed both of those truths to us in Scripture, so we dare not deny one of them simply because we don't understand exactly how God can ordain sin but not be guilty of it.

We do know, however, that God "stands behind good and evil *asymmetrically.*"[12] It is helpful to distinguish at least three kinds of causes (see table 12.1).

Table 12.1   Ultimate, Proximate, and Efficient Causes

Type of Cause	Example 1: Census	Example 2: Death of Christ
The *ultimate* cause ordains or ensures an action.	*God*: "The LORD . . . incited David" to "number Israel and Judah" (2 Sam. 24:1).	*God*: Jesus was "delivered up according to the definite [predetermined (NASB, NET)] plan and foreknowledge of God" (Acts 2:23). The people did "whatever [God's] hand and [God's] plan had predestined to take place" (4:28).
A *proximate* cause influences an action.	*Satan*: "Satan . . . incited David to number Israel" (1 Chron. 21:1).	*Jews*: Jews incited Jesus's death by demanding that Pilate crucify Jesus (see Mark 15:13–14).
An *efficient* cause directly performs an action.	*David*: King David commanded Joab to number the people (2 Sam. 24:2; 1 Chron. 21:2). "I have sinned greatly in what I have done" (2 Sam. 24:10).	*Gentiles*: "The hands of lawless men" (Acts 2:23) and "the Gentiles" (4:27) carried out Jesus's crucifixion. Specifically, "Pontius Pilate" (4:27) ordered it, and the Roman soldiers performed it.

---

12. D. A. Carson, *How Long, O Lord? Reflections on Suffering and Evil*, 2nd ed. (Grand Rapids, MI: Baker Academic, 2006), 189; emphasis original; also 199.

The examples in table 12.1 illustrate three levels of causes (see also 1 Kings 22; Ezek. 14:1–11). God as the ultimate cause accomplishes his purposes through secondary (i.e., proximate and efficient) causes. The secondary causes intend evil, but God intends it for good (cf. Gen. 50:20). The people who freely sin as secondary causes are accountable to God for doing the sinful actions that God ordained they would do. God's meticulous sovereignty and our responsibility are compatible (see chap. 6).

Describing God as the ultimate *cause* may be misleading since *cause* typically means "to make something happen." God is never the efficient cause of evil; he never infuses evil thoughts or intentions into the hearts of sinners. That is why many Calvinists distinguish "between what God causes and what he permits."[13] Horton explains,

> God is not the author of sin, since he does not directly cause or bring it about. (In his treatment in the *Institutes*, Calvin, like Aquinas, employs the Aristotelian categories of primary and secondary causality.) That is, God does not make, create, or coerce creatures toward evil. . . .
>
> The Calvinist says that everything that happens is not only foreknown but determined by God, yet in some cases through his own action (such as working all things together for our good) and in other cases through his permission (such as allowing creatures to commit a particular sin). . . .
>
> While God never causes sin, he is Lord over it, and it can progress no further than his wisdom and goodness will allow.[14]

Berkhof explains that with reference to sin God's decree is "permissive":

13. Paul Helm, "The Augustinian-Calvinist View," in *Divine Foreknowledge: Four Views*, ed. James K. Beilby and Paul R. Eddy, Spectrum Multiview Books (Downers Grove, IL: InterVarsity Press, 2001), 181.

14. Horton, *For Calvinism*, 48, 59, 60; cf. 68–70.

God does not positively work in man "both to will and to do," when man goes contrary to His revealed will. It should be carefully noted, however, that this permissive decree does not imply a passive permission of something which is not under the control of the divine will. It is a decree which renders the future sinful act absolutely certain, but in which God determines (a) not to hinder the sinful self-determination of the finite will; and (b) to regulate and control the result of this sinful self-determination.[15]

The sinless and meticulously sovereign God is the ultimate or primary cause who orchestrates all things—including reprobation. God can righteously see to it that his decree comes to pass through secondary causes such as humans, angels, demons, and natural laws.

It is possible for a cause to bring about an effect without the cause and effect sharing the same qualities. Heat and clay illustrate this. Heat causes wet clay to become dry and hard (e.g., bricks and pottery). Heat can cause hardness, but heat is not hard. Similarly, God is the ultimate cause of sin (i.e., he ordains sin for good and wise purposes), but God is not sinful. God righteously ordains the ends as well as the means to the ends.[16]

Responding with a Prayer

Thank you, Father, that you sovereignly harden the hearts and blind the eyes and deafen the ears of certain sinners, and thank

---

15. Louis Berkhof, *Systematic Theology*, 4th ed. (Grand Rapids, MI: Eerdmans, 1938), 105.

16. See J. Gresham Machen, *Things Unseen: A Systematic Introduction to the Christian Faith and Reformed Theology* (Glenside, PA: Westminster Seminary Press, 2020), 167–74; David E. Alexander and Daniel M. Johnson, eds., *Calvinism and the Problem of Evil* (Eugene, OR: Pickwick, 2016); John MacArthur and Richard Mayhue, eds., *Biblical Doctrine: A Systematic Summary of Bible Truth* (Wheaton, IL: Crossway, 2017), 491–93; Scott Christensen, *What about Evil? A Defense of God's Sovereign Glory* (Phillipsburg, NJ: P&R, 2020), 201–24; Sammons, *Reprobation and God's Sovereignty*, 175–281.

you that you sovereignly soften the hearts and open the eyes and open the ears of certain sinners. We do not fully understand your ways, but we praise you that you are just and good and that you always do what is just and good.

.

13

What Is the Result
of Reprobation?

God sovereignly and justly chose to pass over nonelect sinners and
punish them. The final result of reprobation is heavy, sorrowful,
and terrifying. It is the opposite of eternal life, supreme joy, and
ultimate satisfaction. It is hell. Hell is punishment, destruction,
banishment, and a place of suffering—eternally.[1] At least five terms
describe the destiny that God predetermined for nonelect sinners.

1. Wrath

Paul asks, "What if God, desiring to show *his wrath* and to
make known his power, has endured with much patience *vessels*

---

1. Christopher W. Morgan and Robert A. Peterson, *What Is Hell?*, Basics of the Faith
(Phillipsburg, NJ: P&R, 2010). See also Robert A. Peterson, *Hell on Trial: The Case for
Eternal Punishment* (Phillipsburg, NJ: P&R, 1995); D. A. Carson, "On Banishing the Lake
of Fire," in *The Gagging of God: Christianity Confronts Pluralism* (Grand Rapids, MI:
Zondervan, 1996), 515–36; Christopher W. Morgan and Robert A. Peterson, eds., *Hell
under Fire: Modern Scholarship Reinvents Eternal Punishment* (Grand Rapids, MI: Zondervan, 2004); John Piper, *Let the Nations Be Glad! The Supremacy of God in Missions*, 3rd
ed. (Grand Rapids, MI: Baker Academic, 2010), 133–45; Andrew David Naselli, "Hellfire
and Brimstone: Interpreting the New Testament's Horrific Descriptions of Hell," *9Marks
Journal* 7, no. 4 (2010): 16–19; Denny Burk, "Eternal Conscious Torment," in *Four Views
on Hell*, 2nd ed., ed. Preston Sprinkle, Counterpoints (Grand Rapids, MI: Zondervan, 2016).

of wrath prepared for destruction . . ." (Rom. 9:22). And Paul asserts, "God has not destined us *for wrath*, but to obtain salvation through our Lord Jesus Christ" (1 Thess. 5:9). "Wrath" refers to suffering eternal punishment as "retributive justice"— a justly deserved penalty.[2] Jesus is the one "who delivers us [believers] from the wrath to come" (1 Thess. 1:10; cf. Matt. 3:7; Rom. 2:5, 8; 5:9; Eph. 5:6; Col. 3:6; 1 Thess. 2:16).[3]

2. Destruction

Paul soberly asks, "What if God, desiring to show his wrath and to make known his power, has endured with much patience vessels of wrath *prepared for destruction* . . ." (Rom. 9:22). "Destruction" translates a word (*apōleia*) that commonly occurs in the New Testament for the eternal ruin that unbelievers will experience (e.g., Matt. 7:13; 2 Pet. 2:1; 3:7). The "vessels of wrath" are destined for eternal punishment because they are the opposite of "vessels of mercy," whom God has "prepared beforehand for glory" (Rom. 9:23).[4] As Psalm 92:7 says,

> Though the wicked sprout like grass
> and all evildoers flourish,
> *they are doomed to destruction forever.*[5]

---

2. Gordon D. Fee, *The First and Second Epistles to the Thessalonians*, New International Commentary on the New Testament (Grand Rapids, MI: Eerdmans, 2009), 197.

3. Cf. Benjamin B. Warfield, *The Power of God unto Salvation* (Philadelphia: Presbyterian Board of Publication, 1903), 190.

4. Schreiner writes, "In Paul's writings, both 'wrath' (ὀργή, Rom. 2:5, 8; 5:9; Eph. 5:6; Col. 3:6; 1 Thess. 1:10; 5:9) and 'destruction' (ἀπώλεια, Phil. 1:28; 3:19; 2 Thess. 2:3; 1 Tim. 6:9; cf. the verbal form ἀπολλύναι, *apollynai*, to destroy: 1 Cor. 1:18, 19; 8:11; 10:9, 10; 15:18; 2 Cor. 2:15; 4:3; 2 Thess. 2:10) frequently refer to eschatological judgment. . . . The ἔλεος [mercy] word group often refers to eschatological life, and δόξα [glory] does the same (Rom. 2:7, 10; 5:2; 8:18, 21; 1 Cor. 2:7; 15:41; 2 Cor. 4:17; Eph. 1:18; Phil. 3:21; Col. 1:27; 3:4; 1 Thess. 2:12; 2 Thess. 2:14; 2 Tim. 2:10)." Thomas R. Schreiner, *Romans*, 2nd ed., Baker Exegetical Commentary on the New Testament (Grand Rapids, MI: Baker Academic, 2018), 506.

5. Cf. Richard M. Blaylock, *Vessels of Wrath*, 2 vols. (Eugene, OR: Pickwick, 2023), 1:152–55.

3. Not Obtaining a Right Standing with God

Paul asks, "What then? Israel failed to obtain *what it was seeking.* The elect obtained *it,* but the rest were hardened" (Rom. 11:7). What was Israel seeking? A right standing with God: "Israel . . . pursued a law that would lead to righteousness [but] did not succeed in reaching that law. Why? Because they did not pursue it by faith, but as if it were based on works" (Rom. 9:31–32). Israel failed to obtain a right standing with God. Romans 11:7 teaches that a result of hardening is not obtaining a right standing with God.

4. Condemnation

Jude explains, "Certain people have crept in unnoticed who long ago were designated *for this condemnation*" (Jude 4). "This condemnation" anticipates Jude 5–16 and refers to when God finally condemns unrepentant sinners.[6] Thus, the NET translates, "Certain men have secretly slipped in among you— men who long ago were marked out for *the condemnation I am about to describe.*"

5. The Lake of Fire

John describes a terrifying scene: "If anyone's name was not found written in the book of life, *he was thrown into the lake of fire*" (Rev. 20:15). God wrote the names of specific individuals in the book of life before the foundation of the world, and he passed over the rest (13:8; 17:8). The result of not having one's name in the book of life is being "thrown into the lake of fire" (20:15) and suffering "eternal fire" and "eternal punishment" (Matt. 25:41, 46).

---

6. Cf. Richard J. Bauckham, *2 Peter, Jude,* Word Biblical Commentary 50 (Dallas: Word, 1983), 37; Thomas R. Schreiner, *1 and 2 Peter and Jude,* 2nd ed., Christian Standard Commentary (Nashville: Holman, 2020), 528.

Should We Feel Sorrow about This Reality?

Yes, when we think about the destiny of unbelievers, we should feel great sorrow. That is not *all* we should feel (see the next chapter), but we should genuinely feel deep sorrow. God himself feels sorrow: "As I live, declares the Lord GOD, *I have no pleasure in the death of the wicked*, but that the wicked turn from his way and live" (Ezek. 33:11).[7] Paul writes these God-breathed words about his fellow Israelites:

> I am speaking the truth in Christ—I am not lying; my conscience bears me witness in the Holy Spirit—that *I have great sorrow and unceasing anguish in my heart. For I could wish that I myself were accursed and cut off from Christ for the sake of my brothers*, my kinsmen according to the flesh. (Rom. 9:1–3)

Paul is grieved that so many of his fellow Israelites are rejecting the gospel.[8] Israelites may have questioned the genuineness of Paul's grief since they viewed him as a Gentile sympathizer, but Paul emphasizes his honesty and adds that if it were possible, he would go to hell for his kinsmen! Paul was willing to be "accursed" (Gk. *anathema*) and thus "cut off from Christ" in place of his fellow Israelites who are not saved (cf. Ex. 32:32).

Responding with a Prayer

Father, it grieves me to think of family and friends and neighbors and people all around me who do not love you and are on a path to hell. It causes great sorrow and unceasing anguish in my heart. I beg you to be gracious and merciful—for the sake of your fame. Amen.

---

7. On the two wills of God, see chap. 7 above.

8. Content in this paragraph is adapted from Andrew David Naselli, *From Typology to Doxology: Paul's Use of Isaiah and Job in Romans 11:34–35* (Eugene, OR: Pickwick, 2012), 13–14; used by permission of Wipf and Stock Publishers, www.wipfandstock .com. See also Naselli, *Romans: A Concise Guide to the Greatest Letter Ever Written* (Wheaton, IL: Crossway, 2022), 115.

What Is the Goal of Reprobation?

If it brings God sorrow to pass over nonelect sinners and punish them, then why did he choose to do it? Is his sorrow fake?

God's sorrow is not fake. It is genuine. It is possible for a person to genuinely have two competing desires and to act in accord with one desire without in any way making the other desire fake or false. (See chap. 7.)

What does God value more highly than saving all humans without exception? God in his infinite wisdom ordained election and reprobation to be the way they are because his sovereign choices will glorify him in a way that other situations would not. We do not know all the reasons that God sovereignly and justly chose to pass over nonelect sinners and punish them, but God has revealed two of his goals: (1) to glorify God for his wrath and power and (2) to glorify God for the riches of his glory for vessels of mercy. Those goals are not parallel. The first is subservient to the second. The second is ultimate.

Goal 1: To Glorify God for His Wrath and Power

> For the Scripture says to Pharaoh, "For this very purpose
> I have raised you up, *that I might show my power in you,*
> and *that my name might be proclaimed in all the earth.*" So
> then he has mercy on whomever he wills, and he hardens
> whomever he wills. (Rom. 9:17–18)

Pharaoh dramatically illustrates why God chose to harden
individuals. God raised up Pharaoh for precisely this purpose:
"that I might show my power in you" (9:17). And God dem-
onstrated his power over Pharaoh for this purpose: "that my
name might be proclaimed in all the earth" (9:17)—in other
words, to glorify God. Glorifying God makes much of God by
showing him to be who he is—supremely great and good. God
chose to harden Pharaoh to display his power so that people in
all the earth would make much of God.

> What if God, *desiring to show his wrath* and to *make
> known his power*, has endured with much patience vessels
> of wrath prepared for destruction, in order to make known
> the riches of his glory for vessels of mercy, which he has
> prepared beforehand for glory. (Rom. 9:22–23)

The main clause is "God . . . has endured." There are two
main ways to interpret how "desiring" relates to the main
clause:

1. *Although* (cf. NASB, NIV, NLT). God has endured with
   much patience vessels of wrath prepared for destruction
   although he desired to show his wrath and to make
   known his power.
2. *Because* (cf. NIrV). God has endured with much patience vessels of wrath prepared for destruction *because*
   he desired to show his wrath and to make known his

power. The "because" option makes better sense of how Paul is arguing; it parallels 9:17–18.[1]

We consider 9:22–23 further in the next section, but here note the first two ways that God's sovereign and just choice to pass over nonelect sinners and punish them makes much of God:

1. It displays God's "wrath" against sin and thus glorifies God's justice. Eternally punishing unrepentant sinners in hell is righteous; it shows that God is just.

2. It displays God's "power" over rebellious sinners. The most powerful humans—such as Pharaoh, king of Egypt—are no match for the all-powerful God.[2]

Seven times in the final book of the Bible, people praise God for righteously judging and punishing his enemies. People praise God for his just wrath and invincible power.

[1] And the twenty-four elders who sit on their thrones before God fell on their faces and worshiped God, saying,

> "We give thanks to you, Lord God Almighty,
>   who is and who was,
> for *you have taken your great power*
>   and begun to reign.
> The nations raged,
>   but *your wrath came*,
>   and the time for the dead to be judged,
> and for rewarding your servants, the prophets and
>   saints,
>   and those who fear your name,

---

1. Cf. Douglas J. Moo, *The Letter to the Romans*, 2nd ed., New International Commentary on the New Testament (Grand Rapids, MI: Eerdmans, 2018), 624–25; Thomas R. Schreiner, *Romans*, 2nd ed., Baker Exegetical Commentary on the New Testament (Grand Rapids, MI: Baker Academic, 2018), 501, 507.

2. Cf. Scott Christensen, *What about Evil? A Defense of God's Sovereign Glory* (Phillipsburg, NJ: P&R, 2020), 323–39.

> both small and great,
> and *for destroying the destroyers of the earth*."
>   (Rev. 11:16–18)

[2] And I heard the angel in charge of the waters say,

> "*Just are you*, O Holy One, who is and who was,
>   *for you brought these judgments.*
> For they have shed the blood of saints and prophets,
>   and *you have given them blood to drink.*
> *It is what they deserve!*" (16:5–6)

[3] And I heard the altar saying,

> "Yes, Lord God the Almighty,
>   *true and just are your judgments!*" (16:7)

[4] After this I heard what seemed to be the loud voice of a great multitude in heaven, crying out,

> "Hallelujah!
> Salvation and glory and power belong to our God,
>   *for his judgments are true and just*;
> *for he has judged the great prostitute*
>   who corrupted the earth with her immorality,
> *and has avenged on her the blood of his servants.*"
>   (19:1–2)

[5] Once more they cried out,

> "Hallelujah!
>   *The smoke from her goes up forever and ever.*"
>   (19:3)

[6] And the twenty-four elders and the four living creatures *fell down and worshiped God* who was seated on the throne, saying, "Amen. Hallelujah!" (19:4)

[7] And from the throne came a voice saying,

> "Praise our God,
>   all you his servants,
> you who fear him,
>   small and great." (19:5)

When we praise God today in prayers and songs, we typically praise God for saving us from our sins and from God's wrath. But in Revelation, God's people also praise God for righteously judging and punishing his enemies. When God serves justice by judging and punishing his enemies, he deserves glory for his wrath and power.

Goal 2: To Glorify God for the Riches of His Glory for Vessels of Mercy

> What if God, desiring to show his wrath and to make known his power, has endured with much patience vessels of wrath prepared for destruction, *in order to make known the riches of his glory for vessels of mercy*, which he has prepared beforehand for glory. (Rom. 9:22–23)

Here is how Moo paraphrases 9:22–23:

> What objection can you make if it is in fact the case that God has tolerated with great patience vessels of wrath prepared for destruction when you realize that his purpose in doing so has been to demonstrate his wrath, make known his power, and—especially—to make known the riches of his glory to vessels of mercy, prepared beforehand for glory?[3]

God has the right to immediately condemn sinful humans, and we cannot raise a single objection against it. Piper explains 9:22–23,

---

3. Moo, *Letter to the Romans*, 625.

The word "what" in the phrase "what if" is not there. The sentence is a long *if* clause with no *then* clause. We are expected to supply the part that is missing. Here's my suggestion of what to supply: "*If* God, desiring to show his wrath and to make known his power, has endured with much patience vessels of wrath prepared for destruction, in order to make known the riches of his glory for vessels of mercy, which he has prepared beforehand for glory . . . *then no legitimate objection can be raised.*" That is what the translation "what if" implies as well. "*What if* I have this purpose in showing my wrath and power?" If I do, will you fault me? This is the point Paul has been making in verses 20–21: the potter has a right to show his power and wisdom in any way he considers best for accomplishing his purposes.[4]

So why does God patiently endure sinful humans as they keep breathing his air and rebelling against him—sinners who will experience his wrath and whom he has "prepared for destruction"? Because the whole process makes much of God in at least three ways. We considered the first two ways in the previous section: (1) *it displays God's wrath* against sin and thus glorifies God's justice, and (2) *it displays God's power* over rebellious sinners. Those are subordinate goals for this ultimate goal: (3) *it displays the riches of God's glory for vessels of mercy.*[5]

---

4. John Piper, *Providence* (Wheaton, IL: Crossway, 2021), 108–9; emphasis original.

5. Sammons argues, "It seems likely that [in Romans 9:19–23] Paul intends to emphasize God's activity in the election of the vessels of mercy, reiterating that he is the only active agent in the matter. [John Piper argues,] 'If this is the case, Paul would be implying that not wrath but mercy is the greater, overarching goal for which God does all things.' This is likely why Paul also switches his parallelism throughout Romans 9. First, it was Jacob followed by Esau (9:13). Next, it was Moses (9:15) and Pharaoh (9:17). Then it was mercy followed by hardening (9:18). Then it was honor and dishonor (9:19). Finally, for emphasis, Paul swaps what would be the anticipated order and lists vessels of wrath (9:22) first, before concluding with vessels of mercy (9:23)." Peter Sammons, *Reprobation and God's Sovereignty: Recovering a Biblical Doctrine* (Grand Rapids, MI: Kregel Academic, 2022), 101. This may be why Paul uses the passive voice for vessels of wrath ("prepared for destruction") and the active voice for vessels of mercy ("which he has prepared beforehand for glory").

If reprobation did not exist, then there would be aspects of God's glory that we could not perceive and praise God for. Specifically, God is not only just; he is also merciful. Those whom God foreknew, predestined, and elected are vessels of mercy. If you are a vessel of mercy—someone whom God has enabled to repent and believe—how do you feel about God when you compare yourself to "vessels of wrath prepared for destruction"? You are no better than they are. You deserve the same just condemnation they do. *But God is merciful to you!*

That is why doxologies in the New Testament give glory to God within books that highlight God's wrath and power and especially his mercy. Table 14.1 features some of those doxologies and lists a sampling of passages that feature those themes.

Table 14.1   Doxologies in Books That Highlight God's Wrath and Power and Mercy

Book	Doxologies	God's Wrath and Power	God's Mercy
Romans	"From him and through him and to him are all things. To him be glory forever. Amen" (11:36). "To the only wise God be glory forevermore through Jesus Christ! Amen" (16:27).	1:18, 20; 2:2–3, 5, 8–9; 3:5–6; 9:17, 22; 11:33	3:24; 4:16; 5:6–9, 20–21; 8:32; 9:15–16, 18, 23; 11:30–32; 15:9
Ephesians	"To him be glory in the church and in Christ Jesus throughout all generations, forever and ever. Amen" (3:21).	2:3; 5:6	1:6–8; 2:4–5, 7–8; 3:16
Philippians	"To our God and Father be glory forever and ever. Amen" (4:20).	1:28; 3:21	1:28; 4:19

(Table 14.1 continued)

Book	Doxologies	God's Wrath and Power	God's Mercy
1 Timothy	"To the King of the ages, immortal, invisible, the only God, be honor and glory forever and ever. Amen" (1:17; also 6:15–16).	6:9	1:13, 16
2 Timothy	"To him be the glory forever and ever. Amen" (4:18).	4:8	1:9
1 Peter	"To him belong glory and dominion forever and ever. Amen" (4:11).	1:17; 3:12; 4:5	1:3, 13; 2:10; 5:10
Jude	"Now to him who is able to keep you from stumbling and to present you blameless before the presence of his glory with great joy, to the only God, our Savior, through Jesus Christ our Lord, be glory, majesty, dominion, and authority, before all time and now and forever. Amen" (24–25).	4, 6, 11, 14–15	21
Revelation	"To him who loves us and has freed us from our sins by his blood and made us a kingdom, priests to his God and Father, to him be glory and dominion forever and ever. Amen" (1:5–6; see also 4:8–11; 5:8–3; 7:9–12; 11:15–18; 15:2–4; 16:4–7; 19:1–8).	5:12; 6:16–17; 7:12; 11:18; 12:12; 14:7, 10, 19; 15:1, 7; 16:1, 7, 19; 19:1–2; 20:11–15	1:5; 21:1–22:21

This teaching is hard. Two imperfect illustrations may help.

Viewing a Diamond Ring in a Jewelry Store

About twenty years ago, I shopped for a diamond engagement ring to offer to a godly and beautiful young lady named Jenni. When I inquired about particular diamond rings in jewelry stores, the jewelers would shine bright lights on the diamond ring against the backdrop of a black velvet cloth. Why a black cloth? Because that helps you better appreciate the beauty of a diamond ring. A black cloth contrasts starkly with the diamond ring in ways that help you better treasure the diamond ring. Similarly, one of God's goals for sovereignly and justly choosing to pass over nonelect sinners and punish them is to glorify the riches of his glory for vessels of mercy. Piper summarizes, "The ultimate aim of God is to show mercy. But to do this he must place it against a backdrop of wrath."[6] That's why we can praise God for his mercy and grace.

Feeling Jubilant at the Climax of Epic Stories

How do you feel at the climax of epic stories when the good guys triumph over the bad guys? (Warning: spoilers in the next three paragraphs.)

At the climax of J. R. R. Tolkien's *The Lord of the Rings*, Gollum steals the ring by biting Frodo's finger off but then falls into the fire of Mount Doom. The fire destroys the ring, which destroys Sauron, his Nazgûl, and his evil minions. When we read or watch this story, nobody mourns for Sauron and the evil creatures in Mordor. We cheer! We are jubilant!

At the climax of the blockbuster movie *Star Wars* (now subtitled *Episode IV—A New Hope*), Luke Skywalker is attempting to

---

6. John Piper, *The Justification of God: An Exegetical and Theological Study of Romans 9:1–23*, 2nd ed. (Grand Rapids, MI: Baker Academic, 1993), 220.

destroy the Galactic Empire's Death Star, which is about to destroy the Rebel base. Han Solo and Chewbacca abruptly return and knock Darth Vader's ship off course. That enables Luke to successfully fire a torpedo into the one vulnerable spot of the Death Star, which then explodes. When we watch this story, nobody mourns for the evil people on the Death Star. We cheer! We are jubilant!

At the climax of J. K. Rowling's Harry Potter series, Voldemort shoots a killing curse at Harry and concludes that Harry is finally dead. But as Voldemort and his Death Eaters are attempting to destroy those loyal to Harry, Harry surprises everyone when he removes his invisibility cloak and confronts Voldemort. Harry and Voldemort duel, and Harry's defensive spell causes Voldemort's killing curse to rebound on himself. When we read or watch this story, nobody mourns for Voldemort or his Death Eaters. We cheer! We are jubilant!

That's how we feel at the climax of epic stories when the good guys decisively defeat the bad guys.[7] That's just a taste of how we will feel when God decisively defeats Satan, his demons, and the rebellious offspring of the serpent (i.e., idolatrous and rebellious unbelievers).[8] We will praise God for his just wrath and invincible power.

Two Ways to Respond

How should we respond to this difficult teaching? At least two ways:

1. Be Humbled

The question to ask is not, How could God choose to pass over sinners and eternally punish them? The question to ask is, How

---

7. Cf. Christensen, *What about Evil?*, 226–78.
8. Cf. Andrew David Naselli, *The Serpent and the Serpent Slayer*, Short Studies in Biblical Theology (Wheaton, IL: Crossway, 2020).

could God choose to save *anyone*?[9] Or more personally, How could God choose to save *me*? As Isaac Watts's hymn "How Sweet and Aweful Is the Place" puts it, "Each of us cry, with thankful tongues, / 'Lord, why was I a guest?'"[10]

Don't be like the hypocritical Pharisee: "God, I thank you that I am not like other men, extortioners, unjust, adulterers, or even like this tax collector. I fast twice a week; I give tithes of all that I get" (Luke 18:11–12). If you are a Christian, contrast your eternal destiny with the destiny of hardened sinners who die without trusting Christ. What is the difference between you and them? The difference is that God chose you and not them. Why didn't God choose to pass over you? Why did God choose to save you? Nothing good in you prompted God to choose you (see chap. 4). You deserve exactly the opposite of what you're getting (Titus 3:3–7). There's no place for pride here; you are not smarter or wiser than people who reject God.

This is profoundly humbling, isn't it? It should make you put your hand over your mouth and fall to your knees with thankfulness.

2. Praise God for His Wrath, Power, and Mercy

My mentor Don Carson told me a story about a time he counseled a husband and wife who were wrestling with whether the Bible teaches complementarianism[11] or egalitarianism.[12] They

---

9. Cf. J Gresham Machen, *Things Unseen: A Systematic Introduction to the Christian Faith and Reformed Theology* (Glenside, PA: Westminster Seminary Press, 2020), 180–81.

10. *Sacred Songs and Hymns, on Various Passages of Scripture, Approved by the Synod of Relief; and Recommended to Be Sung in the Congregation under Their Inspection* (Edinburgh: Robertson, 1819), no. 91. I think the verb *forced* later in the hymn poorly represents the Calvinist view of the Spirit's effective grace: "'Twas the same love that spread the feast / that sweetly *forc'd* us in." Later renditions improve the wording by changing "forced" to "drew."

11. See "The Danver's Statement," Council on Biblical Manhood and Womanhood (website), https://cbmw.org/about/danvers-statement/.

12. See the "Mission and Values," Christians for Biblical Equality International (website), https://www.cbeinternational.org/content/cbes-mission.

finally said something like, "We concede that the Bible teaches complementarianism, but we still don't *like* it." They believed it only grudgingly. Carson replied something like, "You're halfway there." His point was that although it is good to believe what the Bible says, it is better to delight in it, to begin to see it how God sees it, to have our hearts aligned in delight with what God's word teaches.

You should cherish everything God reveals in the Bible. It's not okay to say, "The Bible teaches that, but I don't like it."[13] In this case, it's not okay to say, "I believe that God sovereignly and justly chose to pass over nonelect sinners and punish them because the Bible teaches that, but I don't like it." It's a bad sign if you want to apologize for what God has revealed in the Bible. If you don't like the nature and rationale of what God has revealed in his word, then the problem is with *you*—not with God and not with the truth he has revealed.[14]

You should feel deep sorrow when you think about how some people will rebel against the Creator forever and never experience the joy of knowing and loving God (see chap. 13). You should also praise God because God designed reprobation to glorify his wrath, power, and mercy. That is why Jesus praises God for hardening some and not others: "I thank you, Father, Lord of heaven and earth, that you have hidden these things from the wise and understanding and revealed them to little

---

13. See Kevin DeYoung, "I Like What the Bible Teaches," *DeYoung, Restless, and Reformed* (blog), The Gospel Coalition, June 25, 2009, https://www.thegospelcoalition .org/; DeYoung, "Is It Okay for Christians to Believe in the Doctrine of Hell But Not Like It?," *DeYoung, Restless, and Reformed* (blog), The Gospel Coalition, July 12, 2011, https://www.thegospelcoalition.org/.

14. Geerhardus Vos wrote an article in 1900 titled "The Biblical Importance of the Doctrine of Preterition" to respond to some Presbyterians who were removing the doctrine of reprobation from church doctrinal statements. Vos concludes the essay by asking, "Can it be safe for any church to erase from her creed a mode of expressing the divine grace, which God Himself has used to instruct us, on the plea that she deems expedient? Shall man be wiser than God?" Geerhardus Vos, *Redemptive History and Biblical Interpretation: The Shorter Writings of Geerhardus Vos*, ed. Richard B. Gaffin (Phillipsburg, NJ: P&R, 2001), 414.

children; yes, Father, for such was your gracious will" (Matt 11:25–26; Luke 10:21). That's why seven of the doxologies in Revelation praise God for his wrath and power (see above under "Goal 1").

One way you can praise God for sovereignly and justly choosing to pass over nonelect sinners and to punish them is to sing John Piper's hymn based on Romans 9:14–18: "Is There Injustice with Our God?" (to the tune of "O for a Thousand Tongues!"):[15]

Is there injustice with our God
When he decrees our ways?
No! This is but his righteousness
And root of all our praise.

Does he make mercy hang on this:
If we can will or run?
No! He has mercy on his own:
Before the world, it's done!

Did Pharaoh rise and make his name
Renown, and flaunt his mind?
No! He displayed his Maker's fame
And did what was designed.

O that we had a mind to grasp
The depths and riches of
The wisdom of the ways of God
And mysteries of love!

Now let no sin cause you to flee
Or make you suffer loss,
Our God is free, and Christ has died.
Rejoice before his cross!

15. John Piper, "Is There Injustice with Our God?," Desiring God, February 12, 2003, https://www.desiringgod.org/.

Responding with a Prayer

Father, if you have tolerated with great patience vessels of wrath, which you prepared for destruction, in order to show your wrath and make known your power and especially to make known the riches of your glory to vessels of mercy, which you prepared beforehand for glory, then how can I legitimately object? I can't. You are the Potter, and I am the clay. You are the Creator, and I am your creature. You have the right and freedom to do whatever you want with your creatures, and you don't have to explain any of your reasons to me. I praise you for your wrath and power. And I praise you especially for your undeserved kindness to me. Amen.

15

Who Deserves Blame
for Reprobation?

God sovereignly chose not to save certain sinners. He chose to pass over them and punish them. So does that mean that *God* deserves blame for reprobation? No.

Sinners Deserve Blame for Reprobation

> But because of *your* hard and impenitent heart *you* are storing up wrath for yourself on the day of wrath when God's righteous judgment will be revealed. (Rom. 2:5)

> You will say to me then, "Why does he still find fault? For who can resist his will?" But who are you, O man, to answer back to God? Will what is molded say to its molder, "Why have you made me like this?" (Rom. 9:19–20)

Sinful humans (not God) deserve blame for reprobation. An individual nonelect sinner is responsible for his or her reprobation because sinners are responsible for their sins.

It is important to remember the literary context of Romans 9–11.[1] The overarching theme of Romans 9–11 is that God's word has not failed because God has kept, is keeping, and will keep his promises to ethnic Israelites. Paul begins by introducing the tension between God's promises and Israel's plight: God gave Israelites unique privileges, yet they are rejecting the Messiah (9:1–6a). Next Paul addresses God's promises and Israel's unconditional election in the past: God's promises to Israel do not contradict the new twist in salvation history in which God is saving some Israelites and many Gentiles (9:6b–29). Next Paul addresses God's promises and Israel's culpability in the present: Israelites are responsible for not believing in Christ (9:30–10:21). Someone might ask Paul, "Why are *so many* Israelites not part of spiritual Israel?" One might presume that Paul would simply reply, "Because God did not elect them." That is a theologically correct answer, but it is only part of the answer. And perhaps surprisingly, it is not what Paul emphasizes in 9:30–10:21. Paul emphasizes the *human* reason: Israelites are responsible and culpable for not believing in Christ.

- They have not pursued God's righteousness by faith (9:31–32).
- They have stumbled over the stumbling stone (9:32–33).
- They have sought to establish their own righteousness instead of submitting to God's righteousness (10:3–7).
- They have not confessed that Jesus is Lord or believed that God raised him from the dead (10:8–13).
- God has sent preachers, and those preachers have preached, and Israelites have heard the preaching, but

---

1. Content in this paragraph is adapted from Andrew David Naselli, *From Typology to Doxology: Paul's Use of Isaiah and Job in Romans 11:34–35* (Eugene, OR: Pickwick, 2012), 12–24; used by permission of Wipf and Stock Publishers, www.wipfandstock .com. See also Naselli, *Romans: A Concise Guide to the Greatest Letter Ever Written* (Wheaton, IL: Crossway, 2022), 113–28.

many Israelites have not called on the name of the Lord
because they have not believed (10:14–21).

The Israelites, not God, are to blame for their current pre-
dicament. God's sovereignty (9:6b–29) and human responsibility (9:30–10:21) are compatible.

Is That Fair?

In election, sinners get mercy. In reprobation, sinners get justice.

That's fair. God judges sinners justly. God is just and always
does what is just (Gen. 18:25; Deut. 32:4). God is always fair,
and sometimes he is undeservedly kind to individuals (on fairness, see chaps. 5 and 12). The Potter (God) is free to mold the
clay (us) however he wants (on free will, see chap. 6).[2]

Seven Ways to Respond

1. Don't Reject Reprobation because It Seems Unfair to You

Scripture teaches that God sovereignly and justly chose to pass
over nonelect sinners and punish them. Never wish that Scripture does not say what it says. Even though reprobation can
seem horrifying, it is in the Bible, and God is righteous and fair.
You have as much of a right to question God's fairness as a clay
pot has a right to question the potter who molded it.

2. Be Deeply Grateful That God Chose You

If you are a Christian, it is because God sovereignly and graciously chose to save you. God has made known "the riches
of his glory for vessels of mercy, which he has prepared beforehand for glory" (Rom. 9:23). What could make you more
deeply grateful than that?

---

2. Cf. Canons of the Synod of Dort, 1.15; Westminster Confession of Faith, 3.7,
in *Creeds, Confessions, and Catechisms: A Reader's Edition*, ed. Chad Van Dixhoorn
(Wheaton, IL: Crossway, 2022), 141–42, 191.

3. Abominate Sin

God hates sin so much that he is righteously punishing people eternally for it. So don't think, "Since God chose me, I can live however I want." God forbid (Rom. 6:1–2)! God's choosing you should motivate you to be holy (Eph. 1:4).[3]

4. Proclaim the Gospel to Anyone and Everyone

You do not know who the elect are. You get to pray for unbelievers and to proclaim the gospel to anyone and everyone—especially people who seem uninterested or antagonistic and hardened. And you get to band together with fellow Christians to obey your marching orders and proclaim the gospel to everyone—locally and globally (see chap. 8).

5. Flee to Christ

If you are not a Christian, then flee to Christ! You cannot make the excuse, "I want to come to Christ, but he won't let me because he decreed to pass over me and eternally punish me." People reject God because they love sin: "People loved the darkness rather than the light because their works were evil. For everyone who does wicked things hates the light and does not come to the light, lest his works should be exposed" (John 3:19–20). Jesus invites you, "If anyone thirsts, let him come to me and drink" (John 7:37). "Come to me, all who labor and are heavy laden, and I will give you rest" (Matt. 11:28). What will you do with Jesus?[4]

---

3. See Kevin DeYoung, *The Hole in Our Holiness: Filling the Gap between Gospel Passion and the Pursuit of Godliness* (Wheaton, IL: Crossway, 2012).

4. Suggestion: Watch two short videos. (1) John Piper, "The Gospel in 6 Minutes," Desiring God, September 12, 2007, https://www.desiringgod.org/articles/the-gospel-in-6-minutes. (2) John Piper, "The Supremacy of God (Sermon Jam)," Truth Endures, March 26, 2014, YouTube video, https://www.youtube.com/. Three of my former students from Bethlehem College and Seminary collaborated to produce the second video (Brent Fischer, Chris Powers, and Ian Pitkanen).

6. Don't Expect to Understand Every Aspect of Reprobation

"God's hidden decree is not to be searched out but obediently marveled at."[5] Curious minds will inevitably wonder, "How can God be the ultimate cause of reprobation and humans still be responsible for their condemnation?" That's a mystery. I can't fully explain that philosophical tension because the Bible doesn't. (On mystery, see the end of chap. 6.)

7. Trust God

You might be tempted to distrust God when you think about specific unbelievers who are dear to you—a parent, a sibling, a child, a grandparent, a cousin, an aunt, an uncle, a close friend. It might be helpful to remind yourself that you don't know with certainty the ultimate spiritual condition of anyone; only God does. But more importantly, you should *trust God*.

> "The Rock, his work is perfect,
>   for *all his ways are justice.*
> A God of faithfulness and without iniquity,
>   *just and upright is he.*" (Deut. 32:4)

You can't comprehend all the reasons God does what he does, but will you trust his character? Will you trust him? "The very nature of faith," explains John Frame, "is to persevere despite unanswered questions."[6]

Responding with a Prayer

Father, you are just, and you act justly when you condemn sinners. I don't fully understand how your sovereignty is

---

5. Editorial section heading in John Calvin, *Institutes of the Christian Religion*, ed. John T. McNeill, trans. Ford Lewis Battles, 2 vols., Library of Christian Classics (Philadelphia: Westminster, 1960), 3.23.5 (952).

6. John M. Frame, *Apologetics: A Justification of Christian Belief*, ed. Joseph E. Torres, 2nd ed. (Phillipsburg, NJ: P&R, 2015), 179.

compatible with human responsibility, but I trust you that you are always fair. Thank you for being undeservedly kind to me. Would you please be undeservedly kind to my family and friends and neighbors and the nations? I ask in the name of Jesus and for his sake. Amen.

Conclusion

Exult in God as You Take in the View

I opened this book with an invitation to hike up a mountain with me. If you took me up on my offer, then now is the satisfying time to take in the breathtaking panoramic view at the top.

By referring to this point as "the top," I don't mean that in this short book we've exhausted what's true about predestination! We can always go further up and further in. You probably still have unanswered questions about predestination. (I do.)

I pray that God uses this book to help you increasingly treasure God, glorify him for his undeserved kindness to you, glorify him for his wrath and power, and proclaim the gospel freely and boldly. The purpose of studying predestination is not primarily to learn more information. It's to better know and worship the God who predestines. The more you know about God and his ways, the deeper and sweeter will be your praise. So exult in God as you take in the view. See his beauty. Savor him. Praise him. And then complete your joy by sharing it with others.

Responding with a Prayer

Oh, the depth of your riches and wisdom and knowledge! How unsearchable are your judgments and how inscrutable your ways! For who has known your mind? Or who has been your counselor? Or who has given a gift to you with the result that you must repay him? For from you and through you and to you are all things. To you be glory forever. Amen (see Rom. 11:33–36).

Acknowledgments

Thanks to friends for contributing to this book:

1. Don Carson, John Piper, Layton Talbert, Mark Minnick, and others have trained me to exegete God's words and to exult in them—all of them, without shame and without apology.

2. Chancellor John Piper and the other leaders of Bethlehem College and Seminary encourage and empower me to research and write in order to spread a passion for the supremacy of God in all things for the joy of all peoples through Jesus Christ. I finished drafting this book in the first quarter of 2022, during a research sabbatical that the school graciously granted me.

3. North Hills Church in Taylors, South Carolina, generously let my family stay in their missionary house for three months while I worked full time on drafting this book. Pastor Peter Hubbard warmly invited and hosted us.

4. Graham Cole and Oren Martin kindly invited me to write this volume and shared encouraging and sharpening feedback.

5. Some friends graciously offered feedback on drafts of this book, including Doug Becker, Chris Brauns, Phil Brown, Anthony Bushnell, Scott Christensen, Brian Collins, Tom Dodds, John Erickson, Phil Gons, Joshua Greever, David Hanson, Tim Held, Scott Jamison, Kevin Krile, Steven Lee, Charles Naselli, Jenni Naselli, John Piper, Peter Sammons, Michael Southern, Josh Sullivan, Joe Tyrpak, Doug Wilson, and groups of friends

in South Carolina led by Neil Cushman (Bob Jones Seminary), Peter Hubbard (North Hills Church), Trent Hunter (Heritage Bible Church), and Matt Rawlings (Redeeming Grace Church). I also benefitted from feedback when I taught on predestination to my church (summer 2022), DMin students at The Master's Seminary (July 2022), the Campus Outreach staff in Minneapolis (December 2022), and students at Bethlehem College and Seminary (2022–2023).

6. My excellent wife, Jenni, supports the research-writing-teaching-shepherding ministry that God has called me to. She is far more precious than jewels (Prov. 31:10–12).

7. I dedicate this book to Phil Gons, my close friend for over two decades. Phil is Vice President and General Manager of Bible Study Products at Faithlife, makers of Logos Bible Software. Phil helped me use Logos Bible Software to efficiently and thoroughly study predestination for this book. But his help goes back especially to 2002–2005. We did a lot together then—taking PhD courses, teaching Greek to undergraduate students, sharing a room and hundreds of meals, preparing for our PhD comprehensive exams. Exegesis and theology consumed us, and God used Phil to help me see and love what the Bible teaches about predestination.

Phil and I talked a good bit about predestination one semester over twenty years ago while I was taking a systematic theology course from one professor and a soteriology course from another. The first professor argued that reprobation is unbiblical because it isn't preachable; the second professor required us to write a sermon on a topic in soteriology, and I chose to write a sermon on reprobation. I have been meditating on it ever since. This book expands that sermon.

Appendix

Chapter Summary
Questions and Answers

Chapter 1

Question: What is the goal of election?

Answer: The goal of election is for God to save us so that we praise him for his glorious grace.

Chapter 2

Question: When did God choose to save some humans?

Answer: God chose to save some humans before he created the world.

Chapter 3

Question: Did God choose to save *individuals*?

Answer: Yes, God chose to save individuals.

Chapter 4

Question: Did God choose to save individuals based on foreseen faith?

Answer: No, the basis of election is God's forelove.

Chapter 5

Question: Is unconditional election unfair?

Answer: No, unconditional election is merciful and gracious.

Chapter 6

Question: Do we have free will?

Answer: It depends what you mean by "free." We do not have a free will in the sense that we can make equally alternative choices; we have a free will in the sense that we always choose what we most want.

Chapter 7

Question: Does election contradict God's desire that all humans be saved?

Answer: Yes, if we properly distinguish between what God would like to see happen and what God actually wills to happen.

Chapter 8

Question: How does God accomplish his plan to save individuals?

Answer: God accomplishes his sovereign plan to save individuals through Christ's saving work; God applies his sovereign plan to save individuals through the Holy Spirit's regenerating work; and God ordained that individuals would repent and believe through hearing God's word and through prayer.

Chapter 9

Question: How do I know if God has elected me?

Answer: Evidence of election includes your calling, justification, and transformed life.

Chapter 10

Question: Did God elect babies who die?

Answer: Almost certainly. The Bible does not explicitly say, but it implies that God mercifully saves babies who die.

Chapter 11

Question: Who ultimately causes reprobation?

Answer: God ultimately causes reprobation (but not in the same way that he chose to save individuals).

Chapter 12

Question: How does God accomplish reprobation?

Answer: God accomplishes reprobation by hardening hearts, blinding eyes, and deafening ears.

Chapter 13

Question: What is the result of reprobation?

Answer: The result of reprobation is wrath, destruction, not obtaining a right standing with God, condemnation, and the lake of fire—in short, hell.

Chapter 14

Question: What is the purpose of reprobation?

Answer: God sovereignly and justly chose to pass over nonelect sinners and punish them to glorify himself for his wrath and power and especially to glorify himself for the riches of his glory for vessels of mercy.

Chapter 15

Question: Who deserves blame for reprobation?

Answer: Sinful humans (not God) deserve blame for reprobation.

Further Reading

Introductory

Blaylock, Richard M. "The Doctrine of Reprobation." The Gospel Coalition, 2020. https://www.thegospelcoalition.org/essay/doctrine-of-reprobation/. Blaylock concisely explains and defends reprobation (about 2,500 words).

Christensen, Scott. *What about Free Will? Reconciling Our Choices with God's Sovereignty.* Phillipsburg, NJ: P&R, 2016. This is the overall best accessible book on free will that I am aware of. Christensen convincingly defends compatibilism and refutes incompatibilism. He simplifies the sound biblical arguments by luminaries such as Martin Luther (*The Bondage of the Will*) and Jonathan Edwards (*Freedom of the Will*)—as well as more recent theologians such as R. C. Sproul, John Frame, John Feinberg, D. A. Carson, John Piper, and Sam Storms.

Grudem, Wayne. "God's Providence" and "Election and Reprobation." Chapters 16 and 32 in *Systematic Theology: An Introduction to Biblical Doctrine.* 2nd ed. Grand Rapids, MI: Zondervan, 2020. Grudem is well organized, easy to understand, and tethered to the Bible.

Pinson, J. Matthew. *40 Questions about Arminianism.* 40 Questions. Grand Rapids, MI: Kregel Academic, 2022. This is the overall most helpful resource on Arminianism that I am aware of. Most Arminians are Wesleyan; Pinson calls himself a Reformed Arminian. He is *Reformed* in that he claims to be a variety of and not a departure from Reformation theology.[1] Pinson is not a Wesleyan Arminian, but he clarifies, "Wesley's views on predestination, the extent of the atonement, and the resistibility of prevenient grace are stock-in-trade Arminianism. Yet his understanding of the nature of atonement, justification, and continuance in the Christian life differ from that of some other Arminians" (51). Pinson explains those nuances throughout his book as well as how Arminianism in general differs from Calvinism. I think Pinson misrepresents Calvinism at various points, but that does not diminish the book's value for better understanding Arminianism.

Piper, John. *Does God Desire All to Be Saved?* Wheaton, IL: Crossway, 2013. I have probably read this essay slowly about ten times; it strongly influences what I write in chapter 7. Piper originally titled it "Are There Two Wills in God?," and in this sixty-two-page book he expands the original essay from about nine thousand words to seventeen thousand words. Meditating on God's two wills like this leads me to exult in his greatness.

Sproul, R. C. *Chosen by God.* Wheaton, IL: Tyndale House, 1986. A master teacher explains a complex topic simply (not simplistically).

Storms, Sam. *Chosen for Life: The Case for Divine Election.* 2nd Edition. Wheaton, IL: Crossway, 2007. Storms clearly explains and defends God's sovereign election.

Intermediate/Advanced

Bavinck, Herman. "The Divine Counsel." Chapter 7 in *God and Creation.* Vol. 2 of *Reformed Dogmatics.* Edited by John Bolt. Translated by John Vriend. Grand Rapids, MI: Baker Academic,

---

1. Contrary to Pinson, historical theologian Richard Muller argues that on the basis of "documentable theological conviction" Arminus was not Reformed. Richard A. Muller, "Arminius and the Reformed Tradition," *Westminster Theological Journal* 70 (2008): 19–47.

2004. First published in 1895–1901. Bavinck surveys historical theology in more depth than most systematic theologies, and he exegetes relevant texts as he synthesizes what the Bible teaches about predestination.

Blaylock, Richard M. *Vessels of Wrath*. 2 Vols. Eugene, OR: Pickwick, 2023. Blaylock's published PhD dissertation painstakingly analyzes God's reprobating activity in the Bible.

Calvin, John. Book 3, chapters 21–24 in *Institutes of the Christian Religion*. Edited by John T. McNeill. Translated by Ford Lewis Battles. 2 Vols. Library of Christian Classics. Philadelphia: Westminster, 1960. Calvin exalts God and refutes arguments that exalt man.

Edwards, Jonathan. *Freedom of the Will*. Edited by Paul Ramsey. Vol. 1 of *The Works of Jonathan Edwards*. New Haven, CT: Yale University Press, 2009. Edwards is rigorous and cogent. What I write about free will in chapter 6 is my attempt to accessibly repackage what Edwards argues.

Piper, John. *The Justification of God: An Exegetical and Theological Study of Romans 9:1–23*. 2nd Edition. Grand Rapids, MI: Baker Academic, 1993. Piper traces how Paul vindicates God as righteous in the single most important passage on predestination. Piper concludes that according to Romans 9:22–23, "The ultimate aim of God is to show mercy. But to do this he must place it against a backdrop of wrath" (220).

Sammons, Peter. *Reprobation and God's Sovereignty: Recovering a Biblical Doctrine*. Grand Rapids, MI: Kregel Academic, 2022. Sammons revises his penetrating PhD dissertation: "The Decree of Reprobation and Man's Culpability: The Role of God's Use of Secondary Causality" (The Master's Seminary, 2017).

Turretin, Francis. "The Decrees of God in General and Predestination in Particular." Pages 311–430 in vol. 1 of *Institutes of Elenctic Theology*. Edited by James T. Dennison Jr. Translated by George Musgrave Giger. 3 Vols. Phillipsburg, NJ: P&R,

1992–1997. For most modern readers, Turretin's Reformed scholasticism is strange, unfamiliar, and exacting. (Some of my friends think I overdo it with numbered lists in my writing. Turretin makes me feel like a middle way.) But carefully reading Turretin is worth it because he is precise.

General Index

abandonment (by God), 172
Adam and Eve, 92
adoption, 26–28
  as ultimate goal of election, 33
American Revolution, 119
"And Can It Be?" (Wesley hymn),
  73–74
André, John (British major), 119
angels
  and God's glory, 166
  predestination also applies to,
    6n6
Apollinarians, 105
Arians, 104, 105
Arminianism
  and Calvinism, compared, 11–12
  versus Calvinism on God's spe-
    cial grace, 74–75
  the overall best resource on,
    213–14
Arminius, Jacob, 10, 11, 13, 75, 76
Arnold, Benedict, 119
assurance of election, 140–41
atonement
  Arminian versus Calvinist view
    of, 12
  limited, 14
Augustine, 10, 92, 94

babies
  as sinners by nature, not by
    choice, 143–44
  who die, 143–49, 211
    Are they elect?, 143
    David's implication of the
      salvation of, 146–47
    on why God's word is unclear
      on the destiny of, 148
Babylonians, 174
Barsabbas, 169
beast (of Revelation), 38, 39, 158
begun recovery. See moral freedom
Berkhof, Louis, 178–79
Bignon, Guillaume, 83n6
blamelessness, 25
boasting
  on election's goal of preventing
    human, 31–33
  on God's sovereign choice
    removing all grounds for
    human, 63–65
book of life, 38–39, 47, 157, 158,
  183
Boston, Thomas, 92
Brightman, Edgar S., 105t
Bunyan, John, 73, 141

Calvin, John, xviii, 3n2, 9–10, 11, 13, 17, 108, 112

Calvinism
  Arminianism and, compared, 11–12
  versus Arminianism on God's special grace, 74–75
  five points of, 13 (*see* TULIP)
  not to be equated with hyper-Calvinism, 133
  Packer's three-word summary of, 16

Calvinist zeal for evangelism and prayer, 132–34

Carey, William, 133–34

Carson, D. A., 55, 91n11, 103n30, 107, 157, 159–60, 195–96

choices, desires, and the heart, the interrelation of, 95, 95–96

causes
  constraining, 86, 87, 92
  nonconstraining, 86, 87
  three kinds of, 177
  the ultimate, 178

"children of your elect sister," meaning of the phrase, 50n8

Christ. *See* Jesus

Christensen, Scott, 166

Christian Science, 105t

church history, the four broad periods of, 11n15

Clark, Gordon, 105t

compatibilism
  incompatibilism versus, 87–89
  the most remarkable example, 100
  ten reasons for, 96–104

complementarianism, 195–96

condemnation, certain people divinely designated for, 156–58

conditional election, foreknowledge defined according to, 52

conscience, 14, 18, 144

conscious rebellion, 144–45

constraining cause, 86, 87, 92

contradiction(s), 106

conversion, two God-ordained means of, 126

corporate election
  the Arminian view of, 47–48
  the book that makes the strongest case for, 47n3
  versus individual election, 43
  an insurmountable problem of explaining Rom. 9 with, 61
  to save, 45
  to serve, 44
  why we should reject the Arminian view of, 48–50

corruption, an explanation of man's pervasive, 14

creation of the world, on God's election before the, 37–41

Creator-creature distinction, 82–83

Cyrus (king of Persia), 44–45

damnation, 9, 94n17, 170

David (king of Israel)
  on the cause of his census, 177
  on the foreordaining of his days/life, 85
  implication of the salvation of babies, 146–47

day of the Lord, on God's goal to save us on the, 24

death
    of babies. *See* babies
    eternal. *See* eternal death
demons, 174, 179, 194
depravity (of man)
    Arminian versus Calvinist view
        of, 11
    total, 14
desires, choices, and the heart, the
    interrelation of, 95, 95–96
destruction, on God's preparing
    vessels of wrath for, 153–54,
    181–82
determinism, 87, 88, 89, 90,
    91n11
divine passive, 154–55, 157, 158,
    163
Docetists, 105
doctrinal tension
    concerning the person of Christ,
        105
    concerning the problem of evil,
        105
    concerning providence, 105
    concerning the Trinity, 104
Dongell, Joseph, 99–100
double predestination, 160–64,
    165
    five reasons that support non-
        symmetrical, 161–64
    two views on, 160
doxologies in Scripture highlight-
    ing God's wrath, power, and
    mercy, 191–92

early church, 100, 169
Ebionites, 105
economic Trinity, 40
Eddy, Mary Baker, 105

Edwards, Jonathan, 91n12, 95,
    140
effectual call, 123n7
Elder Affirmation of Faith, 18
elect, the meaning of "all the,"
    45
elect Gentiles, 45. *See* Gentiles
election
    Arminian versus Calvinist view
        on God's, 12
    on assurance of one's own,
        137–42
    the basis of God's, 44, 54,
        56–58, 209
    on confirming one's, 140–41
    corporate (*see* corporate
        election)
    defined, 7
    evidence of, 210
        calling and justification, 138
        following Jesus, 139
        a transformed life, 139–40
    and foreseen faith, 67, 209
    four kinds of, 43
    as a gift from God, 32
    goal(s) of, 209
        the eight, 24–35
        the ultimate, 33
    individual. *See* individual
        election
    the most important passage in
        the Bible on, 53
    not an excuse for lawlessness or
        laziness, 141
    not synonymous with *predesti-
        nation*, 6n7
    pleases God, 58
    two objections answers by Paul
        in Romans 9, 59

unconditional. *See* unconditional election

what distinguishes predestination from, 8, 9

elect Israelites, 45. *See* Israelites

"elect lady and her children," meaning of, 50n

entire deprivation. *See* moral freedom

equity, 71

Esau (son of Isaac), 53, 145n3, 153, 190n5

eternal damnation, 9, 170

eternal death, 7, 162–63, 170n1
    and eternal life in Rom. 6:23, 162

eternal life, 7, 9, 46, 50, 55, 56, 66, 119, 126, 139, 158, 162–63, 181
    the meaning of, 66

eternal state. *See* moral ability; moral freedom

evangelism, evangelizing, 128, 130
    that assumes incompatibilism: an example, 97

evil, doctrinal tension concerning the problem of, 105

fairness of God, 69–73

faith
    defined, 123
    election and foreseen, 51–68, 67, 209
    how regeneration enables and causes, 124
    as the means of justification and the evidence of election, 138
    relation of regeneration and repentance to, 12, 75

Finitists, 105

"firstborn among many brothers," 26, 34

foreknowledge
    the basis of God's election, 51
    of Christ by God, 38
    defined according to conditional and unconditional election, 52
    what it means as used in Rom. 8 and 1 Pet., 62

forelove, as basis of God's election, 56–58, 209

foreseen faith, 51–68

Frame, John, 203

freedom
    moral. *See* moral freedom
    natural. *See* natural freedom
    three reasons Walls and Dongell hold to libertarian, 99–100

"Free Grace" (Wesley hymn), 73–74

free will, 79–109
    Arminian versus Calvinist view on man's, 12
    the limits of God's, 103
    the meaning of *free*, 82
    the overall best book on, 86n9, 213
    in what sense we have a, 81–82, 99, 210
    two reasons Olson embraces libertarian, 105

functional Trinity, 40

Gentiles
    are Jesus's "other sheep," 65
    elect, 45
    some appointed to eternal life, 55

glory
  election's goal of eliciting
    praise for God's grace and,
    33–35
  election's goal that we may see
    Jesus's, 29–33
Gnostics, 105
goal(s)
  of election, 209
    the eight, 24–35
    the ultimate, 33
  of God, two, 185–91
God
  on the decisiveness of his sover-
    eign choice, 53–56
  designated certain people for
    condemnation, 156–58
  destined certain people to dis-
    obey the word and stumble,
    154–56
  distinct from his creation, 82–83
  on the fairness of his elective
    mercy, 69–71
  foreknowledge of Christ before
    creation, 38
  foreknew people, 61–63
  hardens hearts, blinds eyes, and
    deafens ears, 170–72
  how he has chosen people
    through history, 32
  on Israel's failure to obtain a
    right standing with, 183
  judges some people more se-
    verely than others, 145
  Piper on the ultimate aim of,
    193, 215
  prepared vessels of wrath for
    destruction, 153–54

on our responsibility to obey (in
  prayer and gospel proclama-
  tion), 128–29
saving and sanctifying work of,
  New Testament portrayal of
  in three tenses, 25
sovereignty of:
  Arminian versus Calvinist
    view of the, 11
  and human freedom simulta-
    neously true, 100–101
  a poor analogy for the, 83
  a useful analogy for the,
    84–85
two goals of, 185–91
the ultimate aim of, 193
who he condemns, 144–45
will of. *See* will
why we should trust, 148, 203
gospel, the
  on election's goal of obedience
    to, 28–29
  encouragement to proclaim the,
    202
  why it is good news, 30
grace
  Arminianism versus Calvinism
    on God's special, 74–75
  Arminian versus Calvinist view
    on the Spirit's, 12
  election based on God's, 58
  God hardens by withholding,
    173
  irresistible, 15
  prevenient. *See* prevenient grace

Hamilton, Jim, 85
hardening (by God), 162, 170–76,
  190n5, 196, 211

Harry Potter series, 111–12, 194

hearing God's word (as a means of conversion), 126–27

heart(s)
  Horton on how God hardens and softens, 176
  the interrelation of choices, desires, and the, 95, 95–96

hell
  on the Bible's ambiguity on whether babies go to, 148
  on what it is, 181
  the righteousness of punishing unrepentant sinners in, 187

heretics, 8n10

Hodge, A. A., 173

holiness
  the meaning of God's, 34
  on election's goal of, 25

Holy Spirit
  and conviction, 140
  the regenerating work of the, 122, 123, 210

Horton, Michael, 161–62, 176, 178

"How Sweet and Aweful Is the Place" (Watts hymn), 195

human(s)
  and angels, how God deemed it best to glorify himself to, 166
  races, the only two, 35
  what God values more highly than saving all, 116–17, 185
  on when God elected to save certain, 37–41, 209
  See also individuals; people

hyper-Calvinism, Calvinism not to be equated with, 133

hyper-Calvinist(s), 133, 134n24, 165

image of God's son: on election's goal of one's conformity to the, 26
  the purpose of that goal, 34

immanent Trinity, 40

incompatibilism
  versus compatibilism, 87–89
  example of a tract that assumes, 97

indeterminism, 87, 88

individual election
  versus corporate election, 43
  an insurmountable problem of explaining Rom. 9 with conditional, 61
  to save, 45–47
  to serve, 44–45

individual(s). *See also* human(s); people
  on God's choosing to save, 43–50; *see also* individual election
  how God accomplishes his plan to save, 122, 210
  the result of God's hardening an, 170

infants. *See* babies

infralapsarianism, 164–66

inheritance (of the elected), 27–28, 33, 55

injustice on God's part, four proofs that there is no, 70

innocence. *See* moral freedom

intermediate stage between being unregenerate and regenerate, 76n7

irresistible grace, 15
Israel
    on their failure to obtain a right
        standing with God, 183
    what God said of their election,
        57. *See also* Istraelites
Israelites
    adults judged, but not their
        children, 145
    elect, 43, 45
    God hardened, blinded, and
        deafened nonelect, 171
    God unconditionally elected
        only some, 53–54
    Paul's grief over the rebellion of
        his fellow, 184
    responsible and culpable for not
        believing in Christ, 200–201

Jacob (patriarch), 54, 145n3, 153,
    190n5
Jehovah's Witnesses, 104
Jeremiah (prophet), 146
Jesus Christ
    appearance (postresurrection) to
        some but not others, 169
    doctrinal tension concerning the
        person of, 105
    on election's goal that we may
        be with, 29–30
    an encouragement to flee to,
        202
    foreknown and loved by God
        before creation, 37–38
    his sheep are his sheep even
        before they believe, 65–67
    the logical connection between
        the elect and being with, 30
    the nine saving events of, 122

no human is saved apart from,
    145–46
the saving work of, 122–23
See also Messiah
John the Baptist, 146
Joseph's brothers, 173
Judaism, 65
Judas (disciple), 49, 102–3, 174
judgment based on degree of rev-
    elation of God, 145

kindness, of God, 69–71

lake of fire, 183, 211
lawlessness, election not an excuse
    for, 141
law of noncontradiction, 108
laziness, election not an excuse
    for, 141
Lewis, C. S
    The Last Battle, 174
    *The Lion, the Witch, and the
        Wardrobe*, 84
    The Magician's Nephew, 131
libertarian freedom, three reasons
    Walls and Dongell hold to,
    99–100
libertarian free will, two reasons
    Olson embraces, 105
limited atonement, 14
Linne, Shai, 121–22
Lord of the Rings (Tolkien), 193
love, God's election based on his
    gracious, 56–57
Luther, Martin, 94, 94n17, 137

MacArthur, John, 144–45
Mark (apostle), 169
Marshall, I. Howard, 112–13,
    113n4

Matthias (apostle), 169

McCall, Tom, 91n11

Menendez, Miguel (coach), 118

mental disabilities, 145, 146

mercy, praise for God's, 191–92, 195–97

Messiah, God's election of the, 44

mighty, on election's goal of shaming the, 31–33

missionaries, 128, 130

missions, 133–34, 134n24

Modalists, 104

Molinism, 87n10

monergism, 123

moral ability, 91–92, 94. *See also* moral freedom

  partial, 93

  state of no, 93

  total, 93

  unconfirmed, 92

moral freedom

  defined, 91–92

  to do what God wants, four possibilities for whether humans have, 92–93

  versus natural freedom, 91–96

Moo, Doug, 9, 162, 170, 189

mystery, 106–8

  defined, 106

natural ability, 91, 94. *See* natural freedom

natural freedom

  defined, 91

  versus moral freedom, 91–96

Nestorians, 105

new heavens and new earth, 30, 103–4

nonconstraining cause, 86, 87

Olson, Roger, 75, 76, 105, 174–75

open theists, 105

original guilt and original sin, 143–44

Osborne, Grant, 52

Packer, J. I., 10, 16, 131–32

pantheists, 105

parable of the laborers in the vineyard, 72–73

paradox, 106

Paul

  on the charge that God is unfair to blame people, 80

  grief over rejection of the gospel, 184

  how he connects election, faith, preaching, and prayer, 127

  and preaching, 126–27

partial regeneration, 76

people

  God foreknew, 61–63

  Paul on the charge of God's unfairness for blaming, 80

  three examples of God's choosing to save groups of, 45

  on why God chooses mostly low-status, 32

  See also human(s); individuals

perseverance

  Arminian versus Calvinist view on the believer's, 12

  of the saints, 5

person of Christ, doctrinal tension concerning the, 105

Pharaoh, 57, 70, 113, 170, 171, 186, 187, 190n5, 197

Pharisee, the hypocritical, 195

Picirilli, Robert, 76
Pilgrim's Progress, The (Bunyan), 141
Piper, John, 8n10, 23, 30, 53, 124–25, 156n3, 189–90, 190n5
  "Is There Injustice with Our God?" (hymn), 197
  on the new birth, 124
  on the ultimate aim of God, 193, 215
  on ultimate self-determination, 90
pleasure, election based on God's good, 58
*post*destination, 66
potter, 46, 80–81, 153, 175, 190, 201
prayer
  as a God-ordained means of conversion, 127–28
  for unbelievers, 131–32
precondemnation, 7n9
predestination
  defined, 7
  on the importance of, 17–18
  on its relation to supralapsarianism and infralapsarianism, 164–66
  not synonymous with *election*, 6n7
  origin of the word (from Greek), 6
  Sproul's definition of, 6n8
  the two main ways theologians have understood, 10–17
  two ways to respond to, 4
  what distinguishes it from election, 8, 9

Presbyterians, Vos's challenge to some irreverent, 196n14
primitive integrity. *See* moral freedom
purpose: on the translation of the word in Eph. 1:5, 58
"pre-regenerating grace," 76
preterition, 7n9
prevenient grace
  author's definitions of, 74, 76
  Brian Shelton's definition of, 75–76
  the effect of, 76
  on whether the view explains how election is unfair, 73–77
problem of evil, doctrinal tension concerning the, 105
providence, doctrinal tension concerning the, 105

races, the only two human, 35
rebellion, on conscious, 144–45
regeneration
  analogies for how it enables and causes faith, 124
  faith, repentance, and (order according to Calvinism, Arminianism), 12, 75
  the means of, 123n7
  partial versus full, 76
  Piper on, 125
  precedes and enables faith, 123
  the work of the Holy Spirit, 123
reprobation
  on the fairness of, 174–76
  how God accomplishes, 169–79, 211
  meaning, 7, 151
  the goal of, 185–98

the most important Biblical passage on election and, 53
the primary means of, 170. *See* hardening
the purpose of, 211
the result of, 181–84, 211
seven proper ways to respond to the doctrines of election and, 201–3
sinners deserve the blame for, 199–201
who ultimately causes, 153–67, 211
Remonstrance, 13
repentance, 115, 117, 125, 126, 127, 128, 135, 140
faith, regeneration, and (order according to Calvinism, Arminianism), 12, 75
right standing with God, 183, 211
Ryland, John, Sr., 133–34

Sabeans, 174
Sabellians, 104
salvation
Christ's saving work in, 122–23
the Spirit's regenerating work in, 123–24
the Father, Son, and Spirit in effecting, 121
the three ways God executes his plan of saving individuals, 122
Samaritans, 65
Sammons, Peter, 172, 190n5
saving events, Christ's nine, 122
Schreiner, Thomas R., 170n2, 182n4
self-examination, 140
semi-Pelagians, 76n7

sheep, 65–67
Shelton, Brian, 75–76
Silas (apostle), 169
sin
encouragement to abominate, 202
how God ordains but is not guilty of, 177–79
how God saves his people from their, 121
sinful people, God's hardening through, 173–74
sinners
deserve the blame for, 199–201
God hardens, deafens, and blinds certain, 171–72
See also sinful people
sons of God
on election's goal of adoption as, 26–28
women as, 27n6
sorrow, 161, 184, 185, 196
sovereignty of God. *See under* God
Spinoza, Benedict, 105
sprinkling with Christ's blood, 28–29
Sproul, R. C., 6n8, 106, 125, 173
Spurgeon, Charles, 56–57, 65–66, 125
Star Wars, 193–94
state of consummate happiness. *See* moral ability; moral freedom
supralapsarianism, 164–65
synergism, 123

Thessalonian believers, 57

total depravity, 14

Trinity
  doctrinal tension concerning
    the, 104
  economic, 40
  functional, 40
  immanent versus economic, 40

tritheists, 104

trusting God, 148, 203

truth, on God's hardening with
  the, 174

TULIP
  logical order of, 16
  meaning of the acronym, 13
  more accurate names for and
    explanations of the five issues
    of, 14–15

unconditional election
  the Arminian view of corporate
    election incompatible with,
    48
  explained, 14
  foreknowledge defined accord-
    ing to conditional and, 52
  the questions in Rom. 9 presup-
    pose, 58–61
  seven arguments that support,
    53–67
  on whether it is unfair, 69–77,
    210

unconfirmed moral ability. See
  under moral ability

universalism, 116

Venema, Cornelis, 137

vessels of wrath for destruction,
  153–54, 181–82

virtues, 140–41

Vos, Geerhardus, 196n14

Walls, Jerry, 99–100

Ware, Bruce, 48, 56

Wesley, Charles, 73–74

Wesley, John, 10, 59n18, 94n15,
  214

wicked people, on God's use of
  in fulfilling his purposes,
  173–74

will
  defined, 86
  free. See free will
  the Spirit's grace and man's
    Calvinism and Arminianism,
    12t
  on the two aspects of God's,
    112–16

wise, on God hiding Jesus's message from the, 159–60

world
  God chose to save humans
    before he created the,
    39–40
  on the meaning of "before
    the foundation of the,"
    37–39

wrath
  on God preparing vessels of,
    153–54, 181–82
  and power and mercy, on prais-
    ing God for his, 195–97
  two illustrations of God's mercy
    on a backdrop of, 193–94
  two ways to respond to God's
    eternal (against sinners),
    194–97

Scripture Index

Genesis
1:1 . . . . .38, 82
4:1 62
6:5 96
18:19 62
18:25 . . . . .148, 176
18:25 201
20:6 173
21:12 54
25:23 54
50:20 . . . . .98, 173, 178

Exodus
2:25 62
4:21 . . . . .113, 171
5:1 113
7:3 . . . . .113, 171, 176
7:16 113
8:1 113
8:10 82
8:15 176
8:20 113
9:1 113
9:12 . . . . .113, 171
9:13 113
9:14 82
9:16 70
10:1 . . . . .113, 171
10:3 113
10:20 . . . . .113, 171
10:27 . . . . .113, 171
11:10 . . . . .113, 171
14:4 171
14:8 . . . . .113, 171
14:17 171
20:12 113
20:13 114
24:3–8 29
32:32 184
32:32–33 158
33:19 70

Leviticus
4:3 25
4:23 25
4:28 25
4:32 25
19:18 99

Deuteronomy
1:39 145
2:30 . . . . .170n1
4:37 57
7:6–8 . . . . .32, 57
9:4–6 32
10:15 57

14:2 44
28:63 113
29:4 171
30:15–20 145
32:4 . . . . .71, 201, 203
33:26 82

Joshua
11:20 176

1 Samuel
2:22–25 113
24:13 96
25:34 173
25:39 173

2 Samuel
6:21 . . . . .45n1
7:22 82
12:15 146
12:18–23 147
18:33 147
24:1 177
24:2 177
24:10 177

1 Kings
8:58 176
22 178

2 Kings
18:4 . . . . .148n7

1 Chronicles
16:13 44
16:31 97
17:20 82
21:1 . . . . .174, 177
21:2 177

Ezra
6:22 . . . . .170n1
7:27 . . . . .170n1

Nehemiah
9:7 . . . . .45n1

Job
1:7–12 174
1:15 174
10:9 . . . . .80, 85
42:2 98

Psalms
1:6 63
13:1 . . . . .80n3
19:1 82
33:8–9 82
47:8 97
51:10 176
67:4 135
69:28 158
69:22–23 171
74:2 39
78:70 . . . . .45n1
79:5 . . . . .80n3
86:8 82
89:4 . . . . .45n1
89:46 . . . . .80n3
92:7 182
95:8 176
97:1 97
99:1 97
105:6 44
105:43 44
106:5 44
106:23 . . . . .45n1
106:37–38 145
115:1 35

115:3..............97
115:3–8..........171
118:22–23........156
119:68 ....148, 176
139:16 85

Proverbs
16:1 ....170n1
16:4 154
16:9 ....100, 170
19:21..............170n1
21:1 ....170n1
31:10–12 208

Isaiah
6:9–10 ....172, 174
7:15–16...........145
10:5–7 ....170n1
29:10..............171
29:16..............81, 85
41:8–9 44
42:1 44
43:20–21 44
43:21..............35
44:6–7 101
44:18..............171
44:24..............82
44:28..............44
45:4 ....44, 45
45:7 ....85, 98
45:7–9 80
45:9 ....81, 85
46:9 82
46:9–10...........98, 101
53:4 114
53:10..............114
56:8 65
57:15..............176
63:17..............176
64:8 ....80, 85

65:9 44
65:15..............44
65:22..............44
66:2 5

Jeremiah
1:5.................63, 146
10:6–7 82
10:12..............82
13:23..............96
18:1–6 ....80, 85
19:4–5 145
31:31–34 176

Lamentations
3:32–33...........113

Ezekiel
11:19..............176
14:1–11...........178
18:23..............113
33:11..............113, 161, 184
36:26..............176

Daniel
4:25 97
4:35 97
10...................115
12:1 158

Hosea
13:5 63

Amos
3:2.................63
3:6.................98

Jonah
2:9.................16n19
4:11 145

Habakkuk
1 174

Haggai
2:23 . . . . .45n1

Malachi
1:2–3 54

Matthew
1:21 159
3:7 182
5:21 114
6:10 120
6:24 94
7:11 . . . . .131, 159
7:12 99
7:13 182
7:23 63
10:29 98
11:20–24 159
11:24 145
11:25–26 . . . . .114, 159, 173,
          197
11:26 159
11:27 45
11:28 . . . . .114, 202
12:18 44
12:33–37 96
13:14–15 . . . . .172, 174
13:35 38
15:4 113
15:14 173
15:18–19 96
18:14 114
19:8 176
19:19 99
20:1–16 . . . . .69, 71, 72
20:14–15 73

21:42 156
22:14 116
22:39 99
23:23 17
23:37 . . . . .114, 119
24:22 5
24:24 5
24:31 5
25:23 30
25:34 . . . . .38, 39
25:41 183
25:46 183
26:23–24 103
26:42 120
28:19–20 128

Mark
4:12 172
13:20 5
13:22 5
13:27 5
15:13–14 177

Luke
1:15 146
6:13 49
8:10 172
9:35 44
10:20 158
10:21 . . . . .114, 159, 173,
          197
11:50 38
11:50–51 . . . . .38n1
13:34 119
16:13 94
18:7 5
18:11–12 195
23:35 44
24:47 128

John

1:1 38
1:3 82
1:9 76
1:13 123
3:3–8 123
3:7 107
3:16 .... 114, 119
3:19–20 202
3:20 176
5:40 93
6 56
6:37 .... 30, 46, 55, 65,
                      138
6:37–40 .... 67, 139
6:37a 55
6:39 .... 30, 55
6:39–40 123
6:40 46
6:44 .... 55, 123, 176
6:63 123
6:63–65 55
6:64 102
6:65 .... 30, 55, 94, 123,
                      176
6:70 50
6:70–71 102
7:37 .... 114, 202
8:34 93
8:44 93
8:47 66
9:39 172
9:41 145
10:1–5 65
10:3–4 65
10:7–10 65
10:11 .... 65, 66
10:11–18 65
10:12–13 65

10:14 65
10:16 .... 65, 66, 130
10:26 .... 7, 65, 66,
                     107
10:26–27 65
10:26–28 130
10:26–30 65
10:27 .... 65, 139
10:27–29 7
10:28 66
10:28–29 .... 101, 139
10:29 .... 30, 55, 67
11:43 .... 15, 124
11:44 124
11:51–52 65
12:32 76
12:37–40 56
12:39–40 172
12:40 176
13:2 .... 103n30
13:11 102
13:18 .... 49, 50
13:18–19 102
13:27 .... 103n30
14:6 145
15:16 64
17 56
17:2 .... 29, 46
17:3 66
17:5 .... 38, 40
17:6 .... 30, 55
17:6–9 .... 29, 46
17:9 .... 30, 55
17:12 .... 102, 174
17:20 .... 29, 46
17:24 .... 29, 30, 37, 38,
                     46, 55
18:9 .... 30, 55

Acts

1:15 102
1:16–17............102
1:23–25............169
2:23 ....100, 107, 156,
                158, 164n18,
                177
2:23a...............114
2:23b...............114
4:12 145
4:27 ....114, 177
4:27–28............100, 107, 156
4:28 ....6, 114, 158,
                164n18, 177
6:1–6..............169
7:51 15
10:39–41 169
13:17..............44
13:48..............46, 50, 55, 126
15:14..............45
15:22–27 169
15:39–40 169
17:24–29 82
17:30..............128
18:9–11............130
20:29–30 157
28:26–27 172

Romans

1 144
1:18 191
1:18–20............144
1:20 ....144, 145, 191
1:24 173
1:26 173
1:28 173
2:2–3..............191
2:4–5..............176

2:5................170n2, 182,
                182n4, 191,
                199
2:7................182n4
2:8................182, 182n4
2:8–9.............191
2:10 ....182n4
3:4................60n19
3:5–6.............191
3:6................60n19
3:10 161
3:11 176
3:24 191
3:31 ....60n19
4:16 191
5:2................182n4
5:6–9.............191
5:9................182, 182n4
5:12–21............143
5:20–21............191
6 ....26, 162
6–7 93
6:1–2.............202
6:2................60n19
6:13 25
6:14 ....61n20
6:15 ....60n19, 61n20
6:23 ....104, 162
7:7................60n19
7:13 ....60n19
8:7................93
8:14–27...........27
8:16–17...........27n6, 28
8:17 27
8:18 ....182n4
8:21 ....182n4
8:23 27
8:28 ....138, 164n18

8:29 ....8, 26, 34, 51,
52, 61, 62
8:29–30............6, 8, 49, 138
8:30 9
8:32 191
8:33 ....5, 9
8:33a..............142
8:33b..............142
9..................53, 61, 69,
190n5
9–11...............200
9:1–3.............184
9:1–4.............161
9:1–6a............200
9:6................53
9:6–8.............45
9:6–13 ....53, 53n5, 58,
59, 60, 69, 70,
79
9:6–18 59
9:6–23 79
9:6–29 ....53n5
9:6b–29...........200, 201
9:7...............54
9:8...............54
9:10–13...........54
9:11 ....54, 153
9:13 ....145n3, 153,
190n5
9:14 ....58, 59, 60,
60n19, 61, 70,
71, 77
9:14–18...........53n5, 59, 69,
70, 79, 197
9:14–23...........59, 69, 79
9:15 ....70, 190n5
9:15–16...........164, 191
9:15–17...........70
9:15–18...........59, 70, 80

9:16 ....70, 79, 153
9:17 ....70, 186, 190n5,
191
9:17–18...........154, 170, 186
9:18 ....70, 163, 164,
176, 190n5,
191
9:18–19...........46
9:19 ....58, 59, 61, 77,
80, 164n18,
190n5
9:19–20...........199
9:19–21...........175
9:19–23...........53n5, 59, 79,
80, 171, 190n5
9:20–23...........153
9:20a.............80
9:20b.............81
9:20b–23 ....80, 85
9:21 ....46, 81, 154,
161
9:22 ....7, 8, 182,
190n5, 191
9:22–23...........81, 117, 154,
163, 186, 189
9:23 ....7, 182, 190n5,
191, 201
9:30–10:21 ....200, 201
9:31–32...........183, 200
9:32–33...........200
10:3–7 200
10:8–13 200
10:14–21 201
10:15.............129
11:1 ....60n19
11:2 ....45, 62
11:5 45
11:5–6 58

11:7 ....7, 45, 170n2, 171, 176, 183
11:7–10 171
11:8 172
11:11 ....60n19
11:25 ....170n2
11:28 45
11:30–32 191
11:35–36 82
11:33 191
11:33–36 206
11:36 ....35, 191
13:9 ....99, 114
15:9 191
16:13 46
16:27 191

1 Corinthians
1:8 25
1:18 ....182n4
1:19 ....182n4
1:12 17
1:21 126
1:26–29 32
1:26–31 ....63, 64
1:27–29 ....64, 67
1:27–30 49
1:29 ....32, 64
1:31 64
2:7 ....6, 40, 182n4
4:7 32
5:7 25
6:9–10 28
6:15 ....60n19
8:3 63
8:6 82
8:11 ....182n4
10:9 ....182n4
10:10 ....182n4

11:12 82
15:3 17
15:18 ....182n4
15:41 ....182n4
15:45–49 26
15:49 26
15:50 28

2 Corinthians
1:11 128
2:15 ....182n4
2:15–16 174
3:3 176
3:14 ....170n2, 176
3:18 26
4:3 ....182n4
4:4–6 34
4:6 ....124, 176
4:16–5:9 26
4:17 ....182n4
5:10 144
11:2 25
13:5 140

Galatians
1:16 128
2:17 ....60n19
3:7 54
3:21 ....60n19
3:29 27
4:5–7 27
4:7 27
4:9 63
5:14 99
5:16–26 93
5:21 28

Ephesians
1:3 33

1:3–4 37
1:3–14 . . . . .9n12, 27n7, 33,
48, 55
1:4 . . . . .8, 25, 25n4, 26,
38, 49, 123,
161, 163, 202
1:4–5 . . . . .9, 26, 55, 56
1:4–6 163
1:4a 33
1:4b–6 33
1:5 . . . . .6, 8, 9n12,
49, 58, 123,
164n18
1:6 33
1:6–8 191
1:7–8 163
1:11 . . . . .6, 27, 55, 98,
164n18
1:11–12 33
1:12 34
1:14 . . . . .27, 27n7
1:18 . . . . .27, 182n4
2:1–10 . . . . .48, 93
2:2 27
2:3 . . . . .27, 191
2:4–5 191
2:7 33
2:7–8 191
2:8–9 . . . . .32, 75
2:11–22 65
3:8 128
3:11 . . . . .41, 164n18
3:16 191
3:21 191
4:18 . . . . .170n2
5:5 27
5:6 . . . . .182, 182n4,
191
5:18–20 128

5:22–32 . . . . .27n6
5:27 . . . . .25, 25n4
5:29 99
6:2 113
6:11–12 137
6:19 134

Philippians
1:9 25
1:28 . . . . .182n4, 191
2:4 99
2:12–13 . . . . .15, 101, 141
2:15 26
3:19 . . . . .182n4
3:21 . . . . .26, 182n4
4:3 158
4:19 191
4:20 191

Colossians
1:16 . . . . .82, 123n5
1:22 25
1:27 . . . . .182n4
3 . . . . .26, 93
3:1–4:1 141
3:3 67
3:4 . . . . .182n4
3:6 . . . . .182, 182n4
3:10 26
3:12 141
4:2–3 128

1 Thessalonians
1:2–10 . . . . .126, 139
1:3 140
1:4 57
1:5 140
1:6 140
1:9–10 140

1:10 ....182, 182n4
2:12 ....182n4
2:13–14............140
2:16 ....24, 182
3:13 25
5:8...................156
5:8–10 24
5:9...................6, 50, 156, 182,
                    182n4

2 Thessalonians
2:3...................182n4
2:8–10 174
2:10 ....24, 182n4
2:13 ....24, 39n2, 50,
                    57
2:13–14............127
2:14 ....182n4
3:1...................127

1 Timothy
1:13, 16............192
1:17 192
2:4...................114, 115
4:1–3...............157
5:21 ....6n6
6:9...................182n4, 192
6:15–16............192

2 Timothy
1:9...................39, 40, 55, 58,
                    163, 192
2:8–10 127
2:10 ....5, 130, 182n4
2:13 103
2:25–26............117
3:13 157
3:16 101
3:16–17............3

4:2...................126
4:8...................192
4:18 192

Titus
1:1...................5, 130
1:2...................103
2:11 76
3:3–7...............195

Hebrews
1:2...................82
2:13 46
3:8...................176
3:13 176
4:3...................38
6:18 103
9:14 25
9:26 38
10:16...............176
10:22...............29
12:24...............29

James
1:13 103
1:18 127
2:5...................32, 50, 64, 68
2:8...................99

1 Peter
1:1–2...............28, 50, 51, 62
1:2...................52
1:3...................123, 192
1:13 192
1:17 192
1:19 25
1:19–20............158
1:20 ....37, 38, 62
2:4...................44

2:6 44
2:6–8 174
2:7 155
2:7–8a 154
2:8 . . . . .8, 155, 156
2:8b 154
2:9 . . . . .45, 124
2:9–10 . . . . .35, 50
2:10 192
2:11 93
3:12 192
4:5 192
4:11 192
5:10 192
5:13 50

2 Peter
1:5–7 141
1:5–11 141
1:11 141
1:20–21 101
2 157
2:1 182
2:3 158
2:4 . . . . .6n6
3:1 115
3:7 182
3:8 115
3:9 114–15
3:13 104
3:14 115
3:17 115

1 John
4:19 . . . . .65, 140

2 John
1 . . . . .50n8
13 . . . . .50n8

3 John
8 130

Jude
4 . . . . .8, 156–57, 183, 192
5–7 157
5–16 183
6 . . . . .6n6, 192
11 192
14–15 192
21 192
24 25
24–25 192

Revelation
1:5 192
3:5 158
4:8–11 192
5:8–3 192
5:9 65
5:12 192
6:16–17 192
7:9–12 192
7:12 192
11:15–18 192
11:16–18 187–88
11:18 192
12:12 192
13:5 174
13:8 . . . . .38, 47, 157, 158, 174, 183
14:7 192
14:10 192
14:19 192
15:1 192
15:2–4 192
15:7 192
16:1 192

16:4–7 192
16:5–6 188
16:7 ....188, 192
16:19...............192
17:8 ....38, 39, 157,
          158, 174, 183
17:12–18 174
17:14..............50
19:1–2 ....188, 192
19:1–8 192
19:3 188

19:4 188
19:5 189
19:7–8 25
20:11–15 192
20:12..............158
20:12–13 144
20:15..............158, 183
21:4 104
21:27..............39, 158
21:1–22:21 192
22:3 104

Short Studies in Systematic Theology

For more information, visit **crossway.org**.